HARVARD STUDIES
IN COMPARATIVE LITERATURE

HARVARD STUDIES
IN COMPARATIVE LITERATURE
FOUNDED BY WILLIAM HENRY SCHOFIELD

· 23 ·

ON TRANSLATION

ON TRANSLATION

- ACHILLES FANG
- DUDLEY FITTS
- JOHN HOLLANDER
- ROLFE HUMPHRIES
- ROMAN JAKOBSON
- DOUGLAS KNIGHT
- RICHMOND LATTIMORE
- JACKSON MATHEWS
- BAYARD QUINCY MORGAN
- EDWIN MUIR
- WILLA MUIR
- VLADIMIR NABOKOV
- EUGENE A. NIDA
- JUSTIN O'BRIEN
- ANTHONY G. OETTINGER
- RENATO POGGIOLI
- WILLARD V. QUINE
- REUBEN A. BROWER, *Editor*

HARVARD UNIVERSITY PRESS

Cambridge, Massachusetts

1 9 5 9

I. A. RICHARDS

hominum poetarumque interpreti

Acknowledgment

The editing of this volume in the *Harvard Studies* was undertaken on the invitation of the Department of Comparative Literature. I am greatly indebted to the Chairman of the Department, Professor Renato Poggioli, and to Professor Harry Levin for generous support and advice at many stages during the preparation of the manuscript. I also want to thank the writers of the papers for their patience and good will in responding to numerous editorial quibbles and queries.

As a matter of record it should be noted that the papers by Richmond Lattimore and Justin O'Brien were in their original form read at a conference of the English Institute, 1954, "Translators on Translating." The paper by Achilles Fang was first published in "Studies in Chinese Thought," *The American Anthropologist*, LV, No. 5, pt. 2 (1953), 263–285, and is reprinted here with the permission of the Editors and the University of Chicago Press. "Seven Agamemnons" was published in the *Journal of the History of Ideas*, VIII, No. 4 (October 1947), 383–405, and is reprinted here with permission of the Editor.

Grateful acknowledgment is made for permission to reprint the following passages: On pages 35–36, "Tuércele el cuello al cisne . . ." by Enrique González Martínez, and, on page 37, "Then twist the neck of this delusive swan" by John Peale Bishop, both from *An Anthology of Contemporary Latin-American Poetry*, edited by Dudley Fitts, copyright 1942 and 1947 by New Directions. Reprinted by permission of New Directions, Norfolk, Connecticut. Selection on page 40 from Dudley Fitts's translation of Aristophanes' *The Frogs*, reprinted by permission of Harcourt, Brace and Company, New York. Passages on pages 50, 52, 53–54 from translations of Euripides' *The Trojan Women*, Aeschylus' *Oresteia: The Libation Bearers*, and Homer's *The Iliad*, respectively, by Richmond Lattimore, reprinted by permission of The University of Chicago Press. On page 57, "Bronze Trumpets and Sea Water," reprinted from *Collected Poems* by Elinor Wylie by permission of the publisher. Copyright 1921, 1932, by Alfred A. Knopf, Inc., New York. Selections on pages 74, 75, 76, 77 from the works of Paul Valéry, translated by Jackson Mathews, reprinted by permission of the Bollingen Foundation, New York. Translation by Fernand Baldensperger on page 83 of lines by Suckling and on page 84 by Keats, reprinted from *D'Edmond Spenser à Alan Seeger*, 1938, volume 13 in the Harvard Studies in Comparative Literature, by permission of the Harvard University Press, Cambridge,

Massachusetts. Passages on pages 176 and 178 from translation of Aeschylus' *Agamemnon* by Louis MacNiece, 1936, reprinted by permission of Harcourt, Brace and Company, New York, and Faber and Faber Ltd., London. Passages on pages 189, 190, 191 from the translation of Aeschylus' *Agamemnon* by Gilbert Murray, 1920, reprinted by permission of George Allen & Unwin Ltd., London. The epigraph on page 210 from A. E. Housman's *Last Poems*, reprinted by permission of Henry Holt and Company, Inc., New York, and The Society of Authors, London. Lines on page 211 from "The Seafarer," from *Personae* by Ezra Pound, copyright 1926, R 1954 by Ezra Pound, reprinted by permission of New Directions, Norfolk, Connecticut, and Shakspear & Parkyn, London. Passage on pages 216–217 from the translation of T. S. Eliot's *The Waste Land* by Ernst Robert Curtius, 1927, reprinted by permission of Suhrkamp Verlag, Frankfurt am Main, publishers of a bilingual edition of Eliot's works.

CONTENTS

Pray Mr. *Lintott* (said I) now you talk of Translators, what is your method of managing them? "Sir (reply'd he) those are the saddest pack of rogues in the world: In a hungry fit, they'll swear they understand all the languages in the universe: I have known one of them take down a *Greek* book upon my counter and cry, Ay this is *Hebrew*, I must read it from the latter end. By G—d I can never be sure in these fellows, for I neither understand *Greek*, *Latin*, *French*, nor *Italian* my self. But this is my way: I agree with them for ten shillings per sheet, with a proviso, that I will have their doings corrected by whom I please; so by one or other they are led at last to the true sense of an author; my judgment giving the negative to all my Translators." But how are you secure that those correctors may not impose upon you? "Why I get any civil gentleman, (especially any *Scotchman*) that comes into my shop, to read the original to me in *English*; by this I know whether my first Translator be deficient, and whether my Corrector merits his money or no?"

Alexander Pope to the Earl of Burlington,
November 1716

ON TRANSLATION

INTRODUCTION

THIS IS a book about a basic process in all writing and thinking and, one is tempted to add, in all experiencing. Whenever we meet an expression in any way foreign to us, whether in the language of signs and gestures or in a written or spoken language, we find ourselves saying more or less consciously, "Oh, he means by that what I mean when I do or say so-and-so." We translate the less familiar by putting the more familiar in its place, and when the right occasion comes along, we are prepared to use or interpret the once foreign gesture or word "like a native." Much of our learning of our own language takes place through similar processes. The child points to a farmer in a hayfield and says — as I once heard a child say — "Man doing!" and the parent, who speaks the foreign language of the adult world, dutifully corrects and translates, "The man is *haying*." The new term is no more accurate than the old, but it happens to be the usual way of describing this action in modern English.

Though some readers may demur at the use of "translation" for such primitive learning activities, all are willing enough to agree that they translate during the earlier stages of acquiring a foreign language, and the more honest will admit that they never stop translating. It is also worth remembering that translating is necessitated not only by differences in the national language of speakers or writers, but also by distance in space and time within a single language. The need for translation between British and American English is well known, and it is equally obvious that the gentleman from Alabama and the citizen of New York often need an interpreter if they are to communicate without friction. As some of the papers in this volume show, it is important to keep these humbler cases in mind if we are to understand what happens in vastly more complicated situations, when for example someone translates from ancient Greek into modern English, or when someone translates from the Hebrew of the Bible into Hiligaynon (a language of the Philippines), or when one translates the language of science and diplomacy from American English into contemporary Russian.

But though the moral of these examples may seem painfully obvious, the question is often asked (I can hear some readers asking it now), "Why a book on translation?" A book on intercultural relations, on linguistics, even on comparative literature, certainly, but on *translation*, the horror of the classroom, the waif of Grub Street, the unacknowledged half-sister of "true" literature? Let us move on with averted if uncomprehending eye to higher things. The simplest general answer, and as good as most general answers, is that to neglect the study of translation is dangerous. A tragi-comic example may bring the point home. In a great American university that has taken the lead along "the *high Priori* Road" (as Pope might call it) of unspecialized education, a Greek scholar of my acquaintance heard an instructor tell a student that such and such a line in the *Antigone* contained "the very essence of Sophocles' meaning in the play." The scholar, fascinated because he did not recognize the sentiment as Sophoclean, consulted the text and found that the line in English was a notorious piece of translator's fudge. An interest in the study of translation, it must be abundantly clear, does not imply a diminished interest in the study of foreign languages, though this is one of the vulgar errors familiar to translators and to all who show some interest in the process.

A more specific answer to the question of "Why a book on translation?" even when put sympathetically, depends on who is asking the question and on the kind of concern he may reveal in asking it. The interest of the literary critic can be assumed and would seem to require no description, since the study of literature necessarily involves some exploration of how it is produced. But in spite of the fact that study of "the creative process" has been a matter of speculation since Plato, and has become increasingly fashionable since Coleridge, it is surprising how little attention has been given to the obscure business of re-enacting someone else's creation. Though the bibliography of studies on translation is much more extensive than is generally realized, a glance through the titles at the end of this volume will show how relatively few major writers or critics have given the problem any long or continuous attention. Translation has as yet no Aristotle or Coleridge. At this point I may appropriately add a gentle caveat for readers who are approaching these essays with over-sanguine hopes of a final illumination. In some two thousand years of study by some of the best minds in the western world, a few good things, but only a few, have been said about the making of literature. It will hardly be surprising if a series of experimental essays in this even darker area do little more than bring out more clearly some of the problems and indicate some of the possible ways of talking more sensibly about their solution. In an area where so little is known, even that little is precious.

The special interest of the student of comparative literature in questions of translation may be assumed with certainty and calls for little demonstration. Though the *comparatiste* must be a master of many languages (not excluding his own), his subject will often be translation in one of its forms. Whether he is studying the effects of English Pre-Romanticism on the Continent, or of German Transcendentalism in England and America, or the Heroic Poem of Tasso as transformed by Spenser and Milton, he is concerned with translation in the narrowest or widest senses, from "metaphrase" to "imitation." For the student of comparative literature in many areas the act of translation is the ideal test case, the laboratory specimen of an "influence" at work. "Poe in France" is Baudelaire's translation of the tales and Mallarmé's of the poetry. From these versions, if anywhere, the *comparatiste* can see what happened to Poe and what happened to French poetic sensibility in the process of give and take between the two languages. For the critic interested primarily in literary traditions and their evolution, the subject of translation has also a special importance, since the study of a particular tradition — say of the pastoral or of tragedy — is in large part a study of successive versions or adaptations of Greek and Roman originals. As recent essays on Chapman, Dryden, and Pope have shown, a translation which was made by a master and which was markedly successful in its time, offers an excellent subject for seeing how a writer responds to alien literary traditions and how he domesticates them by adjudicating between the claims of past and present.

When the explorations of the literary critic lead into areas more properly belonging to the historian of ideas and cultures, translations again offer excellent specimen cases. Because the translator feels a strong pressure to make his importation acceptable to his audience and because with notable exceptions he is rarely one of the great innovators in literature, his style and language often reflect with great clarity the tastes and critical standards of a given literary public. In a translation we may often catch a writer and his readers "off guard," see them unconsciously revealing accepted ideas about the nature of literature or the state or the good life and good manners. Since successful translation depends on a double awareness of the cultural context in which the original was produced and of the context into which it is to be "projected," it will often reveal strikingly the likenesses and differences between two civilizations. Chapman offers illuminating texts for comparing nobility of manners and mind in Heroic Greece and Elizabethan England. A study of the Authorized Version presents similar opportunities for comparing "patriarchal" societies and for understanding how the translators viewed the society of the Old Testament.

To the philosopher with a special interest in language (at the present time, very nearly the definition of a philosopher), the process of translation provides clear examples for defining the nature of meaning and equivalent meanings, and for determining what meaning if any is present in a given statement. It is also hardly surprising that specialists in linguistics should want to study the conditions and modes of translation. And it is no more surprising that the natural scientist, with his growing dependence on investigations reported in many languages, should dream of a time when translation could be produced by mechanical means. The millennium will have come when at last the translator has been eliminated from translation. But as Renato Poggioli reminds us, one of the aims of the good translator is to sacrifice himself so completely to the work that his personality completely disappears.

The connection between the essays in this volume and the interests and disciplines I have been describing will be for the most part self-evident, but some brief remarks on the arrangement of the papers and their general character may be helpful. The book is divided into three parts: I. Translators on Translation; II. Approaches to the Problem; and III. A Critical Bibliography of Works on the Study of Translation. The first part consists of a series of practical reports on the process of translation by a number of distinguished present-day translators. An attempt has been made to represent a wide variety of languages and types of literature: Eugene Nida writes on translating the ancient Biblical languages into some thousand different tongues, including such exotics as Chokwe and Bantu; Dudley Fitts and Richmond Lattimore, on translating Greek drama and Homer (Mr. Fitts also includes examples from Spanish). Rolfe Humphries writes on translation of Virgil, Ovid, and other Latin poets; Justin O'Brien, on the prose of Proust, Camus, and Gide; Jackson Mathews, on the poetry of Valéry, St. John Perse, and others; Vladimir Nabokov, on Pushkin; and Achilles Fang, on translating from Chinese. Edwin and Willa Muir write of their trials in translating Kafka and other modern German novelists. These papers bristle with the particulars that delight and torment the translator's life, particulars that vary distinctly from language to language. Although difference is of the essence in this group of essays, one concern is common to all of them: the necessity of trying to "approximate the form" of the original. (The phrase is taken by Jackson Mathews from Valéry.) One conclusion emerges from their common preoccupation, that the translator is a "creator," that like the original author he is ordering and expressing experience in dramatic and rhythmic speech.

The papers of a more practical cast are not easily separated from the more theoretical papers of the second section, since each of the translators states or implies some general principles or aims drawn from his own experience. While most of the papers of the first part are addressed primarily to understanding the imaginative act of translating, each of the papers that follow in the second part represents one of the other kinds of concern outlined above. Renato Poggioli examines in general terms the critical and interpretive activities of the translator. W. V. Quine defines "empirical meaning" through analyzing the process of translating "a hitherto unknown language," an investigation that leads to conclusions of interest both to the student of foreign languages and to the anthropologist attempting to understand and describe an alien culture. In the next paper, I try to illustrate the usefulness of translations for the historian of literature and the historian of ideas. Douglas Knight, writing of Pope, examines the relation between a translation and the intellectual climate in which it is produced. Roman Jakobson comments on the process of translation as it is viewed by the specialist in linguistics. John Hollander considers the advantages of distinguishing between "translation" and "version" and illustrates the distinction with special reference to the theater. Anthony G. Oettinger gives an account of an experiment in automatic or machine translation. From his study we see clearly the kind of difficulty that staggers the machine, but which the human "operator" handles through the inscrutable processes which the writers of this volume have been attempting to bring more into the light.

Part III, the critical bibliography prepared by B. Q. Morgan, needs no description here. As a final introductory gesture, I might note that the first paper, on translating the Bible, presents an analysis of principles that may serve as an introduction to the book and to further discussion of the basic process of translation.

I

TRANSLATORS ON TRANSLATING

PRINCIPLES OF TRANSLATION AS EXEMPLIFIED BY BIBLE TRANSLATING

EUGENE A. NIDA

In TERMS of the length of tradition, volume of work, and variety of problems, Bible translating is distinctive. Beginning with the translation of the Hebrew Old Testament into Greek in the second and third centuries B.C. and continuing down to the present time, the Scriptures have been translated, at least in part, into 1,109 languages, of which 210 possess the entire Bible and 271 more the New Testament. This means that the major part of the Christian Scriptures exist in the languages of at least 95 per cent of the world's population. Moreover, most of this work has been accomplished in relatively recent times. By the time of the invention of printing, approximately 500 years ago, only 33 languages had anything of the Bible, and even by the beginning of the nineteenth century only 71 languages possessed anything of the Scriptures. However, within the nineteenth century more than 400 languages received something of the Scriptures, and during the first half of the twentieth century some part of the Bible was translated into approximately 500 more languages and dialects. At present the volume of translation and revision is of such magnitude that within the next twenty-five years as much will be published as within the entire nineteenth century, for more than a thousand persons are giving all or a major part of their time to the translation and revision of the Bible in various parts of the world.

The unparalleled range of Bible translating, including as it does not only all the major languages of the world but hundreds of "primitive" tongues, provides a wealth of data and background of experience in the fundamental problems of communication which constitute the basis of the following article.

Practical Nature of Problems in Bible Translating

Whereas for some people translating may be primarily a matter of theoretical interest, the Bible translator must face up to certain immediate problems. For example, if he attempts to translate literally the expression "he beat his breast" (speaking of the repentant Publican,

Luke 18:13), he may discover that, as in the Chokwe language of Central Africa, this phrase actually means "to congratulate oneself" (the equivalent of our "pat himself on the back"). In some instances it is necessary to say "to club one's head."

It is assumed by many people that the repetition of a word will make the meaning more emphatic, but this is not always the case. For example, in Hiligaynon (and a number of other Philippine languages), the very opposite is true. Accordingly, one cannot translate literally "Truly, truly, I say to you," for to say "truly, truly" in Hiligaynon would really mean "perhaps," while saying "truly" once is actually the Biblical equivalent.

Quite without knowing the reasons, we usually insist that, in rendering in another language a sentence such as "he went to town," one must use an active form of the verb meaning "to go." However, in many of the Nilotic languages of the Sudan it would be much more acceptable to say, "the town was gone to by him."

In still other instances one encounters what is regarded by some as a completely distorted orientation of experience. For example, in the Bolivian Quechua language it is quite possible to speak of the future, even as it is in any language, but one speaks of the future as "behind oneself" and the past as "ahead of one." When pressed for an explanation of such an expression, Quechuas have insisted that because one can see "in the mind" what has happened such events must be "in front of one," and that since one cannot "see" the future such events must be "behind one." Such a perspective of the past and the future is every bit as meaningful as our own, and it can certainly not be condemned as distorted. It is simply different from ours.

Accordingly, in such areas as (1) behavior as described by language (e.g., "beating the breast"), (2) semantic patterns (e.g., repetition of constituents), (3) grammatical constructions (e.g., active vs. passive), or (4) idiomatic descriptions of "perspectives," the Bible translator is faced with acute problems demanding answers. He knows full well that reproducing the precise corresponding word may utterly distort the meaning. Accordingly, he has been obliged to adjust the verbal form of the translation to the requirements of the communicative process.

Underlying Principles

Though in many instances the principles underlying Bible translating are only partially recognized or formulated by those engaged in such work, nevertheless the results of any accurate translating reveal the following basic principles:

1. *Language consists of a systematically organized set of oral-aural symbols.* By oral-aural we are simply emphasizing the fact that such symbols not only are uttered by the vocal apparatus of the speaker but are also received and interpreted by the listener. The writing system of any language is a dependent symbolic system and only imperfectly reflects the "spoken-heard" form of language.

2. *Associations between symbols and referents are essentially arbitrary.* Even onomatopoetic forms bear only a "culturally conditioned" resemblance to the sounds which they are designed to imitate. For example, the equivalent of our *tramp-tramp* is *kú· kà·* in Luvale, a Bantu language of Central Africa, and *mingòdongòdona* in Malagasy.

3. *The segmentation of experience by speech symbols is essentially arbitrary.* The different sets of words for color in various languages are perhaps the best ready evidence for such essential arbitrariness. For example, in a high percentage of African languages there are only three "color words," corresponding to our *white, black,* and *red,* which nevertheless divide up the entire spectrum. In the Tarahumara language of Mexico, there are five basic color words, and here "blue" and "green" are subsumed under a single term. The comparison of related sets of words in any field of experience — kinship terms, body parts, or classification of plants — reveals the same essentially arbitrary type of segmentation. Since, therefore, no two languages segment experience in the same way, this means that there can never be a word-for-word type of correspondence which is fully meaningful or accurate.

4. *No two languages exhibit identical systems of organizing symbols into meaningful expressions.* In all grammatical features, that is, order of words, types of dependencies, markers of such dependency relationships, and so on, each language exhibits a distinctive system.

The basic principles of translation mean that no translation in a receptor language can be the exact equivalent of the model in the source language. That is to say, all types of translation involve (1) loss of information, (2) addition of information, and/or (3) skewing of information. To understand clearly the manner in which such

Eugene A. Nida

"distortion" takes place we must examine the ethnolinguistic design of communication.

Ethnolinguistic Design of Communication

By adopting the simpler components of the communication process and relating these to the entire communicative context, we may construct an ethnolinguistic design of communication as shown in Figure 1.

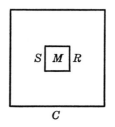

Figure 1

In the diagram of Figure 1 *S* stands for source (the speaker as source and encoder). *M* is the message as expressed in accordance with the particular structure (the inner square in this instance) of the language. The message may include anything from a single word to an entire utterance. *R* is the receptor (including decoder and receiver), and the outer square (designated by *C*) represents the cultural context as a whole, of which the message (as a part of the language) is itself a part and a model (compare similarity of shapes).

It is quite impossible to deal with any language as a linguistic signal without recognizing immediately its essential relationship to the cultural context as a whole. For example, in Hebrew the root * *brk* is used in the meaning of "to bless" and "to curse." Such meanings would only be applicable in a culture in which words in certain socio-religious contexts were regarded as capable of either blessing or cursing, depending upon the purpose of the source. Similarly * *qdš*, which is generally used in the sense of "holy," may also designate a temple prostitute, an association which would be impossible within our own culture, but entirely meaningful in a society which was well acquainted with fertility cults.

This emphasis upon the relationship of *M* to *C* must not, however, constitute an excuse for unwarranted etymologizing, in which meanings are read into words from historically prior usages, for example, treating Greek *ekklesia* "assembly" or "church" as really meaning "called out ones" (a contention of some Bible interpreters) because of an earlier use of the compound word.

Despite the recognition of the close connection between the *M* and *C* (that is, between the realities symbolized by the inner and outer squares), we must at the same time recognize the fact that every *S* (source) and every *R* (receptor) is a different individual in accordance with his background and is hence somewhat diverse in the use and understanding of *M* (the message). If we may describe each person's encoding-decoding mechanism as a kind of linguistic grid based upon the totality of his previous language experience, we must admit that each grid is different in at least some slight degree. This does not make communication impossible, but it removes the possibility of absolute equivalence and opens the way for different understanding of the same message.

In the communicative process, however, *S* and *R* generally recognize these matters of difference and tend to adjust their respective grids so as to communicate more effectively. For example, a speaker adjusts himself to his audience (if he wishes to communicate with any degree of effectiveness) and the audience, in turn, makes allowances for the background of the speaker. Furthermore, each participant in the *S-M-R* process is aware of such adjustments and tends to make reciprocal compensation so as to comprehend more fully and correctly.[1] Communication is thus essentially a two-way process, even though one person might be doing all the speaking.

One of the essential tasks of the Bible translator is to reconstruct the communicative process as evidenced in the written record of the Bible. In other words, he must engage in what is traditionally called exegesis, but not hermeneutics, which is the interpretation of a passage in terms of its relevance to the present-day world, not to the Biblical culture.

One interesting problem in exegesis which may be treated by the method of reconstructing the communicative process is the formal differences between the phrases "kingdom of God" (used exclusively in the Gospel of Luke) and "kingdom of heaven" (used in most contexts in the Gospel of Matthew). Most Biblical scholars have regarded these two phrases as essentially equivalent, but there are some persons who insist that they refer to two different "dispensations." The answer to such a problem consists in reconstructing the facts of the communication: the Jewish taboo avoidance of *Yahweh* (and by extension other terms referring to deity), the substitution of words such as "heaven," "power," and "majesty" for *Yahweh*, the Jewish background of the writer of the Gospel of Matthew, the evident Jewish audience to which the Gospel of Matthew is directed, the Greek background of Luke, the Greco-Roman audience to which the Gospel of Luke was directed, and the complete lack of any substitution device (such as "heaven" for "God") on the part of the Greco-Roman community. These factors in the communication process when considered in the light of the total cultural context make the identification of the two phrases entirely justified.

Two-Language Model of Communication

Up to the present time we have been discussing the translator's task in terms of the Biblical languages, but assuming, for the sake of greater simplicity of statement, that the translator was a part of the Biblical culture. This, of course, is not true, for though he may be well acquainted with numerous aspects of this culture, he is not, nor can he ever be, anything like a fully participating member. Not only can the culture not be fully described, but it can most certainly not be reproduced — despite Alley Oop's time-machine experiences.

The fact that English (the language which we shall, for our present purposes, assume as the language of the translator) is the means by which information concerning the Biblical culture is directly or indirectly gathered, e.g., through commentaries, dictionaries, and learned journals, is described diagrammatically in Figure 2.

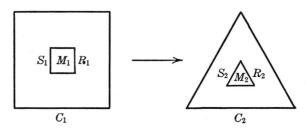

FIGURE 2

In this diagram the squares represent the Biblical language (for the sake of our diagram it makes no essential difference whether we are speaking of Greek, Hebrew, or Aramaic) and the triangles represent the "equivalent" communication in English. The subscript numerals help to identify the different components in these parallel instances of communication. A translator of the New Testament into English assumes the position of R_1, even though he can only approximate the role of a New Testament receptor. At the same time this translator becomes S_2, in that he reproduces M_1 as M_2, so that R_2 may respond in ways essentially similar to those in which the original R_1 responded.

Where there is a time gap between C_1 and C_2 the translator (S_2) can only be a kind of proxy R_1. However, a bilingual translator who participates fully in two linguistic communities may fulfill a dual role by being quite validly both R_1 and S_2.

Figure 2 serves also to emphasize two significant factors: (1) the essential differences in the form between M_1 and M_2, and (2) the relationship of M_1 and M_2 to their respective cultural contexts. Of course, the actual situation is not as simple as the diagram would imply, for nothing so complex as a language-culture relationship can possibly be reduced to a few lines. However, the differences are present and real and can be noted in all phases of the communicative procedure. A few of these differences will enable one to understand more fully certain of the broader implications of what we are only able to hint at here.

Though as English-speaking people we employ a language which is relatively closely related to Greek (certainly in comparison with the differences between English and Hottentot), there are numerous basic differences. In the meanings of words, for example, we have relatively few close correspondences. We use *love* to translate certain aspects of the meanings of at least four different Greek words: *agapaô*, *phileô*, *stergô*, and *eraô*, but these words also correspond to such English meanings as "to like," "to appreciate the value of," "to be friendly with," "to have affection for," and "to have a passion for." Even a first-year Greek student will give the meaning of *logos* as "word," but the Liddell and Scott dictionary lists more than seventy different meanings — and these do not do full justice to the specialized Biblical usage. However, Greek also has two other words, *epos* and *rhêma*, which are likewise translated as "word" in many contexts.

The incommensurability between Greek and English is quite evident in the differences between tense and aspect, a problem which gives constant difficulty to a translator of the New Testament. This problem is made all the more acute by the fact that the Hebrew of the Old Testament employs a tense-aspect system which is quite different from that of the Greek, but which is often reflected in the distinctive Semitic coloring of many New Testament usages.

In the matter of arrangement of words, especially in the marking of long series of dependent phrases and clauses, the English language simply does not have the structural potentialities of Greek. Accordingly, a stretch of speech which may be a perfectly good Greek sentence (consisting, for example, of verses 3–14 of Ephesians 1) can only be rendered intelligibly by several sentences in English.

Whether, then, in terms of the meanings of words or idioms ("heap coals of fire on his head," "bowels of mercy," or "the reins and the heart") or of the grammatical categories or arrangements of words, M_2 differs from M_1. However, this is not the whole story, for most Bible translators are faced not with a two-language but a three-language communication problem.

Three-Language Diagram of Communication

By means of one's own language — which in the case of English bears a close cognate relationship to Greek and reflects a considerable historical connection with the Biblical culture, even as Western culture took over much from the Judaeo-Greco-Roman world — one not only explores the Biblical languages but in large measure tends to mediate these data in communicating into another language. Accordingly, we may diagram this process (Figure 3).

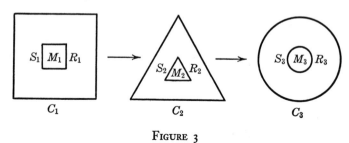

$$C_1 \qquad\qquad C_2 \qquad\qquad C_3$$

FIGURE 3

Of course, there are a number of translators who translate "directly from the original languages," but even then a high percentage of their responses to the forms of the original languages tend to be colored by the medium of study and analysis, namely, their own mother tongue. Their task, however, is to communicate the M_1 in terms of M_3, with the least possible skewing as the result of M_2. The problem is made more difficult in most instances by virtue of the fact that most languages do not have any historical connection with the Biblical languages, either by being members of the same language family or because of historical and cultural associations. However, there is one interesting fact, namely, that the so-called Biblical culture exhibits far more similarities with more other cultures than perhaps any other one culture in the history of civilization. This is not strange, if one takes into consideration the strategic location of this culture in the Middle East, at the "crossroads of the world" and at a point from which radiated so many cultural influences. This fact makes the Bible so much more "translatable" in the many diverse cultures of the world than most books coming out of our own contemporary Western culture. This essential similarity to the cultures of so many peoples helps to explain something of the Bible's wide appeal.

Definition of Translating

A definition of translating will inevitably depend in very large measure upon the purpose to be accomplished by the translation in question. However, since in Bible translating the purpose is not to communicate certain esoteric information about a different culture, but to so communicate that R_3 may be able to respond to M_3 in ways substantially similar to those in which R_1 responded to M_1, a definition of translating which is in accord with the best traditions of Biblical scholarship could be stated as follows: "Translating consists in producing in the receptor language the closest natural equivalent to the message of the source language, first in meaning and secondly in style."

This type of definition recognizes the lack of any absolute correspondence, but it does point up the importance of finding the closest equivalence. By "natural" we mean that the equivalent forms should not be "foreign" either in form (except of course for such inevitable matters as proper names) or meaning. That is to say, a good translation should not reveal its nonnative source.

It is recognized that equivalence in both meaning and style cannot always be retained — in the acrostic poems of the Old Testament, to cite an extreme example. When, therefore, one must be abandoned for the sake of the other, the meaning must have priority over the stylistic forms.

Differences of Formal Structure

In comparing the form of the Biblical message (M_1) with the corresponding form that must be employed in any other language (M_x), we are immediately impressed with the marked formal differences. We cannot, however, consider all these contrasts. Nevertheless, a brief statement of such problems as diversities in (a) word classes, (b) grammatical categories, and (c) arrangements of words can be illustrative of the basic principles involved in determining what is the "closest natural equivalence" in any given situation.

Word Classes

There is a great deal of difference between languages in respect to the word classes that are used to express certain ideas, for so often what is a noun in Greek must be rendered as a verb in other languages, and what is a pronoun in Greek or Hebrew frequently must become a noun in another language. Furthermore, adjectives in Greek or Hebrew are often verb-like words in other languages. Nevertheless, behind this apparent wide discrepancy in the word classes of various languages there are some astonishing similarities. In the first place, most languages described to date have been found to have "object words" (usually treated as noun-like words), "event words" (generally designated as verb-like), and at least some other classes, often pronouns, adjectives, and/or relational particles. What is therefore more significant than the apparent differences between Greek and other languages (such differences are much more evident in New Testament translating than in the Old Testament) is a fundamental agreement between languages as to classes commonly called nouns and verbs.

What we designate as noun-like words and verb-like words are predominantly those which are (1) "object words" with more or less fixed figures or forms, *tree, stick, hill, river, grass, rope, stone, sun, moon, star, canoe, dog, cat, head, foot,* and (2) "event words," *run, walk, jump, swim, see, hear, fight, hit, talk, make,* and *fly.* It is possible that Gestalt psychology can provide certain important clues as to the reasons for this basic dichotomy in languages, though it is recognized that in many languages there is considerable overlapping of classes and shifting of terms from one class to another. The well-defined figure, as compared with the ground (to use Gestalt terminology), could provide us with the core of noun-like words (the so-called "object words"). The less well-defined figures representing movement, becoming, passing, or "eventing" would then be represented by the "event words," namely, the verbs. Certain characteristics held in common by various "object words," for example, *red, yellow, true, good, kind, one,* and *two,* would provide the abstracts generally designated as adjectives, and those designating common features of events, *fast, suddenly, slowly, once,* and *twice,* for instance, would correspond to adverbs, though in this there is also considerable overlapping and shifting of class membership. In addition to the word classes designating objects, events, and abstractions, there are the relationals, which describe relations between objects or between events. If such words are used primarily as relationals between objects, we call them preposition-like words, and if they indicate relations between events, they are generally classed as conjunctions, but here again there is a great deal of overlapping and shifting from one class to another.

The preceding paragraphs must not be interpreted as a defense of the Indo-European word class structure, nor of the fatal error of descriptive methodology in defining a noun as "the name of a person, place, or thing." Furthermore, we are not suggesting that these semantically important classes represent any inevitable direction of development for any language. In the Mayan languages, for example, the equivalents of English adjectives are for the most part a formal subclass of verbs, and the prepositions and conjunctions are predominantly noun-like words, though of a very restricted class. In Tarahumara certain object words (as judged in terms of their present semantic values) are certainly derived from event words, for example, *pačiki* "an ear of corn" (from *pači* "to grow ears of corn") and *remeke* "tortillas" (from *reme* "to make tortillas"). Nevertheless, despite such divergencies there is in most languages a sizable core of words which reflect distinctions explicable in terms of Gestalt psychology. Moreover, whether as major or minor classes, languages do tend to have four principal groups: object words (roughly equivalent to nouns), event words (roughly equivalent to verbs), abstracts (modifiers of object and event words), and relationals (roughly equivalent to prepositions and conjunctions in the Indo-European languages).

For the Bible translator the most serious problem relating to word classes is created by the fact that in Greek, and for that matter in most Indo-European languages, there is a marked tendency to use event words without reference to the objects or persons that may participate in such events. For example, in Mark 1:4 there is the clause "John preached the baptism of repentance unto the forgiveness of sins." All the nouns except *John* are essentially event words, but the participants in the events are not made explicit, and the relationships between the events are very ambiguously indicated. When, as in many languages, this type of expression must be translated not by a series of nouns but by verbs, the problem is difficult; for not only must the participants be explicitly indicated (as required by verb constructions in question), but the relationships between the events must be more explicitly stated. This means that such an expression in many languages must be rendered as "John preached that the people should repent and be baptized so that God would forgive the evil which they had done."

Similarly, it is quite impossible to say in many languages, "God is love." The word indicating "love" is essentially an event word, and it cannot be combined as a kind of predicate complement to a subject by means of a copulative verb. In other words, "love" cannot exist apart from participants. One cannot say, therefore, "God is love" but simply that "God loves." This is, of course, essentially what the Biblical passage means, not that God is to be equated with love, for the expression "God is love" can not be inverted into "Love is God."

Grammatical Categories

When a language possesses certain categories which are not in Greek or Hebrew, the question arises as to whether the translation should conform to the categories of the receptor language. If such categories are obligatory there is really no alternative, unless one wishes to produce a translation which is grammatically incorrect. However, the problem is not quite so simple, for there are two types of factors: (1) the nonexistent, ambiguous, obscure, implicit, or explicit nature of the information in the source language, and (2) the obligatory or optional character of the category in the receptor language.

The following outline indicates those types of situations in the source and receptor languages which give rise to the most common problems of equivalence:

A. *Instances in which M_1 lacks information which is obligatory in M_x.* For example, in Matthew 4:13 there is no information available from the New Testament record as to whether Jesus had ever visited Capernaum prior to his trip recorded at this point. When, as in the Villa Alta dialect of Zapotec, spoken in southern Mexico, it is obligatory to distinguish between actions which occur for the first time with particular participants and those which are repetitious, one must make a decision, despite the lack of data in the source language. Since there is a greater likelihood that Jesus would have visited nearby Capernaum than that he would not have done so, the translation into Villa Alta Zapotec reflects this probability, and there is accordingly a distinct increase in "information" in the translation. When, however, such information is purely optional in a receptor language, it is of course not introduced.

B. *Instances in which information which is obligatory in M_x is obscure in M_1.* The status of Jesus as a rabbi was well recognized by his friends and followers but was openly challenged by others. If, accordingly, we must apply to the Gospel accounts the categories of an honorific system (such as are common in the languages of Southeast Asia), we cannot always be sure precisely what would be the relative social position of Jesus and those who would speak to and of him. Though considerable information is given, there is also real obscurity at many points. If, however, the receptor language requires honorific indicators, they must be added (with at least a partial increase in information).

C. *Instances in which information which is obligatory in M_x is ambiguous in M_1.* Though ambiguities also involve a degree of obscurity, they are different from simple obscurities in that either alternative seems to have almost equal validity. For example, in John 4:12 the Samaritan woman speaks to Jesus of "our father Jacob, who gave us the well." If we apply to this statement the inclusive-exclusive first person plural dichotomy, which occurs in many languages, we can argue almost equally well for the inclusive form (assuming that the woman would be willing to admit that the Jews were also descended from Jacob) or the exclusive form (reflecting something more of the traditional hostility between the Samaritans and the Jews and the evident contrast mentioned in verse 20 of the same chapter). When the inclusive-exclusive distinction is obligatory in the receptor language, the translator must make a decision, and regardless of the results there will be at least a partial increase in information. When, however, the receptor language allows such information to be optional, then the translator should retain the ambiguity of the original.

D. *Instances in which information which must be made explicit in M_x is only implicit in M_1.* When information is implicit in the source language context, but must be made explicit in the receptor language, there is actually no gain in information carried by the message. It is merely carried in a different way — explicitly rather than implicitly. For example, in John 4:20, when the Samaritan woman is reported as saying, "Our fathers worshiped on this mountain; and you say that in Jerusalem is the place where men ought to worship," there is no possible doubt as to the exclusive use of "our." However, this fact is implicitly given, not explicitly so. In many instances, however, what is quite implicitly understood in one language is not so understood in another, especially in those instances where the cultural context is very different. For example, a literal translation (one which translates only the strictly explicit features) of Hebrews 7:3, "He is without father or mother or genealogy, and has neither beginning of days nor end of life. . ." is likely to be understood in many languages as implying that Melchizedek was a theophany, rather than simply a person for whom there is no record of human descent. Accordingly, to avoid serious misunderstanding it is often necessary to make explicit in the receptor language (even on an optional and nonobligatory basis) what is only implicit in the source language.

E. *Instances in which information which is explicit in M_1 must be differently treated in M_x.* Explicit information in the source language should be communicated in the receptor language. There are, however, two exceptions to this general rule. In the first place, the receptor language may not have a corresponding method of indicating such information. For example, in the Greek verb system there are numerous subtle distinctions of aspect which cannot be translated into English without very heavy circumlocutions, which in the end tend to make the aspectual distinctions far more explicit than they were in the source language. Such translations involve a partial increase in information by virtue of their emphasis. In the second place, when the indication of such information is optional in the receptor language, the frequency of occurrence of information of this type may be quite different from what it is in the source language. For example, in Greek and Hebrew number and tense are indicated repeatedly, while in many languages number and tense may be indicated once within a context, but left implicit throughout the rest of the passage in question. It is necessary that a translation indicate such optional factors with a frequency which is comparable with what would normally occur, or the translation becomes unnatural, since the patterns of "redundancy" have been altered.

This outline of criteria for the addition or omission of information is applicable not only to the immediate problem of grammatical categories, but to any and all types of mensurability between the source and receptor languages.

Arrangements of Words

The same principles elaborated in the preceding section with regard to corresponding categories also apply in matters of arrangements of words, whether of order of words or of the number and types of dependencies. Of the numerous problems involved in grammatical arrangements of words, we can only touch briefly upon hypotactic and paratactic constructions. A language with a heavy hypotactic structure (e.g., Greek) simply makes explicit a number of relationships which are left implicit in a language which employs a paratactic type of structure (e.g., Hebrew). Unfortunately, there is a tendency to think that the hypotactic structure is fundamentally superior and that accordingly in translating into a language which has an essentially paratactic structure one should introduce (for example by overworking potential hypotactic patterns and by creating new grammatical forms or arrangements) the same number and types of hypotactic constructions as one finds in Greek. Such a procedure is quite unwarranted, for one should permit to be left implicit in the receptor language what is explicit in the source language if the receptor language in question would normally employ an implicit type of structure. The breaking up of long, involved sentences and the omission of corresponding conjunctions (provided such processes are carried out in conformity with the requirements of the receptor language) do not actually result in any loss of information. It simply means that the information is carried implicitly, rather than explicitly.

Hierarchy of Semantic Constituents

Despite our recognition of the fact that there are no complete synonyms, that is to say, words which may substitute for each other in all possible positions of occurrence, nevertheless, we do recognize that some words are substantially identical with others in the sense that they may be substituted for each other without any appreciable loss or change in meaning within a particular discourse. This is, of course, the experience of everyone who attempts to write without dull repetition of the same words. Not infrequently we need to mention the same referent, but stylistic considerations make it necessary for us to employ some other term which will serve the purpose. A brief examination of this process soon reveals that some words substitute for many words (words such as *thing, matter, object, feature, apparatus, this, he, they, go, come,* and *move* have a wide range of substitution), while other words may substitute for very few words (*raccoon, elephant, thimble, equator, seismograph, crawl, kiss,* and *assassinate*). If we group such words into related series and classify them on the basis of their range of substitution, we soon discover a series of hierarchies, ranging from the most concrete, "low-level" vocabulary at the base (with words having the greatest specificity), and the most generic, "high-level" vocabulary at the top (with words possessing the greatest degree of generality).

For the translator this factor of hierarchical series of concrete-generic vocabulary poses special problems, for though languages exhibit considerable agreement as to the segmentation of experience exhibited by the concrete vocabulary (for such segmentation is dependent largely upon "figure"-"ground" contrasts which are more or less well outlined, in terms of Gestalt psychology), the generic vocabulary, which is dependent upon the recognition of common features, is much more subject to differences of interpretation. Accordingly, it is much easier for the Bible translator to translate the Book of the Revelation, which is filled with symbols, of which the meaning is obscure though the language is specific and concrete, than the Gospel of John, of which the meaning is more evident but the language of a higher hierarchical level.

What makes such high-level generic vocabulary difficult to translate is not the fact that receptor languages lack such vocabulary, but that the generic vocabulary which does exist does not parallel the generic vocabulary of the Bible.

Unfortunately, there are two erroneous (and at the same time contradictory) impressions about so-called primitive languages. One often hears, on the one hand, that a language exhibits a primitive character since the language does not have any generic vocabulary, but only specific terms. On the other hand, people not infrequently lament the fact that a "primitive" language is inadequate as a means of communication because the words in question cover too wide an area of meaning, as for example in Anuak, a language of the Sudan, in which the same word may designate anything made of metal, from a needle to an airplane. The actual situation that one finds in languages is not the real absence of generic vocabulary, but its occurrence on different levels, and with difficult subpatterns of substitution. For example, in Bulu, spoken in the Cameroun, there are at least twenty-five terms for different kinds of baskets but no specific generic term which includes just baskets and nothing else.[2] However, one can refer to such objects by words which would have a higher-level value than our word *basket*, namely, the Bulu equivalent of "thing," "object," or "it." On the other hand, there are not only many different specific words for fruits, but a generic term for fruits as a whole, on a level which more or less corresponds with our term. In Kaka, a related language in the eastern part of the Cameroun, there are two generic terms for fruits, one which includes bananas and pineapples, and another which includes all other kinds of fruits (in terms of our meaning of *fruit*), plus testicles, glands, hearts, kidneys, eyeballs, soccer balls, pills, and the seed of any fruit or plant.

Analytical studies of semantic problems in so-called primitive languages reveal that the general proportion of specific to generic vocabulary is not appreciably different from what it is in the language of so-called civilized societies. The reason for the false impressions about specific and generic vocabulary is that people have wrongly expected generic vocabulary in various languages to exhibit the same degree of correspondence which they have observed in the study of specific vocabulary. Such is simply not the case, nor should one expect this to be so, since specific objects provide a much surer observable base of segmentation than the classification of objects, events, abstracts, and relations, on the basis of shared or unshared features. In other words, the more one depends upon the factors of human "judgment" rather than responses to more or less immediate perception, the greater will be the tendency to diversity.

Areas of Meaning and Amount of Information

The wider the area of meaning of a word (in terms of the wider segment of experience covered by a term) the greater is the likelihood of its statistical frequency of occurrence. This greater statistical frequency means that it tends to have a higher predictability of occurrence and hence greater redundancy. The greater the redundancy the less the information that is actually carried by the unit in question. This means that a translation made up primarily of words with wide areas of meaning does not carry the load of information which is often presumed.

There is, of course, another factor, namely, the transitional probabilities. If, for example, words with wide areas of meaning and hence greater frequency of occurrence in the language occur in unusual combinations and hence have low transitional probabilities in the particular context in question, the signal consisting of these words may still carry considerable information. Nevertheless, a translation made into any artificially restricted vocabulary will inevitably be one which carries less information than the original, unless extensive circumlocutions are employed and the meaning is thus "padded out."

There is a tendency for translators to overwork "good terms." They find certain expressions which may be used in a wide range of situations and hence employ them as frequently as possible. The result is often a marked rise of frequency, in contrast with normal usage, and the resultant loss in information, because of their predictability within the Biblical context. In an analogous manner translators often feel compelled to translate everything in the source language, to the point of employing corresponding expressions in the receptor language with an unnatural frequency. For example, in Greek almost all sentences begin with a connective, and the result is that the connectives have relatively less meaning than the corresponding connectives in English, which occur with much less frequency. If one translates all the Greek connectives, the result is actually overtranslating, for the Greek words (with proportionately less meaning) are translated by corresponding English connectives (with proportionately more meaning). At the same time, while the occurrence of connectives with almost every sentence is a mark of good style in Greek, this is certainly not the case in English. This problem becomes even more acute in a language which is predominantly paratactic in structure.

Endocentric and Exocentric Structures

In the same way that there are endocentric and exocentric constructions on a formal level, there are corresponding structures on a semantic level. For example, it is quite impossible to determine the meaning of "to heap coals of fire on one's head" by knowing the semantic distributions (types of discourse in which such words may be used) of all the component parts. The meaning of this idiom can be determined only by knowing the distribution of the unit as a whole. Accordingly, we regard it as a semantically exocentric expression. Since, however, the majority of expressions in any language are semantically endocentric, not exocentric, those who interpret the source language idioms as rendered in a receptor language are more likely than not to understand the expressions as endocentric rather than as exocentric (unless there are some special markers which provide the clues). That is the reason why, for example, in some of the languages of Congo this expression "heap coals of fire on one's head" was regarded as an excellent new means of torturing people to death, not a means of making them ashamed by being so good to them.

The problem of endocentric interpretation of exocentric expressions can, however, be overcome in part by certain markers. For example, many of the metaphors of the Scriptures — "I am the bread of life," "I am the door," "a camel through a needle's eye" — can be properly understood if they are made into similes — "I am like the bread which gives life," or "I am like a door." By the introduction of the equivalent of "like" the receptor is alerted to the fact that this is a kind of exocentric expression involving a "nonnormal" extension of meaning.

Similarly the context may serve as a guide to interpretation. For example, idioms occurring in a poetical context will be more readily understood in their proper exocentric values, since the total context provides the clue to their correct interpretation.

Relationship of Linguistic Form to Semantic Function

In attempting to discover the closest natural equivalent, whether of meaning or style, one is always faced with the difficulty of finding corresponding forms with analogous semantic functions. On the level of the meaning of words in terms of their referents and their function in the cultural context (space does not permit us to deal with the parallel problems of corresponding styles), one is faced with the following types of situations:

1. *The nonexistence of a term (and its corresponding referent) in the receptor language, but with an equivalent function being performed by another referent.* For example, in some languages there is no word for "snow," for such a phenomenon is outside the realm of the people's experience. However, the widely used equivalent of the phrase "white as snow" is "white as egret feathers." Accordingly, in a translation this different referent with the corresponding function may be introduced. On the other hand, if "white as egret feathers" is not a regular expression for the meaning of very white, then the introduction of "egret feathers" is not an equivalent of "snow," and it

would be more accurate to translate simply as "very, very white." The equivalence of the two expressions "white as snow" and "white as egret feathers" is not primarily a matter of the whiteness of the respective referents, but the recognition of this fact in the traditional use of referents in both the source and the receptor languages, respectively.

2. *The existence of the referent in the receptor language, but with a different function from what it has in the source language.* This means, for example, that "heart" in Greek must often be rendered by "liver," as in the Kabba-Laka language of French Equatorial Africa, by "abdomen," as in Conob, a Mayan language of Guatemala, and by "throat," as in some contexts in Marshallese, a language of the South Pacific. In languages in which "gall" stands for wisdom and a "hard heart" is a symbol of courage, the Bible translator is obliged to make certain adaptations or cause serious misunderstanding.

In some circumstances, however, the referent in the source language is such an integral part of the entire communication that it must be retained and the distinctive functions explained in footnotes. This is true, for example, of such Biblical terms as "sheep," "sacrifices," and "temple."

3. *The nonexistence of the referent in the receptor language and no other referent with a parallel function.* In such circumstances the translator is obliged to borrow foreign words (with or without classifiers) or employ descriptive phrases. For example, he may borrow the names of precious stones, *amethyst, ruby, pearl,* or the names of classes of people, *Pharisees* and *Sadducees.* If he adds a classifier, with resultant expressions such as "valuable stone called amethyst" and "sect called Sadducees," he can do a good deal to compensate for the lack of correspondence between the receptor and the source language. By employing descriptive phrases, he may, for example, translate "phylacteries" as "little leather bundles having holy words written inside" (as has been done in the Navajo translation).

Within the brief scope of this essay it has been impossible to give adequate consideration to a number of significant matters: (1) stylistic parallels, a study for which certain special methods and techniques are required, (2) the influence of a translation of the Bible upon the meanings of words (that is, the important factor of the "Christianization of vocabulary," with a clear recognition of the limitations of such a process), and (3) the precise manner in which new developments in information theory, and in the broader field of cybernetics, are integrally related to Bible translating; though anyone in these fields of study will appreciate the degree to which the above analysis is dependent upon these relatively new disciplines.

In summary, however, it is essential that we point out that in Bible translating, as in almost all fields of translating, the most frequent mistakes result from a failure to make adequate syntactic adjustments in the transference of a message from one language to another. Quite satisfactory equivalents for all the words and even the idioms may have been found, but a person's oversight or inability to rearrange the semantic units in accordance with the different syntactic structure immediately stamps a translation as being "foreign" and unnatural. These most numerous errors are not, however, the most serious, for though they may be wearisome and frustrating, they do not usually result in the serious misunderstandings which arise because of a lack of cultural adjustments.

When there are inadequate equivalents in the formal patterning of sentences (i.e., mistakes in syntax), we generally recognize such faults at once and either excuse them, or at least are able to discount them in trying to ascertain the meaning. Mistakes in cultural equivalence, however, do not carry with them such obvious clues, and hence the lack of agreement is not understood nor the source of the error detectable from the text itself.

Though it is fully recognized that absolute communication is quite impossible, nevertheless, very close approximations to the standard of natural equivalence may be obtained, but only if the translations reflect a high degree of sensitivity to different syntactic structures and result from clear insights into cultural diversities.

NOTES

1. A person with ill-will toward an *S* will purposely not make such an adjustment and will attempt to lift words out of context or not make allowance for background. Similarly, an *S* may have a haughty disregard for *R*, or be more interested in leaving an impression of his erudition than in communicating any set of facts.

2. The following data on Bulu and Kaka were supplied in private correspondence by William D. Reyburn.

THE POETIC NUANCE

DUDLEY FITTS

I SHALL BEGIN with a bit of autobiography that otherwise might not escape the angry paws of time. A few years ago I found myself in the role of Simon Legree to a group of accomplished and amiable writers engaged in translating contemporary Latin-American verse for an anthology of almost gigantic scope. My colleagues read and rendered formidable amounts of poetry in Spanish and Portuguese and French, as did I myself; and each of their translations came to me for final approval, which sometimes meant heartless editing. As I look back upon the job now, I am amazed by the forbearance that my collaborators showed, their generosity in the face of what so often must have seemed arrogance or simple-minded pigheadedness. They all knew more about Latin-American verse than I did, and many of them were serious poets in their own right, yet they were willing to put up with a process that most artists would have found intolerable, the wrenching of their own concepts of translation to fit an aesthetic that was, on the face of it, paradoxical. Since I had planned at the outset to print the original texts on pages facing the translations, and since I had also persuaded myself that any reader interested in so special a work would probably not be entirely illiterate in the foreign languages, I proposed a theory of non-art in the rendering of art. Our versions of the poems were to be as literal as we could make them without descending into the jargon of the interlinear trot. "Line for line and sometimes word for word," I hoped, we might render a text absolutely. If the sonal or otherwise affective qualities of the verse could be accounted for without violating this basic fidelity, so much the better; but my aim was not to write poetry as a substitute for untranslatable poetry. In a sentence that inspired three cases of apoplexy in the Republic of Chile I asserted that "our versions are not poetry, except accidentally"; and I went on to confess that I had editorially spoiled many of my colleagues' happiest effects in the interests of a method *ad litteram expressa*. Aside from the apoplexy and a couple of haughty withdrawals, the project went through successfully enough. Many of my translators will speak to me in the street, and Latin-American verse has not taken permanent injury.

My anthology is mentioned here not because of any contribution it may have made to inter-American enlightenment, but because of the implications of the theory of translation that I then held. In some respects it was, I must admit, a theory of despair. When poets talk about translating poetry, it is usual to begin and to conclude by saying that it can't be done. Certainly I thought then that it could not be done, and I spoke with considerable personal experience to support me. Obviously, if translation means a carrying across, it is nonsense to suppose that we should be satisfied with carrying across anything less than the whole. A poem is a total complex. There are details of it that can be represented adequately in another language, and it was upon these details that I was concentrating in my Latin-American speculations; but no one will mistake the details for the whole, and consequently a translation must fail to the extent that it leaves unaccounted for whatever aspects of the original it is unable to handle. Everyone knows what these aspects are: nuances of diction, of sound, of tone, that make any good poem a discrete experience, an entity somehow different from any other good poem ever written. *Quae cum ita sint*, as the schoolboys say, Herakles might just as well take off that lion skin and lay that shillelagh down.

Yet everyone also knows, paradoxically enough, that there are translations of poetry that do not betray the original, and that some of these may even be improvements upon the original. There is Poe, for instance, to go no farther from home. Poe may not be much to begin with, but he takes on a real authority in a foreign tongue. I can certify, thanks to my Andean researches, that *The Raven* and *Ulalume* and even *Annabel Lee* are very handsome indeed in Spanish, and it may be that in Quechua or Guaraní they would achieve the stature of real poetry. But this is dreaming; what I should like to suggest is the possibility of a parallel art, a technic that will find in the resources of its own language an answer to, and not merely a representation of, the special totality of the original. I can not write exhaustively about this possibility, if for no other reason than that I do not know enough about it; but I hope that I can indicate methods that might be investigated further, and exorcize, by concentrating upon a few details, some of the more insistent bugbears of translation. If in doing so I betray a wild inconsistency with my once puritan stand upon a peak in Darien, I shall account any change one for the better.

In an excellent essay on the difficulties of translating Pushkin,[1] Mr. Vladimir Nabokov states strongly his regard for the thoroughly documented rendering. If I remember his argument correctly, he contemplates a line or two of translation accompanied by notes of every conceivable kind — exegetical, semantic, aesthetic, metrical, historical, sociological — and his printed text would look, I should think, like an eighteenth-century Plato on my own shelves: a snippet or two of precious Greek surrounded by a sea of commentary. A tireless writer of footnotes, I find this concept endearing; but I am not sure that it is anything more. The trouble is that such a translation, though it might give the prose "sense" of the original together with an explanation of whatever goes to lift the prose sense above itself and transmute it into a form of art, might also provide no evidence beyond the saying so that the art was art in the first place. Accordingly one would have to fall back upon Mr. Nabokov's ability as a poet, rather than as an exegete; and this necessity seems to me to beg several questions. If Mr. Nabokov is a poet, well and good; clearly I have no evidence that he is not; but I suggest that if he is, and attuned, moreover, to Pushkin, a great deal of his passion is unnecessary. We need something at once less ambitious and more audacious: another poem. Not a representation, in any formal sense, but a comparable experience.

Comparable to what? To the original, one would hope; but if that is so, we shall have to decide what the original was — and this is by no means an easy thing to do, since it raises all sorts of accidental and subjective considerations. A man may be able to describe the effect that a poem has upon himself; but it is a commonplace that no two persons will be moved in exactly the same way by any one work of art; and if this is true of persons sharing a common social and historical predicament, how will they respond to a work composed perhaps hundreds of years ago and in an entirely unfamiliar setting? We may know what a lyric by Catullus does to us; but if Catullus were living in the next block and celebrating a Lesbia of our own acquaintance, we should not know what his poem did to Lesbia, or even to himself in his relationship to Lesbia. With the real Lesbia dead these two thousand years, the problem seems desperate. Largely, then, we must take the translator on trust, granting him a kind of vatic authority. We do as much, after all, for the original poet. The proviso (and it is a perilous one) must be that the translator prove worthy of that trust. He must be a poet as well as an interpreter. To put it more bluntly, his interpretation must be an act of poetry.

Any such demand as this will cancel a great deal of what passes for translation. The trots will go out with the earnest prose renderings, but no one suspected them of being poetry to begin with. More significantly, the translations in a self-contradictory form will be excluded. I am thinking here of the valuable, almost indispensable prose versions of Homer by Rouse, Rieu, and Chase-Perry; and I exclude them not from daily use, of course — that would be silly as well as ungenerous — but from the presumably ideal state of poetry with which I am now concerned. The canons of that state are strict, and if we apply them we shall not admit any work that falls short of poetic competence. The translation of a poem should be a poem, viable as a poem, and, as a poem, weighable.

i

It is time to get down to cases. I shall take first a poem of relatively low power, since inferior art sometimes gives us a straighter look at the difficulties involved than major work may permit. The late Enrique González Martínez, a Mexican poet whose verse should be better known than it is, once wrote a sonnet that has turned out to be a kind of rallying point for the post-Darío generation of writers in Spanish. It is an *ars poetica* in miniature, the declaration of an aesthetic; and it is one of those germinal poems that illustrate Archibald MacLeish's saying,

> A poem should not mean
> But be.

The sonnet interests me at the moment because it raises certain basic problems that a translator must face. We must always be asking ourselves "What is fidelity?" since so many of our other questions derive from that; at any rate, we must keep it in mind as we investigate González Martínez's contribution to the extensive and respectable corpus of the Swan Myth:

> Tuércele el cuello al cisne de engañoso plumaje
> que da su nota blanca al azul de la fuente;
> él pasea su gracia no más, pero no siente
> el alma de las cosas ni la voz del paisaje.
>
> Huye de toda forma y de todo lenguaje
> que no vayan acordes con el ritmo latente
> de la vida profunda. . . . y adora intensamente
> la vida, y que la vida comprenda tu homenaje.

Mira al sapiente buho cómo tiende las alas
desde el Olimpo, deja el regazo de Palas
y posa en aquel árbol el vuelo taciturno. . . .

El no tiene la gracia del cisne, mas su inquieta
pupila, que se clava en la sombra, interpreta
el misterioso libro del silencio nocturno.

What I find notable in the poem is the anti-poetic quality of a diction ironically at work upon a parcel of images — the Swan, Mount Olympos, Pallas Athene — of moribund conventionality. The force lies in the bland, apparently perfunctory management of the traditional symbols of poetry in an attack upon the spurious elegance of poeticism. One wrings the Swan's neck — presumably encouraged by Verlaine's advice in "Art poétique":

> Prends l'éloquence et tords-lui son cou!

— and then one salutes the descent of a sober dead-pan Owl: all of this in a style so carefully compounded of the lyric and the prosaic that one hardly knows which bird the poet really prefers. González seems to mean that plainness of statement is superior to rhetoric and that poetry should concern itself with the invisible springs of experience rather than its visible and all too easily prettified surface. Whatever prettiness of surface he permits himself, then — and there is quite a lot of it in his first four lines — must be taken either as an example of the qualities that he deprecates, or as an instance of sinning against the very proposition that he is defending. As I have said, this is an inferior poem.

However that may be, our immediate problem is translation. We may as well begin with a classroom exercise. What does González say? Word for word, he "says" this:

Wring the neck of the swan whose cheating plumage contributes a white note to the blue of the fountain. All he does is promenade his grace; he has no feeling for the soul of things or for the voice of the landscape. Flee from any form and from any language that do not chime with the latent beat at the heart of life. . . . Adore life intensely, and may life be sensible of your adoration. See the wise owl, how he stretches his wings and flies down from Olympos, leaving the lap of Pallas, to roost, in silent flight, upon that tree. . . . He has none of the swan's grace; but his restless eye ["pupil": but we are already too much in the classroom], affixed to darkness, interprets the mysterious book of the nocturnal silence.

There we have something; but even in my Simon Legree days I

should not have said that we have a translation of the poem. Accordingly, when we assert that González Martínez "said" whatever our prose paraphrase comes to, we do not really mean that this is the import, or even the content, of his sonnet. Something is missing; and what is missing, of course, is the complex of detail that establishes a poem and distinguishes it from any other kind of utterance. Hence we must consider the various stratagems of the saying, the devices, the tricks of expression; they will get us somewhere, though they will not take us the whole way. For example, what part does meter play in the totality of this poem? What of the contrapuntal effect of the run-on lines, say, in the second quatrain and the second tercet? What of the rhyme, so downright and homespun for a contemporary poet? As for a detail of diction, what shall we make of such a locution as *él pasea su gracia no más*, where the *no más*, instead of the more circumspect *solamente*, enforces an oddly *dégagé* "he-just-walks-around-being-beautiful" tone? (*¡Uf, qué calor! Ascoso, ¿verdá? — ¡Nomá!*) Let us see what another poet has done with all this.

The late John Peale Bishop was kind enough to make a translation of the Swan sonnet to serve as epigraph for the anthology that I have mentioned. The poem went through several versions, finally taking this form:

> Then twist the neck of this delusive swan,
> white stress upon the fountain's overflow,
> that merely drifts in grace and cannot know
> the reeds' green soul and the mute cry of stone.
>
> Avoid all form, all speech, that does not go
> shifting its beat in secret unison
> with life. . . . Love life to adoration!
> Let life accept the homage you bestow.
>
> See how the sapient owl, winging the gap
> from high Olympus, even from Pallas' lap,
> closes upon this tree its noiseless flight. . . .
>
> Here is no swan's grace. But an unquiet stare
> interprets through the penetrable air
> the inscrutable volume of the silent night.

One notices first of all that my literalist preoccupations failed to impress John Bishop. He has not been extravagant, but he has made additions to the original. For instance, there is nothing in the Spanish about the reeds' green soul or the mute cry of stone. These are Bishop's own ideas; but before we condemn them as distortions of González Martínez, we might consider how they came about. The translator felt — it was only an impression, but I think it was right in this case — that a Latin language can be more persuasive than English in dealing with such quasi-particularities as "the soul of things" and "the voice of the landscape," and that in order to achieve something comparable to this incantatory force — always assuming that it is worth achieving — the English demands a harder, more urgent kind of particularity. *El alma de las cosas* is too vague; let's specify a natural "thing" and give it a soul. *La voz del paisaje* could suggest anything from a billboard to a hungry vicuña; let's particularize a part of the landscape and by oxymoron — "mute cry" — provide it with a voice. Similarly with the troublesomely loose "blue of the fountain": the specificity of "overflow" is not in the Spanish, but the word does clarify, naturally and with rhythmic grace, an image that would otherwise be simply clouded. However, the additions are not the only alterations of the original. "This delusive swan" is more compact and more connotative than *el cisne de engañoso plumaje*, and "white stress" ("stress" is a masterly little invention here) works better in the imagination than the neat but rather tentative *nota blanca*. True, the second quatrain of the translation has its embarrassing moments; but they were already with us, ineluctably, in the Spanish. I remember that I did fight a losing battle over "adorati-on," both as a word in itself and as a five-syllabled monstrosity imported for the sake of rhyme; but Mr. Bishop replied tartly that any man confronted by such a philosophic tremolo as *adora intensamente / la vida* had a right to refuge his shame in an Elizabethan caper; and I can not say that he was wrong. At any rate, it is amusing to observe that the flatnesses of the English do not correspond with the conscious flatnesses of the Spanish, but occur where the original most abounds in alien corn: *el regazo de Palas*, for example, which somehow threatens to turn the owl into a cat or a pekinese; and *la vida profunda*, hauntingly set off by the suspension points dear to mystick writers and the authors of perfumery advertisements. On the whole, the Swan's neck is efficiently wrung, by both Señor González Martínez and Mr. Bishop.

The translation is a poem in English. I am willing to accept the idea that in its management of detail, its divergences, its elaborations and subtractions, it may not make the same effect that the Spanish does upon a Spanish reader; but I do not think that we should complain of this or assume that a failure of correspondence means a failure of translation. The alterations and refinements that we have noted are not, in this instance, betrayals. They are the legitimate, even necessary, prerogatives of the translator. Admittedly, in the hands of an incompetent poet they can amount to betrayal, and God knows that there are enough bad poets at large among the translators of poetry; but in the case of the Swan sonnet we have had an expert planning to carry the δύναμις of a poem from one language to another. If in execution he has produced a better poem than the original (and at least the first stanza of the English is superior to the Spanish), I suppose he is answerable for some kind of sin, although I should not care to assess it or expect Enrique González Martínez to feel badly treated in it. Good translation involves more than the communication of ideas and images with which I bludgeoned my unhappy co-anthologists. It is an act of poetry, and I do not now think that it can ever be anything else without risking failure.

ii

We have been working with a conventional set of problems, more or less in the round. *Tuércele el cuello* is right enough for a general demonstration, but I should like to look in a more detailed fashion at certain matters of form, allusion, and tone that I have found fascinating in practice and that may prove useful in discussion. Let us begin abruptly with a specific sorrow: the translation of wit.

A joke can be a nuisance. Nothing is more inert than a witticism that has to be explained. Topicality, the recondite allusion, special jargon — these are matters that can not be handled even in a Nabokovian footnote without inviting the embrace of death. Anyone who has tried to demonstrate that the drunken porter in *Macbeth* is funny will remember how frustrating a job it is, with all the talk about Dr. López and "equivocation" and the farmer that hanged himself in the expectation of plenty. The scene is one of the great dim stretches in Shakespeare, and not all your piety or wit can make it anything else; but at least we have it safely in English. We may be obliged to annotate it, but we need not worry about rendering it into an alien language. If we did, we should immediately run into a special sort of trouble. I propose to stage a clinical exhibition of some aspects of this trouble, taking as examples a notable joke from Aristophanes and an unpleasant little jeer of Martial's. The sobriety of the classics may come as a relief after the Swan of Tlaxcala.

Early in Aristophanes' *Frogs*,[2] Xanthias, a slave, has been torment-
ing his master Dionysos with a wholly imaginary visitation of something called The Empûsa — a dreadful monster that, like Old Man
Proteus, could assume all sorts of arresting shapes. Dionysos, a timid
bravo, has reacted in his usual manner; and suddenly Xanthias takes
pity on him and calls the whole thing off:

> *Xanthias*
>   It's all right, Master.
>
> *Dionysos*
>   What do you mean?
>
> *Xanthias*
>   As Hegélochos would say,
>   'After the storm I see the clam again.'
>   The Empûsa's pushed off.

The quotation from Hegelochos looks like a misprint, or perhaps a
variant of the schoolboy metathesis: "Keep your shirt on, keep clam."
Actually, it is worse than either: Dr. López has been equivocating
again. Let us investigate him for a while. Turning to the Greek, as
even a translator from the Greek must occasionally do, we discover
that what Xanthias actually says is, "After the storm I see once more
the polecat"; an inscrutable remark. The ancient commentators are
helpful, however. It seems that once upon a time there was an actor
named Hegelochos who blew up in his lines during a performance of
the *Orestes* of Euripides — a drama no longer extant, alas — and substituted the word γαλῆν ("polecat," or "weasel," or possibly "mar-
ten") for Euripides' γαλην' ("stillness of the sea," "calm after a
storm"). The slip must have been all but imperceptible, since it involves merely the difference in pitch between ῆ and η; but it was
enough to assure poor Hegelochos of an unenviable kind of immortal-
ity.[3] It also became proverbial, and Xanthias uses it as a limp comment on Dionysos' distress. So much would have been understood,
presumably, by the Greek audience; but what can we do with it
in English? Since the method is comic distortion, the mispronuncia-
tion of a harmless word in such a way as to produce an absurdity,
we need not consult either Dogberry or Mrs. Malaprop in order to
arrive at the *calm:clam* solution: it is a hoary one, certainly, but only
a cad would object to it. The polecat, meanwhile, is departed. But
can we simply let things stand as they are, hoping that the translation
will be funny enough to get us through? I should like to think so;

but there are still customers who will not dare to hear the twenty pairs of pants; * who will suspect the whole thing of being an enigma or a typographical error, and these people must be led through some such process as the one we have just traversed. After that, if they can still do so, let them laugh.

Here we have had an occasion when literal translation would have been useless. "Clam" for "polecat" is no license. It, or something like it — for there must be a happier *trouvaille* — points to the inevitable way out, the only graceful device that will carry the wit of one tradition over into another. The example is crude enough, and the solution is summary; but we may remember it when we come to a problem of greater subtlety.

My specimen from Martial provides such a problem involving considerations of innuendo, of ambiguous intent. The poem[4] is a pleasantry addressed to one Hormus, and it is obscurely in the fine Old Howard tradition:

> Quod nulli calicem tuum propinas,
> humane facis, Horme, non superbe.

That is all. The scene is a dinner table with the toasts going round. *Propinare* is to drink somebody's health: you took a sip and passed your cup to the person you wanted to honor. Martial says that Hormus never does this, that he keeps his cup to himself. Now there are several possible reasons for this unsocial behavior. Hormus may be ignorant; or he may have no friends to toast; or he may like his wine so well that he won't share a drop of it with anyone else, even in courtesy. Any one of these ideas would make a good insulting poem. But Martial, keeping them in the background, invents yet another possibility: Hormus is personally so unclean that even he has enough hygienic sense not to press upon another a cup that he himself has been using. His bad manners are really humanitarianism. . . . Not a very good joke, maybe: one misses the *sal Atticum* that can sometimes preserve even the most somatic of sallies; but it is a better joke than it looks. Two qualities keep it from being just another hiccough: metrical agility and verbal nuance.

The two verses are hendecasyllables counterpoised, the caesura of the second clashing just dissonantly enough with that of the first. Those mistaken enthusiasts who like to think that the classical quantitative meters can be reproduced in English will find that the hen-

* See Note 3, *ad fin.*

decasyllable is particularly troublesome: even Tennyson, whose ear was as keen as that of any poet in the language, did not come off very well with his handful of lines

> All composed in a metre of Catullus,

and Tennyson was not being inhibited at the same time by the necessity to translate. Nevertheless, we can be gallant enough to try:

> Hórmùs, yoú do not páss your cúp when toásting.
> Sóme sày 'rúdeness'; but *I* applaúd your hýgiene.

Well, a charitable man might call them hendecasyllables: each line has eleven syllables, and the stresses are correctly placed. Moreover, the shifting caesura sets up what may well be a delicate tension; and who can fail to be pleased by the *anceps* quality of the final syllables — short against long in quantity (unless the *i* of "toasting" is long by position), short against long in rhyme, with the added attraction of a British dropped *g* to give the composition a *cachet* of elegance? No, I have taken pains with this metrical experiment, but I have taken no comfort from it. Even the most charitable man will perceive at once that the only validity the lines have is that of a literary curiosity. The epigram has lost its point and acquired a battering knob. Martial was amusing himself with the connotations of the word *humane*, but the fun has disappeared in my translation. (I am not definitive, of course. The fun might be kept along with the metrical ingenuity; but I suspect that the technical oddness would shrivel the wit.) *Humane* is, flatly, "human-ly." Greediness is human; so is ignorance; pride (*superbia*) is human too. But "human," in English as in Latin, admits the gentler suggestion "humane": thus Hormus' human-ness is ironically described as an altruistic humanity, the characteristic of being "humane." Moreover, this speculative *humane* remains in suspense until the last word of the poem, where it is negatively defined as *non superbe*: whatever else it may be, it is not "proud." It is better to be a sot or a lout than to be proud; but it is better than any of these things to be considerate of the health of others. There is a real ambiguity here: the joke is not just another comic operation. On the surface we are being told, "Hormus isn't being haughty, he's simply being ornery"; but the latent sneer is a nasty one.[5]

Hendecasyllables may fail us, but we have less arcane resources. One, the eighteenth-century one, would be the heroic couplet. That siren is enticing, and I can imagine how Dr. Johnson would have modulated her song for Martial. But my ears are stuffed with the crass

wax of today: not even Mr. Robert Hillyer or Mr. Roy Campbell
can use the couplet now with complete confidence that he will avoid
the aura of exhumation, and I lack the vanity to presume where
these lyrists have so perilously succeeded. Besides, the heroic couplet
is too self-conscious a medium for my feeling about the poem, hendecasyllables or no hendecasyllables. Yet a compact form is needed.
Shall we turn to the limerick? Its connotations are generally ribald
when they are not Learishly nonsensical,[6] and neither of these tones
is appropriate here. A quatrain in the Long Meter of the hymnbooks
might serve if it did not tempt one to parody. Martial is not parody-
ing anything, unless it be the polite pretense of dinner-table conversation insisting that good old Hormus' motives are of the best. He is
simply being funny; but his fun depends largely upon the composure
of his form, the apparent decorum of his words.

After so long a prelude my own solution will seem dismally tame,
but I offer it anyhow, if only as an example of what not to do:

> You let no one drink from your personal cup, Hormus,
> when the toasts go round the table.
> Haughtiness?
>   Hell, no.
> Humanity.

I have been talking about the importance of form, and now someone
is sure to object that I have come up with a piece that has no form
at all. It is true that for the metrical dance of the original I have
substituted what an impatient reader may take to be a free cadence;
but it is not really free: the lines are measured, scaled down phrase
by phrase in accordance with a symmetrical pattern, and the repetition
of *h* does its part to bring about what the Elizabethans called a
"close." It is not a strict prosody, but neither is it *vers libre*. The
diction, too, has been carefully weighed. One may complain that
"Hell, no" is a gratuitous *cabriole*, unjustified by anything in the
Latin; but although it is clearly jauntier than the Latin, I defend it
on the grounds that Martial himself is committing a kind of solecistic
caper when he forces his hendecasyllables to perform so flatly. Herein
lies the etiquette of the poem. As for verbal expansion, we do have
twenty-eight syllables for the original twenty-two; but that was not
a reasonable objection in the first place. The expansion of image is
more significant: for example, the simple *propinas* becomes "drink
. . . . when the toasts go round the table"; but this is because we
do not observe the Roman custom of passing the cup (unless it be

a general loving-cup), and Martial's insult demands that we have this custom in mind.

This last point is of radical importance. I have been assuming all through this discussion that the original text may contain images, allusions, and the like, that the original audience accepted immediately, but that we, for one reason or another, find difficult. It does seem a pity that a mere joke should demand a Nabokovian apparatus; but actually, the least recondite of our native witticisms may call for something of the sort, although we usually satisfy the need without thinking much about it. Consider one of the finest flowers:

> ℣ Whom was that lady I seen you with last night?
> ℟ That warn't no lady, that wuz my wife.

"Not for philosophy does this rose give a damn," we might say; but as a matter of fact, a man who wanted to express its full aroma in a foreign language would have to go through syntactical and semantic exercises at least as complicated as those that we have undertaken in rendering Martial's little jibe, and I suspect that he would end up writing an exegetical Note. The Nabokov method, as I apprehend it, would translate all these details as "accurately" as possible and leave them *in situ*, relegating the explanation to the Comment. This process postpones comprehension and then threatens to paralyze it. Certainly it involves the loss of epigrammatic wit, where instantaneous recognition is desirable. Can explanation be incorporated with the translation, then, without clogging or sacrificing speed?

In the preface to his translation of the *Iliad* George Chapman points out

. . . . how pedanticall and absurd an affectation it is in the interpretation of any Author (much more of Homer) to turn him word for word, when (according to Horace and other best lawgiuers to translators) it is the part of euery knowing and iudiciall interpreter not to follow the number and order of words but the materiall things themselues, and sentences to weigh diligently, and to clothe and adorne them with words and such a stile and forme of Oration as are most apt for the language into which they are conuerted.

That is it: to weigh the "sentences" — "sentence" here meaning *sententia*, the "sense" of what is being said rather than the syntax, or arrangement of expression — and to find an appropriate "adornment" for them in his own medium. The literal approach may or may not be pedantic and absurd, but it can reduce a poem to debility, if not to downright blankness.

We must sometimes risk blankness. Aristophanes' reference to

Hegelochos may be an instance, and I dare say that there are readers who would be baffled by González Martínez's evocation of Pallas and Olympos. Even ordinary allusions to classical and biblical mythology may be lost today because the symbols themselves no longer seem to matter. It is possible that the time is not distant when

> Of Mans First Disobedience, and the Fruit
> Of that Forbidden Tree

will be as obscure a text as anything that you can dig out of Hesiod or Pindar. Then, unless we are prepared to face

> Sing *Adam*, Muse, in *Genesis* (first writ
> Of *Moses* Screedes) of Mankinde first Create,
> And his Refusall of the Hest eterne,
> By *Iove* proclaim'd, that hee the Tast eschewe
> Of that paine-fruitfull Tree (som say the *Mangoe*,
> Others, that better love the Lord, and bee
> With Holy Light inspired more, affirme
> The *Prune*), the which in *Paradise* upris'n,
> I. e., in *Eden* Parke —

but that way madness lies. If we have forgotten so much that Milton can no longer sing of the Fall of Man without involving himself in an exegetical apparatus, we had better turn for our poetry to his old enemy, Mr. Robert Graves.[7] But I am thinking of something less august. There is an anonymous epigram in the Greek Anthology [8] that says, quite literally,

> The fugitive from the bed of one
> A bed for many has become.

That sounds so Orphic that I think it should be left alone. I can "weigh the sentence," if you like, but I do not see how the explanation can be inflicted upon the text without losing all the force. By the time we have reflected that the girl who owns the bed is named Daphne, and that δάφνη is "laurel" in Greek, and that her bed is made of laurel, and that upon that bed, since she is a gallant lady, she entertains the men who visit her, and that for this reason she is inappropriately named for the original Daphne, a nymph, who, far from being a gallant lady, was so prim that she preferred to be turned into a laurel bush rather than submit to the advances of a god, that god being inflamed Apollo himself — by the time we have pondered all of this, and made a Note of it, the poem will have ceased to exist as a poem about Divine Irony or Poetic Justice and will have become just another heuristic exercise. Yet it is a brilliant little poem, and not even particularly esoteric. My own solution is to give it a pregnant title, *A Whore's Bed of Laurel*, and wait with confidence for the glassy stare.[9]

All of these examples have been jokes of a sadly trifling nature, but the *cruces* that they present are of the kind that must plague the interpreter in any poetry that he undertakes to translate or to explain. No detail is so slight that he can neglect it entirely, but he should remember how few those poets are who have written with absolute clarity for every reader in any time and in any place. He must be enough of a psychologist and literary historian to be able to judge whether or not a passage was obscure to begin with. If it was, it should remain obscure in his translation. He should be enough of a critic himself to be able to discriminate the mechanical operations of his original; and it goes without saying that he must be at least poet enough to make a new poem in the place of the other. Probably he will not often succeed; the pessimists say that he never will; but with insight, and sensitivity, and industry, and luck — luck being as important as anything else — he ought to be able to give an accounting that will neither disgrace his original nor annihilate himself. The way of the translator is hard, but it need not be desperate.

NOTES

1. "Problems of Translation: *Onegin* in English," *Partisan Review*, XXII (1955), 496–512.

2. *Ran.* 302 *sqq.*

3. People are still talking about it. Thus, Van Leeuwen, a modern editor of Aristophanes, makes the following observation, impressively in Latin: "Merry, that keen commentator [*emunctae naris editor*], aptly cites the comparable mishap of a tragic actor who uttered the phrase *Il a vaincu Loth!* ['He has conquered Lot!'], whereupon some joker or other in Nigger Heaven [*in subseliis joci aliquis appetens*] pretended that he had heard him say *Il a vingt culottes!* ['He owns twenty pairs of pants!'], and shouted back at him, 'Give some to the author!' One can well imagine what a laugh [*quantos civerit cachinnos*] this got from the house."

4. *Epig.* II, 15.

5. Cf. Martial, III, 80, for a similar tone, with the admixture of sexual abnormality:

> De nullo quereris, nulli maledicis, Apici:
>   rumor ait linguae te tamen esse malae.
> [You never speak ill of anyone, Apicius;
> and yet, Apicius,
> the story goes that you've a naughty tongue.]

6. Not always: solemnity is possible. One must work for it, however, and I myself have frequently been obliged to retreat into a learned language in order to achieve the high austerity of art, e.g.:

> Erat rex quidam nomine Brutus,
> rubigine linguae imbutus:
> rem λόγῳ gerebat
> ast ἔργον carebat,
> soloecismo salaci cornutus.

7. At the risk of imperfect comprehension, however: for what shall we make of that fine poem *To Juan at the Winter Solstice* without the commentary provided by *The White Goddess?*

8. *AP* IX, 529:

> Λέκτρον ἑνὸς φεύγουσα λέκτρον πολλοῖσιν ἐτύχθην.

9. Allusions may be "difficult" without being essential to the understanding, as in yet another epigram from the Greek (*AP* XI, 201):

> Ἀντιπάτραν γυμνὴν εἴ τις Πάρθοισιν ἔδειξεν,
> ἔκτοθεν ἂν στηλῶν Ἡρακλέους ἔφυγον.

[Send Antipatra naked to meet the Parthian cavalry,
And the Parthian cavalry
Will stampede at once beyond the last horizon.]

We do not have to worry about the Parthian cavalry: any troops would do as well, even the Ancient and Honourable Artillery Company of Massachusetts. My title, *Secret Weapon*, is unnecessary, although it does have a certain amount of topical charm, as does the subdued reference to Mr. Hilton's novel. The only danger is a reader who will not recognize "Antipatra" as a woman's name; but so dim a reader as that has no business sniffing around poetry to begin with. He is the irreducible blank.

PRACTICAL NOTES ON TRANSLATING
GREEK POETRY

THE TRANSLATOR, if he is human, will deal with most problems as he meets them. His principles will come out later, by way of self-explanation, or self-defence. This, at least, is what has happened to me. Still, it is convenient to formulate some of these principles, which were acquired in transit and have not always been consistently followed, as if they were guide-signs toward future practice. And maybe to some extent they will be that.

When I translate a piece of verse into verse, what do I want to do? Take for instance *Agamemnon*. Let me be clear about some of the things I do not want to do. First extreme: I do not want to write a schoolboy's pony, word by word, phrase by phrase. Such a translation would have to be in prose, because English verse, even a verse as free as mine which some friendly critics think is not verse at all, has its own demands, for cadence and color in word chosen and word placed, which will not agree with the "literal" construing. Other extreme: I do not want to take a base of Aeschylus and rewrite it after my own fancy. I do not propose to make Cassandra talk like, and therefore be, either (for example) a half-witted mountain girl who sees things or a confused socialite in need of psychiatry. If she talks as one of these, then one of these is what she is, because what she is is what she talks in this play, and nothing else.

What I wish to emphasize is the difference between the creative verse translation and the new version on an old base. The version of the second type is exemplified in Pound's recent *Women of Trachis* (though more plainly in some of Pound's earlier work) or in Jeffers' *Medea*. I do not have to have any quarrel with them. They are interesting, and the modern *Medea* at least is actable. But, in view of present reputations, I must say that I do not think either is really a translation. David Grene's *Oedipus the King* is Sophocles plus Grene; I even think that Gilbert Murray's now unfashionable *Antigone* is Sophocles plus Murray (plus also, if you must, Swinburne, Wilde, and Lewis Campbell); but Pound's *Women of Trachis* is zero plus Pound. That Pound's work is, to modern ears, and probably simply is, a better piece of English versification than Murray's is beside the point. Admire it, as Pound, if you can or must, or feel you ought to; it gives no Sophocles.

For different reasons, the last might also be said about Jeffers' *Medea*. He is a better translator than Pound, and probably his *Medea* is an improvement on Euripides (Euripides did better elsewhere). Still, there is a great deal in Jeffers which was never in Euripides. Jeffers has, for instance, fussed with the Aegeus scene, and made a bad implausible scene into a bad plausible one (perhaps so as to give Florence Reed material unsuited to Judith Anderson; this is *not* an improvement). More characteristically, the scores of animals, mostly wild, who stalk through Jeffers' play, are his own heraldic symbols. At line 2 the gray fish-hawk nests in the pines that made Argo. "My falcons," says Medea to her children. Jason is a tame stallion. Add tiger, hound, wolf, toad, serpent, etc. The Greek has only the lioness, and it is no compliment to Medea to call her that. What Euripides knew of brute nature, he mostly disliked. Jeffers loves it. This changes his heroine and his play. I understand he has tampered even further with the original Hippolytus in his new *Cretan Woman*, which I have still not read or seen. He is not likely to have improved *Hippolytus*.

Right or wrong, I think verse translation is something else. It is author plus translator. But the translator cannot put his author bodily into English. He must use all his talents, his understanding of the language and of the meaning of his original and his own skill in verse, to make a new piece of verse-work which represents, to him, what the original would be, might be, or ought to be, must be, in English. This will be neither the original-in-English only, nor the author-helped-by-original only, but a product rather than a sum of the two.

How best, then? Do not be afraid of your author. Grant that you are not as good a poet as your original, your Pindar, Simonides, Sophocles, forget it; sorrow over the fact will not help your translation. Do not, of course, patronize him either. No, but if you honestly find him less good than his own standard, should you improve him?

This is more difficult. But, in the first place, what you are improving may be, not the Greek, but just your own English version. "Blue-snooded Theba," writes a fine modern critic for a phrase κυανάμπυκα Θήβαν in one of Pindar's fragments. That seems to be just what the phrase means. Then, in Third Pythian, where the ampyx is gold, not blue, ought I to speak of gold-snooded Muses? I feel forced. Even if the unhappy phoneme *sn* plus long *u*-sound has not killed the word snood, even if there are no words in the language unusable for poetry (a very noble thought) I cannot handle snood in a noun-adjective compound here. It makes the gaudiest kind of poesy. What I find I wrote is "gold-chapleted." It is not accurate and it is not good and I am not proud of it. The alternatives are merely preposterous. Pound renders Sophocles' δασύστερνος of the centaur Nessus "with hair on his chest" and a contemporary critic finds this so good that he waves it at us as a reason among many reasons for all translators to take Pound as our model. To me, it seems that one moderately powerful four-syllable Greek word turns into a flabby phrase of five English monosyllables which wouldn't startle any bourgeois worthy of the name, though it looks as if it were meant to do just that. Pound's phrase is accurate enough, merely not good. Greek noun-adjective compounds are indeed troublesome. καλλίσφυρος ("with lovely ankles"?), βαθύζωνος ("deep-girdled" or what?) and numerous others, native to Greek, unnatural to English, represent a series of hazards for us to fall over as we come to them, as best we can.

Only, observe: all this breaking of the heart and beating of the breast goes on in *English*. There is nothing whatever wrong with our original χρυσάμπυξ. Greek welds words where English has to string them.

We come next to a hard question. Grant that I cannot deal successfully with χρυσάμπυξ, *why don't I just leave it out?* I should say, because Pindar had an adjective here, and to present the bare Muses is glaring misrepresentation. But will that satisfy anyone but me?

Let us take a larger instance, a characteristic passage from Euripides. There is a place in his *Trojan Women* where Hecuba, in the depth of her despair, explains to Andromache how words fail her, thus:

> I have never been inside the hull of a ship, but know
> what I know only by hearsay and from painted scenes,
> yet think that seamen, while the gale blows moderately,
> take pains to spare unnecessary work, and send
> one man to the steering oar, another aloft, and crews
> to pump the bilge from the hold. But when the tempest comes,
> and seas wash over the decks they lose their nerve, and let
> her go by the run at the waves' will, leaving all to chance.
> So I, in this succession of disasters, swamped,
> battered by this storm immortally inspired, have lost
> my lips' control and let them go, say anything
> they will.

After this disclaimer, she proceeds to argue rationally. It all seems to mean she has reached the point of sheer helplessness that sailors reach when their ship is obviously foundering at sea: nothing they can do will do any good, so they might as well stop trying to work the ship and give up; nothing Hecuba can say will do any good, so she might as well stop trying to speak sensibly, and say whatever comes to her mouth. But Hecuba, who of all tragic characters is least likely ever to have been to sea, is made, by an unspeakable little touch of misapplied realism, to explain that she doesn't really know what she is talking about when she talks about ships. All she knows is as much as Hippolytus knew about love, that is, she has heard some stories and seen some pictures. The passage is hopelessly bad: bad writing, bad drama, bad taste, the mobled queen at her mobledest.

What shall I do with it? Leave it out? *No.* But might I skip the grotesque introduction and strip the rest to a quick paraphrase, as:

> I feel like a sailor helpless in a sinking ship. What
> is the use of trying to do anything or say anything?
> But still, I'll try to talk sense. Listen, Andromache . . .

Perhaps this is neater, certainly yes, but the trouble is that *The Trojan Women* is an untidy play. There is no plot, and the length of it has to be filled with rhetorical arguments and declamations, some in worse taste than the one I have just been crucifying. Cassandra enters raving in white satin, explains that she is going to be sane, for a spell, so that she can expound a few points, argues like a school debater that the Trojans are really better off than the Greeks, then exits raving again. Hecuba can not speak of little Astyanax's archery without mentioning that the Trojans never carried athletic competition to excess. There are streaks of bad writing throughout this play. But again, the trouble is that in spite of it all, this is a great tragedy, though it isn't a neat one. To hack it up or streamline it would improve the neatness, but Euripides' play would be gone. The translator may have to swallow hard, but he must translate in full. If he can't, he had better leave Euripides alone. Euripides is not for perfectionists.

Then, besides such long fills, there are those padded lines whose spirit has been caught by A. E. Housman:

> May I then enter, passing through the door?

Dialogue is handed out a line at a time. If the speaker has to say more than fills a line, he must squeeze it, if less, more painfully, stretch.

The hand of Procrustes may be felt in my version of the recognition scene in the *Libation Bearers* of Aeschylus:

Electra
> Someone has cut a strand of hair and laid it on
> the tomb.

Chorus
>   What man? Or was it some deep-waisted girl?

Electra
> There is a mark, which makes it plain for any to guess.

Chorus
> Explain, and let your youth instruct my elder age.

Electra
> No one could have cut off this strand, except myself.

Chorus
> Those others, whom it would have become, are full of hate.

Electra
> Yet here it is, and for appearance matches well . . .

Chorus
> With whose hair? Tell me. This is what I long to know . . .

Electra
> With my own hair. It is almost exactly like.

Chorus
> Can it then be a secret gift from Orestes?

Electra
> It seems that it must be nobody's hair but his.

Chorus
> Did Orestes dare to come back here? How could this be?

Electra
> He sent this severed strand, to do my father grace.

Euripides saw long ago that the recognition by a lock of hair is silly, that the subsequent tokens, a footprint and a piece of childish weaving, are sillier. Surely, this passage in Greek is poor, and surely my English is worse. So shall I try recasting, thus:

Electra
> Someone has cut a strand of hair and laid it on
> the tomb.

Chorus
> Whose is it?

Electra

I can not understand it. This is no slave or hired
bodyguard. Nobody here has hair like that, except me.

Chorus

Clytaemestra and Aegisthus do. But they wouldn't put
it on Agamemnon's tomb. Could it be Orestes?

Electra

It must be.

Chorus

Does this mean he has come back?

Electra

No. It means he has sent his hair as a token of
respect for Agamemnon. If he came back, he would
not need to. So it means he is not coming back.

Is this an improvement? It says, I think, what Aeschylus meant to
say. If so, it says it more clearly. It is certainly snappier, although
while I lopped some lines I pulled others. The unsatisfactory result
is that, apart from the question of liberties taken with line distribution,
the lines as given do not belong with this play as written or with this
play as translated. First I quoted the scene out of context, and context is all. Then I made a brisk, lucid, reasonable exchange between
Electra and the chorus, for a scene of mechanism which cannot stand
being made brisk and lucid because it is not really very reasonable.
It can only stand as a clumsy bridge, an old wooden bridge, between
the impressive prologue and the still more impressive invocation
scene to follow. It expresses the kind of naïve charade which Aeschylus even so late was still capable of writing, and it is bad with a strictly
Aeschylean badness which does not damage the play as a whole, any
more than the armed rhinoceros damages *Macbeth* or Ossa like a wart
damages *Hamlet*.

I have been arguing against simplification or streamlining. There
is another kind of mistranslation, by improvement or simplification,
nowhere better to be seen than at the end of *Iliad* VIII in Pope's
famous version. First, let me give my own version, simply to show
the plain sense:

Such in their numbers blazed the watchfires the Trojans were
burning

between the waters of Xanthos and the ships, before Ilion.
A thousand fires were burning there in the plain, and beside
each

one sat fifty men in the flare of the blazing firelight.
And standing each beside his chariot, champing white barley
and oats, the horses waited for the dawn to mount to her
                                                    high place.

Now Pope:

> So many flames before proud Ilion blaze,
> And lighten glimmering Xanthus with their rays:
> The long reflections of the distant fires
> Gleam on the walls, and tremble on the spires.
> A thousand piles the dusky horrors gild,
> And shoot a shady lustre o'er the field.
> Full fifty guards each flaming pile attend,
> Whose umber'd arms, by fits, thick flashes send.
> Loud neigh the coursers o'er their heaps of corn,
> And ardent warriors wait the rising morn.

To this, apply Richard Bentley's "very pretty, but you must not call it Homer" or "the verses are good verses but the work is not Homer," whichever it was that Bentley said. He, the greatest classicist of his day, thought Pope had written a pretty poem but a bad translation. Why did Bentley say it isn't Homer? Surely, not because it is done in precise heroic couplets, because neither Bentley nor Pope would have considered any verse form more appropriate — almost inevitable, the numbers Pope lisped as second nature. And why ever called heroic if not for heroic poetry just like this? What is not Homeric is the way Pope has seen this night of war. The bare darkness has sprouted spires, because Pope saw a piece of antiquity, and antiquity needs a gothic gloom of buildings, preferably ruined, if not ruined at least dimly seen. The passage is better than very pretty; until the last few lines, it is sheer poetry. But it is non-Homeric in a deeper sense than can be told in a count of additions made. The gothic features dreamed into this stretch of translation make it an antiquarian piece; to Homer, the passage was not antiquarian at all, not even traditional or formulaic, but bold, realistic, modern, and incidentally, only half as long as the translation. Homer's warriors are not ardent and his horses do not neigh (they eat). Pope's spires and walls here are his own version of Jeffers' hawks, wolves, and stallions.

No translator, however, can escape being colored by his own time, and it is wrong to try too hard to cut free from this influence. One can not translate in a vacuum. This does not matter too much, for it is the *Iliad* and the *Oresteia* and the *Third Pythian* which are in-destructible and will continue to shake off one translation after an-other, translations which, when timely, for that very reason will later drop on to the accumulated pile of antiques. But these originals are not antiques and never will be.

The principal problem remains the problem I should have begun with, the problem of meter inseparable from the problem of word choice. Despite anything I may have said, the way toward making the best translation is to write in verse which is of our time. I do not mean this in any narrow sense. Contemporary verse offers a variety of variable forms unmatched, I think, in the history of our language; certainly it offers the chance of success in media far more variable than those which were thought available to Pope, or to Dryden either, or even to the Elizabethans.

The tendency, for most Greek verse, is now toward loose-beaten variations on a base of iambic blank, whose vagaries have been blessed with orthodoxy through the efforts of our founding fathers. This can work very well, but my own preference is for a medium based on the meter of the original, which I follow line by line wherever possi-ble. For short and simple stanzas like those of Sappho and Anacreon, the verse forms are almost entirely recoverable. This is partly true also for the six-beat iambics of drama. Hexameter is harder, and the heavy polysyllabic strophes of choral lyric are harder still, or im-possible, though they still must be tried. The major difficulty is in the texture of the language. First, the rudimentary inflections of English nouns and verbs make it hard to achieve those massive periods with suspension of main verb or subject which characterize Pindar. Second, English is resolutely monosyllabic, and Greek is not. This makes for trouble even in the simple iambics of tragic monologue. For instance, in a 49-line passage of *Trojan Women* I have, trans-lating as faithfully as I could, used 464 words to render Euripides' 255. Worse, of my words a monstrous 84 per cent are monosyllables, while Euripides has 27 per cent monosyllables, 38 per cent disyllables, and 26 per cent trisyllables. Mine reads differently, *of course*.

Necessarily, then, my translation fails to reproduce the Greek meter. It was bound to. So why try it? Maybe, I should say, precisely *because* I was bound to fail, because I should not care to succeed. We want a re-creation, not a reproduction. The shape of the original serves as what archers call point of aim. You do not propose to hit your point of aim, and if you do, you make a wretched shot, but you use it as the guide toward the mark you mean to hit but can not aim at directly. You should come out with something that reads as modern English verse, and yet not like any modern English verse ever yet written; at best, infected with some vital germination from contact with the great aliens; or at least, if nothing so positive has been granted, guarded by the form-base from the pompous or the ponderous as we find it in pseudo-Milton or pseudo-Shakespeare, and from the querulous, fatigued, self-pitiful progress of pseudo-Eliot, pseudo-Auden, or pseudo-Pound. What we get is a piece of pseudo-Greek, maybe, but not really, for it is not exactly trying to be Greek, and if vicious, at least with shining new vices all its own.

The line-by-line and base of original metric help also to keep translation from straying off into free variation, which should be done by deliberate choice, not by drift. This is where I began and where I must now end. Among the multiple objects which the translator of Greek poetry must keep simultaneously in mind, the chief one is perhaps this: to make from the Greek poem a poem in English which, while giving a high minimum of the meaning of the Greek, is still a new English poem, which would not be the kind of poem it is if it were not translating the Greek which it translates.

LATIN AND ENGLISH VERSE — SOME PRACTICAL CONSIDERATIONS

ROLFE HUMPHRIES

ELINOR WYLIE has a poem on the subject: *Bronze Trumpets and Sea-Water: On Turning Latin Into English* —

> Alembics turn to stranger things
> Strange things, but never, while we live,
> Shall magic turn this bronze that sings
> To singing water in a sieve.
>
> The trumpeters of Caesar's guard
> Salute his rigorous bastions
> With ordered bruit; the bronze is hard,
> Though there is silver in the bronze.
>
> Our mutable speech is like the sea,
> Curled wave and shattering thunder-fit;
> Dangle in strings of sand shall he
> Who smoothes the ripples out of it.

Now, like many other poems, this one Has a Lot of Truth in it, but Does Not Tell the Whole Story. Dryden and Pope, for example, managed to smooth quite a few ripples out of it; much of *Paradise Lost* resembles blocks of basalt masonry rather than the wonder of running water. On the other hand, Tibullus does not assay too much bronze, being *tener* all over the place. But, in general, the poem out-lines the main difficulty clearly enough — to keep the translation from Latin into English sounding a little harder, more bronzen, more (as Garrod has said) with the sound of a great nation in it than our mutable speech naturally contrives.

One difficulty everybody begins by talking about, the difficulty of converting quantitative to accentual meters. This difficulty, I believe, is greatly exaggerated. For one thing, Latin meters contain a large element of the accentual; in the hexameter, for example, one of the chief effects comes from the way in which, early in the verse, the accent pulls against the quantity, and, later, coincides with it. *Per contra*, in English verse, there is considerable use of quantity, and stress, much more often than not, falls on syllables long to the ear, if not long by mathematics.

By quantity we mean, I take it, a measurement of syllables, a decision as to whether they are long or short, and an arrangement in this or that pattern. In Latin the definition is perfectly clear: a long syllable is one which contains a long vowel or a diphthong, or a short vowel immediately followed by two or more consonants, a mute followed by a liquid (this may be old-fashioned terminology) being a possible exception. In English we have no such arbitrary distinction as to what makes a syllable long, what makes one short; no one who has aspired to writing quantitative verse ever gets around to defining his terms. Bridges' version of the *Aeneid* simply will not scan if you apply the Latin rules; Tennyson's "Look, I come to the test, a tiny poem/ all composed in a meter of Catullus" would need a north-country drawling of the first word, *Looook*, to make a long syllable of it. The Latin rule of thumb that a macron takes twice as long as a breve strikes me as pure convention; does any one believe that it takes twice as long as to say "My hats are" as "A hat is"? I have heard one theory to the effect that a monosyllable is long when it ends with a voiced consonant, short otherwise: thus, *hum* would be a long, *hut* short. What about *Huh?* That the man did not say. Our whole approach to this problem, when not dilettante and intuitive, has been, I think, empirical rather than scientific. Perhaps what is needed is for the poet to go around to an electronics man and get him to bread-board up some sort of instrument that can measure for him accurate-ly, and can tell him, finally, whether it takes longer to say *wire* than *ire* and *choir* than *wire*, and if so exactly how much; we might then have the basis for a system. Meanwhile, playing it loosely or strictly by ear, we can nevertheless feel reasonably sure that the effects of quantitative verse, if not the nomenclature, are to be found in English poetry. (W. H. D. Rouse used to be very fond of showing this with all sorts of samples from English songs.) Take a line of Keats' — "Robs not one light seed from the feather'd grass." Technically, iambic pentameter; at least that is the dominating meter of the poem in which the line is found. Actually, only an idiot, or a school teacher more obtuse than most, would insist that the line be read

(a)   ∪ | ∪ | ∪ | ∪ | ∪ |.

What it really goes like is the following:

(b) | | | | | ∪ ∪ | ∪ |.

If we follow the rules of classical prosody, we get

(c)   — — — — — — ∪ ∪ — ∪

which is certainly closer to (b) than to (a) above.

One more example, this time from Shakespeare — "Fear no more
the heat o' the sun/ Nor the furious winter's rages." Here there is a
little more room for difference of opinion as to stress and slack; I
would read

(a) | | | ∪ | ∪ ∪ |
      | ∪ | ∪ | ∪ | ∪

but I realize somebody else might make the second line come out

(b)   ∪ ∪ | ∪ ∪ | ∪ | ∪.

Classical prosody would leave no room for doubt, and not be far off
from either

(c)   — — — ∪ — ∪ ∪ ∪
         — ∪ — ∪ — — — — ∪.

So the English translator, whether he intends to or not, is bound to
bring over some quantitative effects; he cannot help having some
alternation between his long and short syllables, some counterpointing of length against stress, some coincidence of brevity and slack.

The trouble, I think, is not so much that we are accentual and the
Latins quantitative, but that their system permits, insists on, within
the line, a much greater variety among the feet. Once we start out
in iambic pentameter, every foot is going to be an iamb, dactylic
hexameter means five dactyls one after the other, and probably a
trochee, as the closest approximation, at the end of the verse. We
have no line that encourages the variety of the Hendecasyllabic: Spondee, Dactyl, Trochee, Trochee, Spondee or Trochee; nor the Sapphic:
Trochee, Spondee, Dactyl, Trochee, Trochee or Spondee. This does
not seem to me at all a question of quantitative *vs.* accentual; rather
of our ears' being too insistent on establishing a regular alternate
swat, once we get the thing under way: no reason at all, except lazi-
ness, why a man can't write accentual alcaics. Our great masters, of
course, are always contending against this monotony: they write two
eighth-notes for a quarter-note, substitute a rest for a half-bar; they
are always varying and counterpointing the ground rhythms; is "O
it came o'er my ear like the sweet sound?" to be read as straight
iambic pentameter, ta-DUM, ta-DUM, ta-DUM, and so on, or in three

groups of threes "O it came   o'er my ear   like the sweet" with a long close on "sound," drawn out? And, in the line, there are all sorts of secondary stresses for which we have no satisfactory identifying apparatus.

A good translation from Latin into English verse ought, for the sake of the contemporary reader, to sound, on the whole, more familiar than strange; yet in justice to the original, some hint, at least, of his quality, some *soupçon* of his foreign accent, must be kept. The problem is one of proportion, and a very nice problem it is. Take hexameters, for instance: in Latin, the verses run along, hardly any two identical; of the first seven verses in the *Aeneid*, the second comes out the same as the fourth, no other two alike. In *Evangeline*, I doubt there's anywhere near that much variety. I do not, however, hold that a translator would be well advised, though it might be within his powers as well as those of the monkeys in the British Museum, to present America with a version of the *Aeneid* that scanned line for line with Virgil's. Mr. Lattimore's *Iliad*, which I admire very much, does bother my ear at times because the strange seems to over-ride the familiar; on the other hand, I could find fault with my own version of Ovidian elegiacs as being a little too glib and easy-running. Working on Juvenal, I decided on hexameters, but this, in our usage, is a meter which is apt to run away with you, and unless I watch my step, my Juvenal — *horresco referens!* — might come out sounding like Longfellow. So I go back, pull up, force myself to write spondees (which do not come natural in English), roughen up the line with iambs even, get the run-ons to jar more, and hope, in the end, he won't sound like Ovid.

In poems of any length, the tradition of our language seems to prefer the pentameter line to the hexameter, whether in blank verse, in heroic couplets, or the rhymed stanzas of Spenser or Byron. This leads into another vexing problem, the matter of comparative length. The line, of course, is always a unit (and I wish people would remember that when they read aloud), and so to render line for line is, of course, the greater accuracy. Gilbert Highet is correct in saying that "If a translator takes a poem ten lines long, and turns it into a version containing sixteen lines, he has altered its proportions and sacrificed an important element of its art." Mr. Day Lewis, comparing my version of the *Aeneid* with his own, which used six-beat lines against my five-beat method, raised rather the same point; the shoe would have been on the other foot if I had used octometers. But there is a problem here not entirely related to the choice between pentameter and hexameter. The fact is that the translator from the Latin, to a greater degree than the man who is working from the Greek, is bound to use more words than the original. It seems like such a minor point, that Latin has no articles, whether definite or indefinite! (Greek, at least, has ὁ δέ, ὁ μέν, κτλ., a full set of particles as well as articles.) Latin can express a subject and predicate in one word, Latin does not have to use all those miserable little space-taking pronouns, articles, prepositions — he, she, it, the, an, a, of, to — words that, before you know it, creep in, like the termites they are, to eat away the whole fiber of a line. A youth in a seminar of mine at Yale, a year or so back, contended that the thing to do was use no articles whatsoever, and illustrated with a version of Catullus' poem on the death of his brother —

> Forced through many peoples much sea
> I've come brother to these "sad rites"
> to give last gifts of Death to you,
> speak nevertheless to mute ash
> since Fortune took yourself from me
> poor brother snatched suddenly from me.
> Now then through these which ancestors
> first custom hands down as funeral gifts
> accept much moistened with brother's tears
> But forever brother "hail and farewell."

I must say this doesn't seem to work, either.

Latin, an inflected language, makes possible effects that are impossible in our word-order English. Words not in agreement can be placed side by side for ironic effect; images can carry from one word to the next, the memory, the lingering overtone of the first making a chord, or a prism, with the second; the line, or the stanza, can be full of ambiguities or surprises, matters held in suspense, judgment on them changed as we go along, and the resolution not coming till the very end. Horace is the master of these effects, and the utter despair of all translators (except those who make him out a light-verse comic).

Nunc et latentis (somebody's hiding) *proditor* (somebody's betraying) *intimo* (something here about intimacy — betrayed?) *gratus* (the betrayer is welcomed, or maybe pleasing) *puellae* (to the girl, or maybe it's the betrayer of the girl) *risus* (Oh! now we see it's the girl's laugh giving her away) *ab angulo* (and now its's clear and we see how *intimo* fitted in).

Horace is full of such examples. To take a less complicated specimen,
examine an epigram of Martial

> Dicis amore tui bellas ardere puellas
> Qui faciem sub aqua, Sexte, natantis habes!

where most of the effect (overlooking, for the moment, the neat
playing off of *ardere* against *sub aqua*) lies in the postponement, till
the very last letter, of the knockout punch. I think it would be a fair
test of a student's understanding of the nature of Martial and epigram
to write this couplet on the board, with the last word omitted, and
ask him to supply it. Virgil's *Tendebantque manus ripae ulterioris
amore* conveys much, not all, of its emotional impact by the delay of
the last word; with the long *ulterioris* ahead of it, the yearning, the
longing, the desperate reaching out, stretching so far, has much more
impact than the mere picture of the souls holding out their hands in
love for the farther bank. ". . . .Their hands, in longing,/ Reach
out for the farther shore. . ." is the way I rendered it, and now that
I am talking about it, I don't think that's any too good. May I revise
— "Their hands reach out/ For the farther shore, in longing" —
that's a little, not much better; it still misses the long wait of a longer
equivalent for *ulterioris*, and Oh above all, it misses the sighing echo
of *ulterioris amore*.

That brings us to another responsibility, the obligation of the translator to try to keep the sound of the Latin, the effects that depend,
for their full value, on the emphasis of the sound. Our first impulse
is to think of English, compared with the Romance tongues, as an
ugly, unmusical language, too full of gutturals, like German or
Welsh, or too much mush and potatoes in the mouth, no lovely vowel
music (and never mind about Housman or Tennyson). Actually, I
think (some scholar ought to check this), English has more vowel
sounds than Latin; I know we have at least one it does not have, the
repulsive A as in hat. Where the trouble really lies is in our proportion
of vowels to consonants; my rough guess is that Latin, by and large,
runs to not more than two consonants to one vowel or diphthong,
whereas English, to cite an extreme example, deliberately wrought
by Housman, can pile things up like this —

> And then the clock collected in the tower
> ITS STRENGTH AND STRUCK.

We have to *hear* the Latin, to *listen, listen, listen* for the play of
sound, for instances like Catullus' *Diversae variae viae reportant,*

where the intricate linking of the v and r consonants and the variation on the short i vowels and the ae diphthong is like the Welsh *cynghanedd*. What can we do, in *Vivamus, mea Lesbia, atque amemus*, with the abrupt axe-stroke of *lux* at the end of the line, with *nox* the first word of the next, and then, by contrast, the interminable effect of the long u in *una*, and the long words running on in *perpetua dormienda?* "Light/night" won't do it — a little too shrill, t not as final a severance as x, and then *perpetua una dormienda*. Better give up. My Yale youth (op. cit.) obviously either did not notice, or was not impressed by, the music of the Catullus elegy — the dominance of the m consonant, the *ah* and *oo* vowel sounds, the dreadful choking up of *et mutam nequicquam alloquerer cinerem*, the sinking thump of *adempte*. The translator should read every line aloud; he should saturate himself with the cadence and rhythms; is it asking too much of him to lend an ear? Or to have one?

A more prosaic problem. Proper names, whether of personages or places. We all know how, as soon as a word begins with a capital letter, boys and girls get the absolute horrors and tie their tongues all up in knots over words that would bother them no whit in lower case. They prove stumbling-blocks to the translator, too; for one thing, quite a few of them won't scan if you've changed the meter around. But the problem is more troublesome than that. In Ovid's story of Phaethon, for example, should we bring over the name of every single burning river and mountain? The purist will answer in the affirmative; but here is where one will get you ten if you are positive that *l'homme moyen sensible* is not going to do some skipping. Some names, whether of place or person, let's face it, mean nothing to us in allusion or connotation, and one of our obligations to the original author is not to bore his audience. I like to think that one of the passages Virgil, had he lived long enough, might have stricken from the *Aeneid* is X, 747–754,

> Caedicus Alcathoum obtruncat, Sacrator Hydaspen,
> Partheniumque Rapo et praedurum viribus Orsen,
> Messapus Cloniumque Lycaoniumque Ericeten
> illum infrenis equi lapsu tellure iacentem,
> hunc peditem. pedes et Lycius processerat Agis;
> quem tamen haud expers Valerus virtutis avitae
> deiecit; at Thronium Salius, Saliumque Nealces
> insignis iaculo et longe fallente sagitta.

The confidence with which commentators can identify this one or that one as Trojan or Rutulian never ceases to amaze. I am sure, in my translation of the *Aeneid*, I was tempted to skip these lines, but on looking it up, I find I have the names all in there, all fifteen of them. My usual method is not so scrupulous. I will, at least, suggest a catalogue, but am apt to abridge it; occasionally I will include, in the text proper, material that would otherwise have to go in an eye-dropping footnote, occasionally I will substitute the general for the specific, "mountain" for *Othrys*, "wine" for *Lageos*, modernize the name of a town, writing Yerevan for Artaxata at the end of Juvenal's second satire.

This leads into the business of solecisms, anachronisms, improprieties, neologisms, and archaicisms. In only the last of these need we commit meticulous avoidance. On very rare occasions your original author deliberately perpetrates an archaicism; mostly he does not think of himself as a classic, but as a modern. And even if you do follow him closely in his performance (but how can you archaicize *Ast olli* in translation?), you cannot be sure the reader does not ascribe to you, rather than to your original, his peculiar effect. In this connection, the problems of the second person singular have bothered me no little. I am sure that Bridges' version of *Aen.* VI, 377 — *sed cape dicta memor duri solacia casus* — "Let my sooth a litel thy cruel destiny comfort," and the Loeb Library translator's rendition of stanza XI of the Pervigilium Veneris — *ipsa vellet te rogare, si pudicam flecteret/ipsa vellet ut venires, si deceret virginem* — "Herself she would ask thee, if she might bend thy virginity; thyself she would thou camest [sic and ! !] if that were meet for a maiden" — I am sure that these are dead wrong. On the other hand, our *You* seems, at times, a little crude and impolite, especially in a prayer, with a relative clause ensuing: "Apollo, you who. . ." Yoo hoo, Apollo! I think the neatest way to get out of this is by turning the modifying clauses into nouns — "Apollo, always our pitier," some such device.

It seems to me that in all the respects above, save archaicisms, we need to remind ourselves that the great writers commit these torts, if so they be, sometimes, perhaps, through ignorance, more often through deliberate hatred of nicety and wanton exuberance of strength. Virgil makes contemporaries of Aeneas and Dido; Shakespeare gives Bohemia a sea-coast and makes coral plural; Shelley tells the West wind to "be thou me." And we really have no way of knowing with assurance the extent to which their use of vernacular, of slang, of neologisms, of words coined by themselves made such expressions an

authentic and respectable part of our idiom. The Loeb Library translators are mostly, it seems to me, shockingly shocked by grossness;
they emasculate their originals by making the specific general, by
ambiguous vagueness, by omissions. To render the grosser epigrams
of Martial into Italian instead of English is peculiarly comic, but at
least it affords an opportunity for academic jokes, "Oh, the reason
they do that is because they think Italian is the only language God
can't understand." But when it comes to the point, as it does in the
edition of Juvenal, of putting the word as *d—n* — well, really! This
kind of a translator should be locked up in a cage with an original
author, preferably carnivorous.

Do writers ever know, beyond the immediate circle of peers and
friends whose approval they covet, the nature and scope of their
audience? The translator can pin-point his own circle of readers
perhaps a little more closely. He knows that at one pole he will find,
and must at least make some effort to please, the scholars. These men,
in many ways, know more than he does, and he must benefit by their
superior wisdom. Yet they are not easy to please; some of them, one
suspects, resent his intrusion. A vested interest of theirs, it seems, is
somehow threatened; their proprietary rights include every variant
reading, including the conflicting ones. They are peculiarly prone to
resent liberties, to insist on literalness, even at the expense of literacy.
The translator should not thumb his nose at them, but he may,
occasionally, have to shrug his shoulders; their eyes and noses, poor
chaps, are sometimes so much better than their ears. On the other
hand, we must not dash madly from them only to fall into the embrace of the vulgar popularizers, the boys who really ham it up
pandering to what they conceive to be the modern taste. (Horace,
more than any one else, has been the victim of this approach.) The
translator hopes, for his author's as well as his royalties' sake, that he
will reach many readers who do not have the original language; he
hopes that his work will not entirely satisfy them, that across their
consciences there will occasionally flutter a nuance of regret that
they could not have read the author in his own language.

In the final analysis, the man whose praise the translator must
solicit above all others is the original author. Not long ago, talking
about translation to the students and faculty of St. John's in Annapolis, I confessed that my conscience was not entirely easy about
having turned Ovid's chariot-races (*Amores* III, 2), into American
flat races, working in even the stable-colors carried by Nashua. This

horrified some devotees of the Great Books, I cannot say beyond words, but the more they protested, the less anxious my conscience became. I felt surer by the minute that could I sit down beside Ovid and say "Look, chum, we don't have this kind of race here any more, but we do have something more or less equivalent; come on out to Belmont with me and see. And, anyway, it isn't the kind of racing that's important, it's what the boy and girl in the grandstand are doing, isn't it? Would you mind if I tried it this way?" — I would have received his blessing. On the other hand, I know I must not do things that would make my author, in so far as I can understand him beyond the text, in so far as I can, with my imagination, enter into his spirit, cringe, wince, or look for the nearest exit. I know I can never do him complete justice; if there are rare moments when I think I can improve on him, and not violate his spirit, I must not, out of modesty, refrain, for I shall already have weakened so many passages that the debt is still all on my side. What I do, I do with a double knowledge of my inadequacy, looking toward him in the past, looking, beyond our day, to the future when men will think my work not at all in the idiom of their time. It will all have to be done over again, anyway; *post mea mansurum fata superstes opus!* is a prayer the translator knows can never be answered with any excessive life expectancy.

THIRD THOUGHTS ON TRANSLATING POETRY

"I, too, dislike it."

JACKSON MATHEWS

ONE THING seems clear: to translate a poem whole is to compose another poem. A whole translation will be faithful to the *matter*, and it will "approximate the form," of the original; and it will have a life of its own, which is the voice of the translator. The difference from original work lies mainly in the restriction of working upon matter that is already composed.

The translator may misread his model in a number of ways; he may not see what is to be seen nor hear what is to be heard in it. But if he does see and hear clearly and fully, he will hold the original poem in a sort of colloidal suspension in his mind — I mean a fluid state in which the syntax, all the rigid features of the original dissolve, and yet its movements and inner structures persist and operate. It is out of these that he must make another poem that will speak, or sing, with his own voice.

Probably not very much that is useful can be said about the requirement to be faithful. Deciding to translate a poem is, at the start, a matter of perceiving *what* the translator hopes to be faithful to. But in being faithful, he must not give the effect of being so, that is deadly. It also makes for unfaithful translation, for no such effect could have been in the original poem. It is only on later examination, by comparison, that a translated poem should appear to be faithful; but that is another matter, it is not reading the poem. Being faithful without seeming to be — that is one of the "secrets," one of the special joys of this labor. A translator should make a good lover.

In the "approximation of form" (a term I have borrowed from Valéry) the motive is invention, not imitation. The translator has to invent formal effects in his own language that give a sense of those produced by the original in its own. This is working by analogy. The temptation is much greater in poetry than in prose to fall under the spell of the model, to try to imitate its obvious features, even its syntax, or to mimic the voice of the other poet. The usual mistake is to believe that the form of the model must somehow be copied; for example, that the French alexandrine, having twelve syllables, must be rendered in English by a twelve-syllable (or a six-beat) line. This is the error of literalness. It badly marred, as I have said elsewhere, the translations from Baudelaire done by Edna St. Vincent Millay and George Dillon. My feeling is that a well-managed pentameter is the only English line, for very complex historical, physical, and other reasons, that can approximate the effects of the alexandrine. The opposite mistake is to pay too little attention to the form of the model. Although Day Lewis' translation of the *Cimetière marin* has its charms as an English poem, I have always held against it, as a translation, that it gives too little sense of formal relation to the original.

Every language has its own forms, actual and possible: those which poets have already found and used, and those still to be found. The forms come from the sounds, rhythms, meanings, and all the relations that poets can discover among these and bring into perceptible existence. It is the business of poets to find the combinations, and that means inventing them.

The possibilities of form as they are felt by poets at any moment in the life of a language make what might be called the metrical situation. This sort of generalized formative impulse does seem to exist as part of a poet's awareness of himself and other poets. Whether he thinks much about it or not, and however he may feel it, or feel about it, he is generally aware of it. For instance, the situation in America now seems to be one of fairly free play within fairly settled forms. But since the impulse to invention is rare and personal, there is a constant tendency for forms to settle more and more. A slack formality is always ready to take the upper hand, and stasis in these matters is bound to bring on crisis. In France at the moment, the situation seems to be turning with the younger poets toward a renewed impulse to form, after a period of "poems in prose," which itself was in part a rejection of Valéry and an effort to survive his impact.

Just as every way of translating poetry is partial, every way of judging the results is partial. It is one of the most hazardous, and it nearly always appears to others as the most whimsical, of all literary judgments. Yet the final test of a translated poem must be *does it speak, does it sing?* In spite of the restrictions under which he works, in spite of his sense of fidelity to another poem, a translator is bound to sound out for himself. The poem he is writing is also his own. In it he is obliged to take over, to give a sense of command, to make his creative will felt. His instruments are style and his own voice. These can set him free to compose. The model, if it is to be translated, simply has to take the consequences of being transmuted into another voice, which is its new life. Every saddened reader knows that what a poem is most in danger of losing in translation is its life.

Ezra Pound's way of being faithful, or unfaithful, in his Chinese translations has excited a good deal of comment but has scarcely been defined. I am told that Pound has never wanted to learn Chinese as a language, that he does not speak it and has little interest in hearing it spoken. This helps to understand his use of it. His interest is in good part etymological. How could the roots of a language not be one of the richest sources of its poetry? A poet must be at least an amateur philologist; he may be a learned one and be a better poet for it.

What has long absorbed Pound's interest is the Chinese written character. Chinese may be unique in the way its etymologies have been transmitted — preserved and not preserved in the compound vestigial images that make up its ideograms. Pound has explored these written signs for traces of the pictures that went into their formation — the old *Imagiste* engaged in a kind of etymological archaeology. What he has hunted for are the shadowy images, the shades that may or may not haunt the penumbra of the Chinese mind. Whether the Chinese themselves are generally aware of these when they speak or read does not matter to Pound; he is persuaded that they are there waiting to be brought back to light. He is doing what he has always believed to be the business of poetry, taking care of language. Revivifying the faded image, reviving the meanings lost in banality and dead usage: he has taken Rémy de Gourmont's idea of language and put it to the test of a whole gamut of uses. Pound's method with Chinese aims to make the far past of words active, which generally means translating *everything that is left out* in ordinary modern usage. The fact that he has worked with ancient texts should help justify the technique. Yet no wonder so many Chinese say he is wrong — he tells them that their words mean more than they think.

Etymological method is by no means peculiar to Chinese or to Ezra Pound; poetry in any language doubtless has its ways of invoking the past of words. What gives the peculiar sense of depth to the language of Paul Valéry, particularly in his poems but in his prose also, is his way of bringing etymologies into play. To look into his words is to look down through their history — like looking into a well, measuring its depth by the distance from ourselves at which we see ourselves reflected.

Pound is a master of rhythmic invention in verse; there is probably no one who would want to dispute this. Yet how wrong he has been at moments about language. Consider a remark of his on rhythm: "Let the candidate fill his mind with the finest cadences he can discover, preferably in a foreign language, so that the meaning of the words may be less likely to divert his attention from the movement." (*A Few Don'ts.*) This is a misapprehension of the way sound and sense work together, but it is a worse mistake about the very nature of rhythm in language. Rhythm is the one feature of a foreign language that we can probably never learn to hear *purely*. Rhythm and the meaning of rhythm lie too deep in us. They are absorbed into the habits of the body and the uses of the voice along with all our earliest apprehensions of ourselves and the world. Rhythm forms the sensibility, becomes part of the personality; and one's sense of rhythm is shaped once and for all on one's native tongue. If one happens to have several "native" tongues, the sensibility responds I suppose like Babel, with confusion, and one's sense of language fails to take on the *meaning of rhythm*. It may have been this experience with English that kept Santayana from becoming a poet, his sensibility having been formed in Spanish. He felt that it was so, and said so in a preface to his *Poems*, written in 1922: "Even if my temperament had been naturally warmer, the fact that the English language (and I can write no other with assurance) was not my mother-tongue would of itself preclude any inspired use of it on my part; its roots do not quite reach to my centre. I never drank in in childhood the homely cadences and ditties which in pure spontaneous poetry set the essential key." Whatever one may think of his notion of "pure spontaneous poetry," Santayana was not wrong about the "cadences" of language. And I do not think that the example of Conrad contradicts this point; Santayana also wrote fine English prose. It is a matter rather of the difference between the uses of rhythm in prose and in poetry. Once a sensibility has been deeply formed in a language, it is bound to hear other languages comparatively, to feel their rhythms against the background of its own. A one-language poet does not have this comparative measure in mind (and body). Some poets feel that it is better not to learn a foreign language at all, that its rhythms are likely to impair or at least to conflict with their own. The danger for a one-language poet is that he may not become conscious enough of his own language, of language as objective matter to be worked upon.

It seems to me, in short, that Pound has always thought about the music of poetry too much in terms of music, too little in terms of language. This is a habit he probably picked up from some of the later French Symbolists, maybe Albert Mockel. It was not an error that Mallarmé would have made, whose idea was to "take back from music" what he knew belonged to language. Pound on the French poets says almost nothing about Mallarmé and Baudelaire.

I should now like to look closely at a little known translation. The first publication of Part I of *The Hollow Men* was accompanied by this "adaptation" into French by St. John Perse (*Commerce*, Paris, 1924).

Aumône aux hommes de peu de poids

Nous sommes les hommes sans substance,
Nous sommes les hommes faits de paille.
Pressés en foule fraternelle,
têtes bourrées de paille. Hélas!
Nos voix stériles, si tout bas
nous murmurons en foule,
sont voix plus douces et plus vaines
que le souffle du vent parmi l'herbe stérile,
que la course des rats sur les débris de verre,
dans nos caves stériles.

Ombres sans forme, nuances sans couleur,
force sans mouvement et geste qui ne bouge . . .

Ceux qui s'en furent
droit devant eux, vers l'autre Royaume de la Mort,
songeant à nous, s'ils songent à rien, n'évoquent point des âmes
violentes et perdues, mais seulement
les hommes sans substance,
les hommes faits de paille.

The translation is admirable. The voice of St. John Perse is heard in the first words, *Aumône aux hommes de peu de poids*; and continues to sound unmistakably in *sont voix plus douces et plus vaines, geste qui ne bouge, ceux qui s'en furent droit devant eux*. There is constant invention of figure and form; and yet everyone who has the

English poem in his ear — and who does not? — will feel at once the strong formal relation to it.

As usual, the points of "departure" from the original are the points of interest. It is probably impossible to waken in French the historical allusions in the phrase "a penny for the Old Guy"; these are difficult to catch in America and it is doubtful how immediately effective they are even in London. Perse has simply turned the line into one of his own, bearing directly on the subject of the poem. The only question about it is whether, lacking the ambiguities of the English phrase, it doesn't contradict some of the poem's intentions?

Pressés en foule fraternelle is not the same figure as helpless scarecrows "leaning together," supported by nothing but one another. Yet Perse's figure comes nearer than one might think, at a first glance, to producing the same effect as the other. *Foule fraternelle* is doubtless the French equivalent of "souls" without individuality, instinctively forming a crowd to keep from feeling "lost"; and *fraternelle* renders the notion of leaning on one another. The reader who takes this sort of alteration of figure to be a mistranslation has much to learn about translating poetry. The figure is faithful in the full sense.

The only phrase in the French text that seems to me a mistranslation is *s'ils songent à rien*. Here one's attention is misdirected. The comment falls upon "those who have crossed with direct eyes," whereas it should fall on "the hollow men"; and the devastating effect of the words "if at all" is lost.

A nicety of formal invention may be observed in the line ending with *n'évoquent point des âmes* in relation to the next; these lines in French do not exactly coincide with the English but create the right effect — being faithful, as they should be, by analogy.

There is one departure that seems to derive from an essential difference between English and French. *La course des rats sur les débris de verre* is a correct translation of "rats' feet over broken glass," but it substitutes motion for matter. It seems that French will not tolerate the kind of concreteness which consists in bringing the rats' *feet* into central focus, which is just what makes the English line. This case may be in part explained, if the point is not too boring, by the static nature of French prepositions. In English, motion in the figure is expressed by "over," but in French the motion is transferred characteristically to the noun, *la course*. Imagine if you can a literal French version: *les pattes de rats sur les débris de verre*. Here the rats stand still, if they are there at all, which is doubtful — as in a bad snapshot, they can hardly be seen for their feet. The line is clearly impossible.

It may be worthwhile to give another example of this "essential difference" between two languages. I am reminded of Gide's handling of a famous figure in *Hamlet*: "O most wicked speed, to post with such dexterity to incestuous sheets!" Gide was clearly much puzzled, perhaps annoyed and even repelled by the figure and wit in the phrase "to post with such dexterity." He first translated the line, *ô hâte abominable, à se glisser entre des draps incestueux*, skimping the figure altogether, making haste to get the lady into bed more fittingly than by posting. But he was not satisfied, for in a later edition *à se glisser* becomes *à s'embusquer*, which is certainly livelier, more concrete, but it is only a little closer to Shakespeare, and it contradicts the bald-faced public aspect of the Queen's marriage. I take it that the odd mixture of suggestions that flicker through the English phrase (lady on horseback, a quick and clever gallop into bed) is to the French "logic of imagination" and taste repellent and indigestible.

What Paul Valéry has written about poetry is surely the most penetrating account a poet ever made of how he wrote his poems. His ideas on translation will illuminate and, I believe, support much of what I have been saying.

Like nearly everyone else who has thought about the translation of poetry while doing it, Valéry was of two minds: he thought poems were untranslatable; and he thought translation was the nearest thing to writing "pure poetry." But perhaps these are not contradictory notions. If the translation of poetry is impossible, perhaps it is so exactly in the same sense that "pure poetry" is impossible. "I use the word pure," said Valéry, "in the sense in which the physicist speaks of pure water. I mean that the question arises of knowing whether one can manage to construct one of those works which may be pure of all nonpoetic elements. I have always held, and I still hold, that this aim is impossible to reach and that poetry is always a striving after this purely ideal state."

Poetry is a kind of writing that uses all the resources of language. It is involved bodily in the particular language of which it is made, and does not evolve out of it, as prose tries to do and seems to do. Painters, sculptors, and musicians can be understood beyond the borders of their own country, but a poet, as Valéry says, is never profoundly, intimately, and completely understood and felt but by his own people: he is inseparable from the speech of his nation. . . . The prose writer, the novelist, the philosopher, can be translated, and often are, without too much damage. But to the poet belongs the privilege and inevitable disadvantage that his work cannot be translated either into prose or into a foreign language. A true poet is strictly untranslatable. . . .

On the other hand, the impossibility of translating poetry has never kept translators from their labor. Rather the contrary, it may well be what keeps them at it. Translations after all do exist and do continue to be made, and Valéry admired some of them as some of the finest poetry in his language. In a late essay (1941) on some seventeenth-century translations from St. John of the Cross made by a certain Father Cyprian, he wrote:

> This former Inspector of Finances . . . turned Carmelite was accomplished in the fine art of writing verse in the pure state. I say *writing verse in the pure state*, and by that I mean that in the work I am discussing, his share is limited to fashioning the form. All the rest — ideas, images, and choice of terms — belongs to St. John of the Cross. The translation being extremely faithful, there remained for the versifier only the very restricted freedom jealously allowed him by the severity of our language and the strict rules of our prosody. . . . His originality is to admit of none, and yet he makes a kind of masterpiece by producing poems whose substance is not his own and each word of which is prescribed by a given text. I can hardly refrain from claiming that the merit of so successfully completing such a task is greater (as it is rarer) than that of an author entirely free to choose his means.

I know of no other passage anywhere that holds quite so much cheer for the translator of poetry. The right sort of praise, knowing praise, of translation surely must be the rarest article in all of literary criticism.

At moments Valéry seemed to think of translation as the model of all writing:

> Writing anything at all, as soon as the act of writing requires a certain amount of thought and is not a mechanical and unbroken inscribing of spontaneous inner speech, is a work of translation exactly comparable to that of transmuting a text from one language into another. [Or again] The poet is a peculiar type of translator, who translates ordinary speech, modified by emotion, into "language of the gods," and his inner labor consists less of seeking words for his ideas than of seeking ideas for his words and paramount rhythms.

It would seem then that Valéry considered the translator as an original artist working (like a Chinese miniaturist) within severer limits and for this reason composing in a purer medium than an original poet. The translator's contribution is in the inventions of form, and this for Valéry is the essence of the matter. His respect for "the inventors" is even more exaggerated than Pound's, as we see in this bit of fancy:

> Sometimes I am the kind of man who, if he met the inventor of the sonnet in the underworld, would say to him with great respect (if there is any left, in the other world):
> "My dear colleague, I salute you most humbly. I do not know the worth of your verses, which I have not read, but I would wager that they are worthless, for the odds always are that verses are bad; but however bad they are, however flat, insipid, shallow, stupid, and naïvely made they may be, I still hold you in my heart above all other poets on earth and in Hades! . . . You invented a *form*, and the greatest poets have adapted themselves to that form."

But to return to Father Cyprian's own inventions, Valéry wrote of them:

> It is impossible to be more faithful — even though our reverend translator has modified the form of the stanza. He has adopted our octosyllabics instead of following the variations of the original meter. . . . Unlike other translators (particularly in the 16th and 19th centuries), he has not attempted to impose on French what French does not itself impose on or propose to the French ear. This is really to *translate*, which is to reconstitute as nearly as possible the *effect* of a certain *cause* (here, a text in Spanish) by means of *another cause* (a text in French).

But Valéry did not write about translation without having tried it himself. He turned to it on occasion, for use, practice, or pleasure, throughout his life. A youthful notebook is filled with passages translated from Leonardo's manuscripts; among his early poems are two sonnets, one from Petrarch, another from Dante Rossetti; later on he translated some of Poe's *Marginalia* and Thomas Hardy's last poem, *Felling a Tree* (*Commerce*, 1927). This is by no means a complete list. One of his last important works was a full rendering of the *Eclogues* of Virgil. And the account he gave, in "Variations on the Eclogues," of how he went about them makes one of the finest modern essays on the art of translation.

As always with poetry, Valéry's mind moved behind the finished poem toward the moment and the act of writing it. It was the act of composition itself, from its beginnings in sensibility down to the finally composed (but never "finished") poem, that held his mind more than anything else. He had spent much of his life observing this process in himself. In order to translate the *Eclogues*, he felt that he must "observe," by imagining it, the same process in Virgil — a technique he had used long before in describing the "method" of Leonardo. The intimidating age and fame of the poems he was to translate did not balk him, though he recognized in irony his presumption in treating these famous poems as if they were his own. "At moments, as I fiddled with my translation, I caught myself wanting to change something in the venerable text. It was a naïve and unconscious identification with the imagined state of mind of a writer of the Augustan age. . . . I could not help looking at the text of the *Eclogues*, as I translated them, with the same critical eye as at French verse, my own or another's."

Valéry's method was to imagine the moment of composition, the "still fluid state" of mind of the young Virgil, who was working at a time when Latin poets were already highly "conscious of the means" of their art. And he did not fail to draw the analogy with his own beginnings, relying on his experience in the craft of poetry to help him to imagine the "nascent state" of those other poems now "crystallized in their fame." He put the matter this way:

> The work of translation, done with regard for a certain approximation of form, causes us in some way to try walking in the tracks left by the author; and not to fashion one text upon another, but from the latter to work back to the virtual time of its formation, to the phase when the mind is in the same state as an orchestra whose instruments begin to waken, calling to each other and seeking harmony before beginning their concert. From this imagined living state one must make one's way down toward its resolution in a work in a different tongue.

The aim then was "a certain approximation of form." We have seen, in the case of Father Cyprian's *Canticles*, that Valéry understood this clause to mean the invention of forms suited to the translator's own language and related to the original by an analogy of effects.

> Having sworn on this childhood Virgil to be as faithful as possible to the text of these occasional pieces which 19 centuries of fame have rendered venerable and almost sacred . . . I decided to write a line for a line, an alexandrine opposite each hexameter. However, I did not even consider making the alexandrines rhyme for this would undoubtedly have led me to make too free with the text. . . .

> > Hic tamen hanc mecum poteras requiescere noctem
> > Fronde super viridi. Sunt nobis mitia poma,
> > Castaneae molles et pressi copia lactis;
> > Et jam summa procul villarum culmina fumant,
> > Majoresque cadunt altis de montibus umbrae.

Reste encor cette nuit. Dors là tout près de moi
Sur ce feuillage frais. Nous aurons de bons fruits,
Fromage en abondance et de tendres châtaignes.
Vois: au lointain déjà les toits des fermes fument
Et les ombres des monts grandissent jusqu'à nous.

Valéry wanted his lines to reconstruct with as little loss as possible the *sense* of Virgil's lines, but that sense had to be wed to the *sound* of the French line, for Valéry was composing in French. His lines had to sing in French, for Virgil's had sung in Latin. That was his first consideration; it is the consideration *sine qua non* in being faithful, as it is the basis of all analogy of forms in two languages.

A few words on a practical point. I have insisted, elsewhere, that verse translations should not be printed facing their models. The life is knocked out of translated poems by the kind of misreading they get under these circumstances; they can never get a whole hearing for themselves.

There would seem to be only two alternatives: to leave the originals out, which gives the impression of shirking comparison, or to divide the book in halves, one of translations, the other of originals, which is not a happy solution for the book.

Actually there is a third alternative, which I now believe is the right solution. Verse translations should be given the position of privilege, by themselves, and followed by the originals with facing prose translations, the three in one volume. My point is that the true place and function of prose translations is to come between verse translations and their models, forming a kind of bodyguard for the verse. The reason is that prose translations define and illustrate what the verse is *not* trying to do. They take the onus off the verse of being expected to say exactly what the original says, which no verse translation can do and live. Verse translations will equally define and illustrate the limited function of prose translations, and prevent anyone from taking them for poems — avoiding in this way the dangers of prose paraphrase.

Could it be that the antique question, should verse be translated into verse or into prose, has found its answer: *both?*

FROM FRENCH TO ENGLISH

JUSTIN O'BRIEN

As a translator I am an amateur. So was Jacques Amyot who contributed signally in the Renaissance to forging a French prose style by translating Plutarch; so was Sir Thomas North who in turn translated Amyot so well that even Shakespeare could quote an English Plutarch without amending a word. When John Wyclif worked on the first complete rendering of the Bible into English, he doubtless considered himself an amateur — as his model, Saint Jerome, probably also did after his long labors had produced the Vulgate.

The truth is that no one *wants* to be a professional translator — partly because the guild enjoys no particular dignity or respect and partly because the occasional translator is generally better than the one who, making a living at his task, is obliged to accept almost any assignment. Now God forbid that, having said as much, I should lose my amateur standing by these remarks on the art of translating.

Some years ago Valery Larbaud, the subtle creator of A. O. Barnabooth and introducer of Joyce's *Ulysses* to the world, who had spent long years translating into French Samuel Butler, Hawthorne, Sir Thomas Browne, and many others, thought of writing an essay to be entitled (I am translating here myself) "On the Eminent Dignity of Translators in the Republic of Letters." Obviously, it would have been something of a parody of Bossuet's famous sermon "On the Eminent Dignity of the Poor in the Church" and its development, Larbaud tells us, would have run rather like this:

> The translator is unappreciated; he is seated in the lowest position; he lives so to speak on alms; he is willing to perform the humblest functions and to play the most unobtrusive parts. "Be of service" is his motto, and he asks nothing for himself, priding himself on being faithful to his chosen masters, faithful even to the point of suppressing his own intellectual personality. To pay no attention to him, to refuse him all consideration, to name him, most often, only to accuse him — generally without proof — of having betrayed the writer he aimed to interpret, to scorn him even when his work satisfies us amounts to holding in contempt the most precious qualities and the rarest virtues: abnegation, patience, charity itself, and scrupulous integrity, intelligence, subtlety, broad knowledge, a rich and ready memory — virtues and qualities some of which may be wanting in the best minds, but which are never found united in mediocrity.

I already feel ennobled simply from having set down these richly charged words in the manner of the silver-tongued Bossuet. Larbaud never did write the projected *pastiche* to glorify the humble servant of literature, but he saved this heady outline and incorporated it into a long essay entitled "The Patron Saint of Translators" devoted — of course — to the career of Saint Jerome. From the various writings of Jerome he pieced together a prayer which, addressed to that patron, should be on the lips of every translator as he sits down, surrounded by his dictionaries, reference books, and scratch pads, to his selfless task: *O Doctor Optime, aggrediar opus difficillimum . . . Nunc te precor ut me orationibus tuis juves, quo possim eodem spiritu quo scripti sunt libri in Latinum transferre sermonem.* For the pleasure of translating this pious prayer I shall proceed as if my readers did not understand Latin: "Excellent Doctor, light of the Holy Church, Blessed Jerome, I am about to undertake a task full of difficulties, and even now I beg you to aid me with your prayers in order that I may translate this work into English [for obviously we should have to supply *Anglicum* instead of Jerome's *Latinum* or Larbaud's *Gallicum*] in the very spirit in which it was composed."

Hilaire Belloc felt much as Larbaud did. He began his Taylorian Lecture of 1931 by saying:

> The art of translation is a subsidiary art, and derivative. On this account it has never been granted the dignity of original work, and has suffered too much in the general judgment of letters. This natural under-estimation of its value has had the bad practical effect of lowering the standard demanded, and in some periods has almost destroyed the art altogether.

But it is not my aim to deliver a panegyric on the unjustly neglected translator. Rather, mine is the more modest assignment of relating some of my experiences in translating from French to English. Perhaps one should say from French to American in view of the vast difference in idioms. English reviewers (and there would be much to say of American translators and English reviewers) have more than once deplored what they call "transatlanticisms" whereas American reviewers sometimes complain that Sartre's street-urchins have been given a Kensington accent.

It is only fair to state that what I have to say divides itself (as translators from the French are regularly supposed to say) into three parts: (1) Why translate? (2) Who should translate? and (3) How to translate?

The first question is readily answered. We can begin by rejecting all vulgar considerations of gain, because, although people have made small sums through translating, I doubt if anyone whose name we can remember ever *began* translating for that reason. Unfortunately publishers know this too. No, I am speaking about those who feel a *vocation* to translate. Four considerations can enter into the decision to translate, and the first of these is the desire to exercise one's faculties while perfecting one's knowledge of a foreign language. Just think of all the maiden ladies in Victorian parsonages throughout the English counties and our New England states filling the attic with neatly penned versions, an occupation which passed the time of day in those happy, pre-television times.

In my generation we began learning a foreign language by painfully rendering word for word a simple text of Maupassant, Daudet, Schiller, or Manzoni. Then, just as we were acquiring skill at this stultifying maneuver, we suddenly became self-conscious about the "direct method" which aimed to make us *think* in French, German, or Italian. Direct translation by means of a bilingual vocabulary was rigorously outlawed. Finally, our formal schooling over and still unable to formulate even rudimentary thoughts in any tongue but our own, we thought we could revert to our early experience and make satisfactory versions of the writers we were then discovering. The results were most often disastrous, though the exercise may well have been salutary. I began in this way as a very young man during a holiday at Portofino Mare (two decades before the Roman branch of Hollywood discovered that picturesque seaport) by doing a few pages of Valery Larbaud every day. Naturally, I was rather proud of the result — until, on the recommendation of a friend of the writer, I sent Larbaud the typescript. It came back with interfoliated sheets of blue writing-paper watermarked "Smithson's," one to each page, which clearly revealed that Larbaud not only possessed his own language but also appreciated the subtleties of mine far better than I. It was a humbling experience, the effects of which lasted almost twenty years.

An equally disinterested reason for translating is the hope of penetrating more deeply into an alien civilization. Goethe once remarked that through translation one's awareness of the untranslatable reveals the differences between cultures. Certainly the Abbé Prévost recognized this after putting into French Richardson's *History of Sir Charles Grandison*, for he wrote in his preface: "I have suppressed or reduced to the common customs of Europe everything in the customs of England that might be shocking to other nations." That was the France of the Bourbons, but a hundred years later the shoe was on the other foot, and Sir Lascelles Wraxall, writing in the age of Victoria, apologized for having cut two or three pages in his translation of *Les Misérables* "because," he said, "the French is a bolder language than the English, and I could not find the proper equivalents in which to convey Cambronne's extraordinary reply and the conclusions which Victor Hugo draws from it." The sophisticated writer of today, however, knows what Hugo did not know and leaves nothing to chance. In one of Jean Cocteau's plays a Hollywood-bound starlet, whom we have learned to detest in the course of three acts, leaves the stage definitively after shouting the *mot de Cambronne* and slamming the door. Now, Cocteau in his notes on the roles writes: "Sortie de Liane. Une langue qui ne possède pas un mot analogue à ce mot qu'elle jette avec une violence terrible qui lui enlève toute vulgarité, devra le remplacer par quelque insulte courte et injuste." If there is any justice in the author's assumption that his play will someday be translated, I can suggest to the English-language translator just the word for this particular scene: it is quite obviously *bitch* . . . monosyllabic, unjust under the circumstances, and ideally suited to accompany the slam of a door.

Sometimes such an experience may even lead to the conclusion that certain works had best *not* be translated. Raymond Guérin, writing in *La Parisienne* of January 1954, wondered why Maupassant is so exaggeratedly admired outside of his native country and concluded that the very banality of his thought and poverty of his style had facilitated his credit abroad. The mere fact that Maupassant's work is more easily accessible to a foreigner than that of Rabelais, Racine, or Proust leads M. Guérin to the generalization that "the most convincing criterion of the quality of a work is the fact that it can only be translated with difficulty," for if it passes readily into another language without losing its essence, then it must have no particular essence or at least not one of the rarest. And finally the critic concludes: "If Americans [we are the barbarians, of course] . . . if Americans want to be capable of enjoying Fargue or Breton, Michaux or Follain, let them learn to read the text. And we likewise, if Chaucer or Forster attracts us!" We must credit him with an interesting, if unorthodox, choice of American authors. This is a defensible point of view, and certain recent American translations of French poets encourage one to agree with M. Guérin. Yet, on the other hand, if the published translation reads "throat high suspended" (instead of "high hung breast") for *gorge haut suspendue* (as in one volume) or (as in another) "horses on a frieze" for *chevaux de frise* (a military term long common in English and regularly given in our dictionaries), obviously it will take some preparation before even those who might seem most qualified will be able to read those poets in the original. Still, it just happens that Henri Michaux — one of the poets mentioned by the French critic as having a very special flavor — has been particularly well translated here.

Remember also that if such an attitude as this were carried to its logical conclusion it would prevent the translation of any but the writers with the least rare essence. As George Sampson stated: "You have only to consider how much of the world's literature is translation to see that theoretical objections to translation are empty air."

The third reason for translating, which is also an excuse for beating in the doors of publishers with one's manuscript, is the laudable desire to communicate, to share one's enthusiasm for an unjustly neglected writer or work. This is at once the commonest and the most sophisticated motivation. All translation is an interpretation, an explication, of a beloved text. Hence the act of translation appeals to anyone possessing the instincts of the teacher. But the would-be translator should beware, for the shelves of remaindered items groan under the weight of translations for which America was not ready. In this sense the French critic was right and, barring such happy exceptions as the meeting of H. J. Kaplan and Raymond Queneau, of Sylvia Beach and Henri Michaux, of Jackson Mathews and René Char, many titles had better be left to those who can read them in the original.

The fourth reason for translating — let's be frank — is that it offers a way of enjoying, with but little creative effort and less creative power, a position on the fringe of Beautiful Letters. Translation is, after all, a legitimate form of plagiarism, ever offering the hope of rising to fame on borrowed wings.

So much for the *why* of translation. As for the second question — *who* should translate? — I can be quite categorical and therefore briefer. Inasmuch as translation is the carrying over into a new form of something already existing in another form, the original matter must be re-created and yet remain recognizably the same matter. If I read you the following lines in the French of Fernand Baldensperger:

Pourquoi donc si blême et si jaune, amant?
    Pourquoi donc si blême?
Serait-ce, cruelle à tout bien portant,
    L'air souffrant qu'Elle aime?
    Pourquoi donc si blême?

You will recognize at once Suckling's lines beginning

Why so pale and wan, fond lover?

It is, furthermore, axiomatic that the ideal translator should work from a language he knows well into his own, native language. Indeed, a double rule might be laid down for translators: (1) that they must possess perfectly the language *from which* they are working (in the case of a living language they should be able to speak and write it fluently) and (2) that they must control even more intimately all the resources of the language *into which* they are translating.

Insufficient knowledge of the foreign language produced such howlers as I have already mentioned. If the one translator had ever looked at the advertisements in any popular French magazine, he would have known that *soutien-gorge* has nothing to do with what we call the throat; and if the other had noticed the juxtaposition of barbed wire with his *chevaux de frise*, he would not have thought of sculpture. Some years ago a justly respected American poet rendered into English an even more honored French poet, stumbling over almost every deceptive cognate in the long list of "false friends," mistaking the antecedents of pronouns, generally so clear in French, and jumbling the tenses of the original in such a way as to make the already obscure original seem limpid. The publisher, I believe, soon withdrew the book from circulation — but not before the *New Yorker* had hailed this "admirable translation" and the New York *Times* had praised the translator's "great service in making [this French poem] so easily available to American readers." You see, then, why I insist upon the obvious.

Yet it is manifestly unjust to dismiss a translation, as certain critics have lately tended to dismiss Scott Moncrieff's version of Proust, because of occasional misunderstood words or phrases when other, more essential qualities are preserved. Guiding a French illustrator through the volumes of Proust, I fell upon some examples that shocked me. The artist being French, we were working from the original, although the paintings were to accompany the English version. Only

after he had depicted Marcel's first view of the little Gilberte over
the hawthorn hedge holding a *bêche de jardinage* or garden-spade in
her hand did we discover that Scott Moncrieff had her holding a
"trowel." The illustrator simply painted a somewhat higher hedge —
so that we shall never know what Gilberte has in her hand. In another
case Scott Moncrieff had transformed a part in the back of a dandy's
head to a pleat down the back of his greatcoat. But these are petty
contresens, and probably every translator who has ever worked has
been guilty of some such. Dryden, who had encountered these problems himself, insisted that the translator who would express himself
as vividly as if he were writing an original "must never dwell on the
words of his author." In fact, absolute verbal accuracy is less desirable
than reproducing the tone of voice and rhythm of the original.

One can, indeed, go one step further and say with Alan Conder,
who is responsible for some of the best English versions of French
poems, that "to single out a particularly happy line in a poem and to
expect to find its perfect counterpart in an English version is, to say
the least, somewhat unreasonable." Some loss in melody or evocative
power or both is almost inevitable. Perhaps I can illustrate more
clearly by moving from English to French and citing another example
by Fernand Baldensperger, who was responsible for the rendering of
Suckling quoted earlier. Everyone knows the opening of Keats'
sonnet:

> When I have fears that I may cease to be
> Before my pen has glean'd my teeming brain . . .

This is the way the French poet has valiantly approximated it, and I
doubt if his lines would satisfy anyone brought up on the English:

> Quand j'ai peur de finir ma carrière, avant
> Que ma plume ait glané le rêve qui m'enivre . . .

No, it is the whole poem that matters and on its success the translator must be judged. This time, without giving the French original
at all, let me offer two versions of a pithy quatrain so that you may
judge which you prefer: Henry Carrington translated it thus:

> You everywhere speak ill of me;
> I everywhere speak well of you.
> But lo! our common failure see:
> None thinks what either utters true.

And Alan Conder gave it this form:

To all men thou dost slander me;
To all men I speak well of thee.
How sad to think we're dubbed a pair
Of arrant liars everywhere.

Is there not something snappier, more truly epigrammatic, about one of these versions? And don't you feel, once you have read it, that there is no real need to know the original?

But I am getting away from the purely linguistic qualifications of the translator, and so much the better. I hope I suggested earlier that one should *never translate anything one does not admire*. If possible, a natural affinity should exist between translator and translated. When Rainer Maria Rilke, who was to re-create in German some of Paul Valéry's most beautiful poems, first read the French poet, he wrote to a friend that he had discovered an *alter ego*. Of course we cannot all hope to bring to our French poet what Rilke brought to the interpretation of Valéry, but we can at least choose a subject, or victim, who is greatly congenial to us. André Gide, admired in France for his sensitive versions of Shakespeare, Blake, and Conrad, once reflected that if he had been Napoleon he would have imposed on each writer worthy of the honor the task of enriching his own literature with the translation of some foreign work having an affinity with his own talent. Thus, for instance, André Maurois might be asked to do *Tristram Shandy*. Such a system would simultaneously be a boon to literature and to the individual writer, who would unquestionably gain both in mastery of his craft and in humility. Of course some central office would have to record each would-be translator's choice and examine his qualifications; otherwise certain periods in the last seventy-five years would have seen a general rush to do Nietzsche or Dostoevsky or Ibsen and today everyone might want to translate Kafka or Camus.

Still, without such a system and without Gide miscast as Napoleon, is it too much to ask that the translator possess a somewhat similar cultural background to that of the author he is translating? If he does not have it, at least he should be willing and readily able to make up for this deficiency. In other words, he ought to have read most of the books his author has read, heard the same music (if music matters to that author), seen the same works of art (if works of art matter), and been in the same places. Not long ago an American publisher brought out (I can't imagine why) a group of mediocre and long outdated essays by François Mauriac entitled *Proust's Way*. The

translator, evidently not familiar with Proust, had not checked with
the standard English version of his work. Consequently, each time
Mauriac referred to that section of Proust known in English as *Swann
in Love*, it came out as *One of Swann's Loves*. I did something similar
when I had Gide refer to Bach's *Inventions for Two Voices* when the
title should have read *Two-Part Inventions*. But, inasmuch as the title
occurred only once and was not the principal subject even of the
passage concerned, I like to think that my mistake was not so serious.
For some time, after all — possibly even for years — the translator
will have to identify himself with his chosen author, submerging his
personality in that of another. And one always hopes that he can do
so without having to indulge in the contortions of the rubber-man
from the circus.

It should be clear that I have gradually slid from my second point
to the third. But such confusion between the *who* and the *how* is
inherent in the subject, for once the ideal translator is found, he or
she will find his own method of working. In truth, it is certainly
presumptuous and most likely useless to attempt to draw up a set of
rules. One translator, who had worked chiefly on and in verse, said
that it is "as impossible to suggest any guidance for translators as it
would be to write a primer for poets."

Yet, while hesitating to prescribe, I can at least outline my own
method — which has the advantage of agreeing in the main with the
modus operandi of other translators whose work I admire. To begin
with, the tools used by anyone working from French to English are
not numerous; all the standard dictionaries, both French and English,
plus (despite all the unpleasant things everyone has said about bilingual
dictionaries) the two-volume one by J. E. Mansion, published in
England by Harrap and here by D. C. Heath, on condition that it
not be relied on slavishly. In addition, Roget's *Thesaurus* for that
elusive synonym or antonym, and Fowler's *Modern English Usage*
(to which may well be added the companion *Modern American
Usage* by Horwill). Not long ago, for instance, I paused over this
expression in Camus' *Mythe de Sisyphe*: ". . . le décalage constant
entre ce que nous imaginons savoir et ce que nous savons réelle-
ment. . ." I knew what *décalage* means — one of those learned-seem-
ing words which nevertheless figure in the vocabulary of every
Frenchman. The first thing that came to mind was "gap" or "interval,"
neither of which would do. A glance at Mansion proved of no help
at all, for his dictionary gave merely "staggering, shifting, displace-

ment, difference of phase (of current), etc." The elusive term — *hiatus* — leaped out of the pages of Roget and I translated the phrase as ". . . the regular hiatus between what we fancy we know and what we really know. . ."

These are not the only essential tools. In a *Partisan Review* article on this same subject, my colleague Jacques Barzun says: "It is a sign of the unprofessional character of the business that no translator with whom I have talked had ever heard of *Les Faux Amis* by Koessler and Derocquigny or *Le Mot Juste* by J. G. Anderson." Alas, the two aids he mentions are probably as neglected as he says, yet it is hard to imagine a conscientious translator from the French who does not keep at his elbow those illuminating collections of deceptive cognates, unless — and this is even better — he has to a large extent absorbed their contents long before he even thought of translating.

Everyone who deals with French has his own list of those bothersome near-homonyms which generally present a quite different meaning in French and English: *confier* and "confide," *demander* and "demand," *prétendre* and "pretend," *sympathique* and "sympathetic." (Some years ago while preparing a special issue in honor of André Gide, an undergraduate editor asked me to secure a letter from the elderly writer, which Gide gave on condition that I should translate it. The closing read *en toute sympathie*, which I transposed into something equally anodyne involving the word "sincerely." What was my horror on publication day to find that the zealous editors had changed this to read: "With every sympathy" as if they had collectively lost their grandmother!)

To expatiate on such ambiguous false friends, however, is only to emphasize a point that is even more false — that translation is largely a matter of verbal equivalences. It most certainly is *not*, and everything I have said so far should only reinforce this statement. In the July 1954 issue of *Les lettres nouvelles*, Edmond Jabès has a rather haunting sentence: "Les mots qui se cherchent ont le regard triste des amants séparés." I should translate this as "Words looking for each other wear the sad expression of separated lovers" and assume that the author was thinking of pairs of words in a single language: adjective and noun, verb and adverb, verb and preposition, for instance. The quest of the *mot juste* has driven many a writer — witness Flaubert — to the verge of madness. As a child, Gide rebelled against a dogmatic teacher who tried to convince him that certain words were made to go together by natural affinity and consecrated custom. But, like most real poets, the boy insisted on the virtue of "bad company" among verbal frequentations. It is doubtless this kind of thing that M. Jabès had in mind; yet his remark enlivened by its memorable metaphor could apply also to translation — the equivalent in one language of a word in another language. Such an equivalent in the particular context of the moment, with all its connotations or Empsonian ambiguities, *does* exist. The translator feels he has it on the tip of his tongue, on the point of his pen, but somehow it does not come forth. Forget — this is my advice in such cases — forget the problem and the anguish written on the face of the lover bereft; leave a blank and the first time you reread your work, before the final typing of course, the desired expression will slip as if automatically into the blank space you have hopefully left for it.

But such a thoroughly recalcitrant expression is the exception. Even as he picks up a text and reads it for the first time, I like to think, the experienced translator will understand it fully and feel as if he *could* re-express it smoothly in his own language. When he thinks for the moment solely in the language of the original — French for our purpose — nothing remains obscure to him; it is only when he reverts to English that the difficulties begin. In my own practice, four steps make up the act of translating. First, I read and reread the text as a whole to absorb it and, as it were, make it part of myself; this is where some sort of identification with the author takes place. Proceeding, I do this specifically for each chapter, paragraph, and sentence as I come to it. Secondly, I write out the best version I can make, after weighing all possible alternatives that come to mind. Theatrical producers, I am told, will often contract for what they call a "rough translation" which they can then give to some playwright, ignorant of French, so that he can make from it a smooth and free "adaptation." Yet there is no such thing as a "rough translation" from the point of view of the translator. Each of us makes the best version of which he is capable, and it is as fantastic to think of a translator as to think of a poet producing on command either a "cheap product" or a "quality product." Thirdly, after putting the first version aside for a time, I come back to it and read it through without reference to the original, making changes wherever necessary. This is the point where at least one reading aloud is essential, for the final translation must stand on its own. In the fourth place and as an ultimate precaution, I check the resultant second version with the original text, the details of which I have by then happily forgotten, just to catch any passage where I may have deviated too far from the text.

Even with such cautious checking and re-rechecking, errors will persist. I recall with recurrent blushes a dreadful one early in the second volume of *The Journals of André Gide*. At the end of a discussion of the contribution to French literature made by Jewish writers, Gide insisted upon the non-French characteristics of such writers. The whole passage is potential dynamite because it suggests an intellectual form of anti-semitism. Not unaware of this, I got the idea that he looked on such writers as really thinking in a different, a foreign, language and having to translate their thoughts into French. Accordingly, this is what I made Gide say: "I do not deny, indeed, the great worth of certain Jewish works, for example the plays of Porto-Riche. But how much more willingly I should admire them if they did not come to us in translation!" Not until after the book was in print did I recognize that he had actually written: ". . . if only they came to us in translation!" Obviously this made more sense, even if it did not substantially change the underlying thought. My only consolation was that I had at least preserved Gide's feeling that there was something decidedly foreign about such writers. When I apologized to my victim for having distorted his expression, he replied that the fault was his for having originally written a very poor sentence that could lead to such a misunderstanding. Later, I was relieved to come across this remark of his, written in 1928 when he could not have been thinking of my as yet uncommitted *contresens*: "Often, most always, it is the least well written sentences, the ones the author wrote most hastily, that cause the translator the most trouble."

However ungracious it may be for the translator to blame his faults upon the ambiguities of the text, he would often be justified in doing so. Translating a group of essays by Albert Camus, I was momentarily stopped by one construction occurring in a particularly evocative and poetic passage. Describing the carefree life of naked Algerian youths swimming and paddling all morning under the hot sun, he records in a typically Camusian question their return to shore at noon: "Et lorsque, le battement cadencé de la double pagaie aux ailes couleur de fruit suspendu brusquement, nous glissons longuement dans l'eau calme de la darse, comment n'être pas sûr que je mène à travers les eaux lisses une fauve cargaison de dieux où je reconnais mes frères?" To visualize this scene properly the translator should be familiar with those bright narrow canoes or *périssoires* propelled by a double-headed paddle. He does not have to know Algiers, for he could have seen the same thing anywhere along the south coast of France. As the canoe approaches you with the rapid and regular beating of its paddle describing a flashing semi-circle over the paddler's head, it almost seems propelled by wings. But in this illusion or metaphor it is the canoe that has wings, not the paddle. The paddle *is* the wings. Beautiful as Camus' image is, it would have been clearer in French, and therefore easier to put into English, if he had not attributed the colorful wings to the paddle. In any case, this is the way I rendered his sentence: "And when, having suddenly interrupted the cadenced beat of the double paddle's bright-colored wings, we glide slowly in the calm water of the inner harbor, how can I fail to feel that I am piloting through the smooth waters a savage cargo of gods, in whom I recognize my brothers?" For the moment at least, I am satisfied with this version.

"In general," Gide wrote in 1928, "I deplore that spitefulness that tries to discredit a translation (perhaps excellent in other regards) because here and there slight mistranslations have slipped in. . . . It is always easy to alert the public against very obvious errors, often mere trifles. The fundamental virtues are the hardest to appreciate and to point out." Each year the jury of the Denise Clairouin Award used to examine — and probably still does — the annual output of published translations from the French in order to grant the best of them a prize. Hardly a single contestant, when closely scrutinized by a group of experts, failed to reveal certain awkwardly stiff passages and even downright mistranslations. But the jury focused its attention on the translator's success in catching the tone of voice, in reproducing the intentions of the original.

Sometimes the most difficult passages to put into English are the deceptively simple ones. Paul Valéry, for example, recognized the subtle problems raised by the intentional flatness of the opening paragraph of his *Soirée avec Monsieur Teste* and even challenged one translator to find an appropriate equivalent for the initial sentence — "La bêtise n'est pas mon fort." This is the direct and admirable version by Jackson Mathews, who, I wager, spent some time turning that paragraph over in his mind:

Stupidity is not my strong point. I have seen many persons; I have visited several nations; I have taken part in divers enterprises without liking them; I have eaten nearly every day; I have touched women. I now recall several hundred faces, two or three great events, and perhaps the substance of twenty books. I have not retained the best nor the worst of these things. What could stick, did.

Now, that paragraph was dreadfully important for establishing the tone of the whole little book, and, once he had heard Monsieur Teste's dry voice in English, Mr. Mathews merely had to maintain that tone to the end.

In the same vein, let me take a passage from Proust that I included in a collection of what I rashly called his "Maxims." In my version it reads: "For lack of a congenial society, the artist often lives in isolation, with an aloofness which is variously called: by society people pose and lack of breeding, by the authorities a dangerous attitude, by his neighbors madness, by his family selfishness and pride." A comparison of this with the original might make it appear rather free at first glance, but had I translated *faute d'une société supportable* as "failing society that was endurable" (instead of "for lack of a congenial society") and *sauvagerie* as "savagery" (rather than "isolation") and *un mauvais esprit* as "a recalcitrant spirit" (instead of "a dangerous attitude"), I should have failed to make Proust speak clear English in this instance. A friend, thoroughly conversant with French, to whom I read this page asked why I had gone out of my way to choose such unsatisfactorily literal expressions to contrast with my freer version. When he learned that they all came from Scott Moncrieff's rendering of the same original, he exclaimed: "Then why don't you say so?" Well, I *am* now saying so.

Ronald Knox, who spent nine years retranslating the entire Bible and recorded some of his difficulties quite fascinatingly in *The Trials of a Translator*, states that in all translation three things are expected of the translator: "You must find out," he says, "what the original means; you must try to express in your own language what the other man was trying to express in his. . . . Nor is it enough to find out what the man said, you must find out why he said it; you must reproduce, not only the sense, but the emphasis of his words." A good example occurs in two versions of Gide's early satire of stagnation and acceptance entitled *Paludes* (*Marshlands* in English). When asked "Of what are you complaining?" the agitated agitator replies in the original: "Je me plains de ce que personne ne se plaigne." In English, version A reads flatly: "I am complaining because no one complains," missing not only the emphasis but even the sense of his words; whereas version B reads correctly: "I am complaining of the fact that no one complains." The difference may seem slight at first, but in this central statement which sums up the whole little treatise it marks the distance between a careless approximation that misses the point and an exact equivalent.

Above all, translation must speak to us not only in English words but also in the most appropriate English or American idioms. And if it does not do this, it falls short of its primary purpose, which is simply to introduce us to a new writer or a new work that without such a translation we might never know.

TRANSLATING FROM THE GERMAN

EDWIN MUIR AND WILLA MUIR

I

TRANSLATION is obviously a difficult art: I use that word, for if translation is not an art it can hardly be called translation. Yet it is a secondary art, and at best can strive for but never reach a final perfection. My own experience is mainly of translation from the German, and there, as a beginnning, one must change the order of the words, and to do that with a great prose work is to commit an irremediable yet unavoidable injury against it. I am thinking of Franz Kafka, whom my wife and I spent years in translating. The word order of Kafka is naked and infallible; it not only expresses his meaning but is involved as part of it; only in that order could he have said what he had to say. Yet the fine order has to be disarranged, the original edifice of the sentence dismantled and put up again. And the result can never be quite satisfactory, simply because the words run differently.

No other modern writer has made them run more easily and naturally than Kafka, so easily and naturally, indeed, that his style never strikes one as being acquired by study and practice, but simply to be there, like the intonation of a voice. So our main problem was to write an English prose as natural in the English way as his was in his own way. For there is a great diversity of modern German prose, from the sophisticatedly top-heavy, and sometimes merely heavy, prose of Thomas Mann, to the sweetly flowing and labyrinthine prose of Hugo von Hofmannsthal. With Mann, the translator must reproduce the accent of a writer engaged continually in building up his own style, sometimes succeeding and sometimes calamitously failing to render some rare attempted felicity, always at a strain, unless at moments when the writer exhibits, a little complacently perhaps, but forgivably, his own astonishing skill. The translator must reproduce the effort and the performance at the same time. In Kafka the effect is there without any visible sign of the effort.

Translation has obviously to face degrees of difficulty. It must be easier — though it cannot be easy — to translate Jane Austen than the later Henry James; the technical problem must be more complicated. A German translator of James would be forced to contort his own language, and perhaps himself.

The late Hermann Broch's fine trilogy, *The Sleepwalkers*, almost reduced my wife and myself to that pass. Those who have read it will remember that the first book is written in one style, the second in another, and the third in a whole medley of styles, the object being to reproduce by these verbal fluctuations a sense of the disintegration of values in Germany in the years leading up to and following the first World War. This must have been a difficult feat for Broch himself, and so difficulty itself became an essential quality of his prose; his attempt to express the almost inexpressible. He had to show the writer battling with his own style, and indicate his intention as part of his performance. With Kafka one is conscious only of the performance.

How to translate poetry, where the actual words, the music, and the movement signify so much more than they do in prose, I find it hard to understand. The verse translator obviously must be allowed far more freedom (including freedom to invent) than the translator of prose. Perhaps the final thing that one can ask from a translation of poetry is that it should be a good poem in English. A prose translation rendered back into its own language should be quite recognizable as a cousin of its original. But Chapman's Homer, and Pope's, turned into ancient Greek, if that were imaginable, would not be Homer at all. Yet Chapman's *Iliad* is a great poem. There are advantages in this impossibility of translating poetry: scores of Homers and Dantes and Shakespeares and Goethes scattered over the world, all different while in their origin the same. Verse translation does sometimes produce great literature.

E. M.

II

I remember once saying that doing a job of translation was like breaking stones, but of course I was wrong to say so. Translating from a foreign language into one's mother tongue is as fatiguing as breaking stones, but there the resemblance ceases. One is not dealing with blocks of words that have to be trimmed into other shapes, one is struggling with something at once more recalcitrant and more fluid, the spirit of a language, which makes thought flow into molds that are quite different from those of one's native speech. The very shape of thought has to be changed in translation, and that seems to me more difficult than rendering words and idioms into their equivalents.

The German language, for instance, is supposed to be not unlike English, and word for word there are many resemblances. *Ein Glas*

Bier can be recognized by an Englishman without translation. Yet a German paragraph is quite unlike an English paragraph; even a German sentence is unlike an English one. At its source the thought which flows into either is differently controlled and directed. From its first word a classical German sentence is purposively controlled until the verbs come down at the end of it to clinch the statement; one cannot be sure of the meaning, however one may guess, until these verbs are reached. The English statement has not this control; it cannot wait, or does not choose to wait, for the end of the sentence to convey its meaning. It runs on discursively, perhaps qualifying or changing its meaning, and uses verbs as they come in what seems to the English their natural order. To construct an English sentence is not unlike stringing beads one after the other. But to construct a German sentence — what image can best describe that?

Before I suggest an image I ought to say that the last war prejudiced me, I think, against the German language. I find myself disliking the purposive control, the will power dominating the German sentence. I dislike its subordination of everything to these hammer-blow verbs; I dislike its weight and its clotted abstractions. I have the feeling that the shape of the German language affects the thought of those who use it and disposes them to overvalue authoritative statement, will power, and purposive drive. In its emphasis on subordination and control it is not so ruthless as Latin, but both in Latin and in German the structure of the language, I am inclined to think, conditions the kind of thought that it expresses. And so it must have an organic relation to the aspirations and imaginative constructions of those who use it. A language which emphasizes control and rigid subordination must tend to shape what we call *Macht-Menschen*. The drive, the straight purposive drive, of Latin, for instance, is remarkably like the straight purposive drive of the Roman roads. One might hazard a guess that from the use of *ut* with the subjunctive one could deduce the Roman Empire. Could one then deduce Hitler's Reich from the less ruthless shape of the German sentence? I think one could, and I think that is why I have come to dislike it.

The German sentence is less ruthless than the Latin sentence, but it is also less realistic. The Romans preferred concrete statements to abstract ones, while the Germans roll compound words into sausages of abstraction, and then roll these sausages into bigger ones. This predilection for the sausage shape cannot be fortuitous. It must have some relation to the German love of *Wurst* and *Dachshunds*. And why did the Germans invent the Zeppelin? Nor should we forget that the favorite German word of abuse is *Scheiss*. One can tell that the Germans are very bowel-conscious, or as the psychoanalysts say, anal-erotic. So the right image for the German sentence, I suggest, is that of a great gut, a bowel, which deposits at the end of it a sediment of verbs. Is not this like the Reich desired by Hitler, who planned to make mincemeat of Europe?

I should like to suggest, too, that Austrians use the German language quite differently. They write a less rigid, less clotted, more supple German which I, for one, find much easier to translate into good English, and I am not prejudiced against it. But to turn classical German into sound democratic English — there is the difficulty.

W. M.

THE SERVILE PATH

VLADIMIR NABOKOV

PUSHKIN'S novel in verse *Eugene Onegin* was begun 9 May 1823 (Old Style), in Kishinev, and completed 5 October 1831, in Tsarskoe Selo. During the poet's lifetime it went through three editions: 1825– 1832, 1833, and 1837.

For the last five or six years I have been engaged in translating and annotating it. The work is now finished. In my translation I have sacrificed to total accuracy and completeness of meaning every element of form save the iambic rhythm, the retention of which assisted rather than impaired fidelity.

In a recent article [1] I mentioned some of the complications attending the turning of *Eugene Onegin* into English, such as the need to cope with a constant intrusion of gallicisms and of borrowings from French poets. My main contention was, and is, that the translator, in order to be lucidly faithful to his text, should be aware of this or that authorial reminiscence, imitation, or direct translation from another language into that of the text, and that this awareness may not only save him from committing howlers, or from bungling the rendering of stylistic details, but also guide him in the choice of the best wording where several are possible. The English translator of *Eugene Onegin* would seem to need not only a Russian's knowledge of Russian but also Pushkin's knowledge of French.

1. The French middleman

Russian commentators keep overlooking the significant fact that in Pushkin's day Russian writers knew the literatures of England, Germany, and Italy, as well as the works of the Ancients, not from original texts but from the stupendous exertions of French paraphrasts. The ignoble Russian adaptations of popular European novels were read only by the lower classes, while, on the other hand, the admirable melodies of Zhukovski's versions of English and German poems won such triumphs for Russian letters as to make negligible the loss Schiller or Gray suffered in adaptation. As a rule, the St. Petersburg fashionable, the ennuied Hussar, the civilized squire, the provincial miss in her linden-shaded chateau of painted wood — all read Shakespeare and Sterne, Richardson and Scott, Moore and Byron, as well as the

German novelists (Goethe, August Lafontaine), in French versions, and French versions only.

In consequence, Shakespeare is really Letourneur, Byron and Moore are Pichot, Scott is Dufauconpret, Sterne is Frenais, and so on. In *Eugene Onegin* there are numerous references to foreign books; but one should constantly bear in mind that what Pushkin and his Tatiana Larin read is not the real Richardson but the French versions by the monstrously prolific Abbé Antoine François Prévost, such as *Lettres angloises, ou Histoire de Miss Clarisse Harlove* [sic], Londres, 1751, 6 vols.; and *Nouvelles lettres angloises, ou Histoire du chevalier Grandisson* [sic], *par l'auteur de "Pamela" et de "Clarisse,"* Amsterdam, 1755, 4 vols.; and that Pushkin and his Onegin admired not *Melmoth the Wanderer*, Edinburgh, 1820, 4 vols., by Rev. Charles Robert Maturin (an Irish clergyman), but *"Melmoth ou l'Homme errant" par Mathurin* [sic] *traduit librement de l'anglais par Jean Cohen,* 6 vols., Paris, 1821.

For some quaint reason, it often happened among fashionable Russian families of the early eighteen-hundreds that, while children of both sexes were taught French in infancy, only the girls had English governesses. But even then French versions of English works were so much easier to obtain than the English originals that the chances were the Russian trilingual lady would go for relaxation to the French hack. Pushkin's heroine, Tatiana, belonging as she did to a provincial family, had no English, though she quite certainly had had a French governess just before the curtain of the romance gently rose. Pushkin's sister Olga had at one time received lessons from a Miss or Mrs. Bailey, but it is absolutely certain that when in May 1820 our poet left St. Petersburg for seven years, he was able to decipher English only in so far as this could be done through a French medium, with the addition of the kind of school Latin anyone possessed in those days, and some stale crumbs of school German. Like most Russians, Pushkin was a poor linguist: even the natural and fluent French he had learned as an infant lacks (judging by his letters and manuscript notes) personal tang, being strictly limited to a brilliant command of eighteenth-century ready-made phrases and slightly dated idioms. When he tried to teach himself English — as he fitfully did at various odd moments between the early eighteen-twenties and the end of his life — he never went beyond the beginner's stage, and his attempts (hampered rather than aided by the promptings of an English-French dictionary) to translate passages from Wordsworth (1833) or Byron

(1836) are embodied in a few disjointed sentences that prove him unable to understand the simplest English locutions. In the years when he began writing *Onegin* he could not pronounce English vowels, and not only misspelled the "Childe" of Byron's title in the French popular way ("Child") but sounded the "i" as in "chilled" — which is only one step removed from the French pronunciation: "shilled."

French versions of fragments of the four cantos of *Childe Harold*, as well as passages from *The Prisoner of Chillon, The Corsair,* and *The Giaour,* had appeared in *La Bibliothèque universelle de Genève,* series *littérature,* as early as 1817–1819. It is on these versions that in Russia the poet Vyazemski, or in France the poets Lamartine and Alfred de Vigny, were obliged to depend. By the beginning of 1820, eager Russian readers had already at their disposal the first four volumes (1819) of Amédée Pichot's and Euzèbe de Salle's anonymous first edition of Byron's works in French. For the second edition, the translators used the joint pseudonym "A.E. de Chastopalli," which is an imperfect anagram of their names. In the course of the third edition A.P. and E.d.S. quarreled, and beginning with the eighth volume (1821), Pichot becomes alone responsible for the translation.

The first four editions of the monumental and mediocre prose versions of the *Oeuvres de lord Byron* (all brought out by Ladvocat in Paris) came out between 1819 and 1825.

Pushkin read the first two cantos of *Le Pélérinage,* probably in Pyatigorsk (North Caucasus), in the summer of 1820. He read its last two cantos, and the first two of *Don Juan,* either at Kamenka (Province of Kiev) during the following winter, or in Kishinev, 1821–1822. He found the two cantos of *Don Juan* that he already knew and three more in Volume 6 of Pichot's fourth edition, which he read in Odessa or at Mihaylovskoe (Province of Pskov) not later than October 1824. Through the good offices of his country neighbor Annette Osipov and her cousin Anna Kern, he obtained from Riga the remaining eleven cantos, in Volume 7 of the same edition, in December 1825.

2. *Pichotism*

The English translator of Pushkin must be very careful in distinguishing between his author's debt to Byron and his debt to Pichot. Thus in Volume 2 of Pichot's 1822 edition the title of Byron's romaunt appears as *Childe-Harold, poème romantique;* and *this* explains why Pushkin, in a celebrated letter from Odessa, in the spring of 1824, terms *Eugene Onegin*, which he was then writing, "the motley strophes of a romantic poem," романтической поэмы.

Another pretty example of Pichot's influence sneaking past that of Byron is furnished by *Eugene Onegin*, One, XLVII, in which are described Onegin's and Pushkin's strolls along the Palace Quay, in "a reverie of retrospection and regret" (as Jane Austen might have put it). The stanza echoes thematically Canto Two, XXIV, of *Childe Harold's Pilgrimage*; but Pushkin's line 4 about "the gay glass of the waters" which "does not reflect Diana's face" (supplanting the "Dian's wave-reflected sphere" of Byron) is a cliché due to Pichot's wretched version ". . . le disque de Diane qui se réfléchit dans le miroir [!] de l'océan." Thus a paraphrast, while betraying one poet, misleads another.

On the other hand, despite Hamlet's coming to Pushkin and to his characters through Letourneur,[2] I think that, with a little tact, and while remaining absolutely faithful to Pushkin's text, we still can give a tinge of the basic Shakespeare to Lenski's little soliloquy in Two, XXXV, over the tomb of Brigadier Larin:

> "Poor Yorick!" mournfully he uttered, "he
> hath borne me in his arms.
> How oft I played in childhood
> with his Ochákov medal!

> "Poor Yorick!" молвил он уныло,
> Он на руках меня держал.
> Как часто в детстве я играл
> Его Очаковской медалью!

The quotation, of course, does not come directly from the original, as Russian commentators have taken for granted. To it Pushkin affixed the note "Poor Yorick: Hamlet's exclamation over the fool's skull (see Shakespeare and Sterne)." Says Brodski, in his incredibly vulgar and misleading commentary to "Eugene Onegin" (Leningrad, third edition, 1950): "By referring to Sterne. . . . Pushkin subtly discloses his ironic attitude to Lenski's applying the name of an English fool to Brigadier Larin." Alas, poor Brodski! Pushkin's note comes straight from a note (pages 386–387) in the French version of *Hamlet*, edition 1821: "Alas, poor Yorick! Tout le monde se souvient et du chapitre de Sterne où il cite ce passage et comment, dans le Voyage sentimental, il s'est à ce propos donné à lui-même le nom de Yorick."

3. *French formulas*

The English translator should realize that a number of words borrowed by Pushkin from the lexicon of Batyushkov and other minor poets are meant to render in Russian definite lyrical terms found in Parny and in other French elegists. To cite only a few at random: умиление is "attendrissement," нега is "mollesse," любезный is "aimable," жар is "ardeur," бред is "délire," пламень is "flamme," ветреный is "frivole" or "volage," залог is "gage," досуг is "loisir," бурный is "turbulent," лоно is "sein," сладострастие is "volupté" and so forth.

The English translator will have to find exact equivalents for such ready-made French locutions in Russian garb as (again I can list only a few) "âme novice" (неопытная душа), "belle âme" (прекрасная душа), "espérance flatteuse" (лестная надежда), "heureux talent" (щастливый талант), "sentiment mesquin" (мелкое чувство), "vivement touché" (живо тронут), "fausse honte" (ложный стыд), "grands droits" (большие права), "femme à la mode" (модная жена), "neveux d'Apollon" (внуки Аполлона), "sein de la tranquillité" (лоно тишины), "par la force des choses" (силою вещей), "par le suprême vouloir" (всевышней волею), "sans art" (без искусства), and many other similar expressions which *Eugene Onegin* shares with French works of the time.

The English translator will have trouble with the frequently used даль, "le lointain," "l'éloignement," the poetry of distance rather than distance itself. He will be exasperated by the recurrence of кипит, "bouillonne," in such phrases as кровь кипит, "le sang bouillonne," which implies the passion of love, not the passion of anger. From the lexicon of pastoral poesy comes the special use of поля, "les champs," "la campagne," in the sense of champaign, open country, which may include forests (Karamzin, in the seventeen-nineties, had attempted to render "la campagne" by the Russicism чистое поле), and thence, too, comes the idyllic (evoking knights turned eremites) "désert," old-fashioned "desart," "beau désert," прекрасная пустыня, "the beautiful wild." A stale metaphor of French rhetorics, "moisson," жатва, occurs in Two, XXXVIII, while замок in Two, II, is merely the usual attempt to translate "château" (in the sense of manor house). Речи is in certain cases not "speeches," but French "accents." The madrigalic надменные (красавицы) means not merely the "haughty (fair)," but is an onomatope of "inhumaines." The

German baker's бумажный колпак in One, XXXV, is of course not a "paper cap" but a "bonnet de coton."

It is curious how indifferent Pushkin is to the banality of a form in French, provided that it can be neatly and euphonically rendered in Russian. Thus in One, XXXII, he uses рой желаний, swarm of Desires, or Ardors, long after Gresset's "l'essaim des folâtres amours," Parny's "l'essaim des voluptés," Bertin's "tendre essaim des désirs," Ducis' "des plaisirs le dangereux essaim," [3] and many others, had become trite. Indeed, Laharpe, in his *Cours de littérature*, has occasion (in a critique of Roucher's *Les Mois*) to deplore the "retour fréquent de mots parasites /tels que/ 'essaims'/etc./, termes communs trop souvent répétés."

4. Translation of translations

An interesting situation arises when, in alluding to an author, Pushkin uses a phrase which constitutes a parody of that author's diction. Yet even more interesting are such passages where the aped phrase is found to occur in the Russian version of the French translation of an English author, so that in result Pushkin's pastiche (which *we* have to render in English) is three times removed from its model! What should the translator do in the following case:

The second stanza of Chapter Eight of the established text turns on Pushkin's recollection of Derzhavin's praise. The principal edition retains only the first quatrain of the stanza. A fair copy in Pushkin's hand provides us with the expunged remainder wherein three other writers are alluded to, Dmitriev, Karamzin, and Zhukovski. The line about Dmitriev reads:

And Dmitrev [*sic*] was not our detractor

Now, if we turn to Dmitriev's colorless version (1798), in alexandrine couplets, of Pope's *Epistle to Dr. Arbuthnot* (1734), we discover in the second hemistich of Dmitriev's line 176 the model of Pushkin's phrase:

Kongrév applauded me, *Svift* was not my detractor

Dmitriev, who had no English, used a French translation of Pope (probably La Porte's), and this explains the Gallic garb of Congreve (which Dmitriev mentally rhymes with grève). If we look up Pope's text, we find that Dmitriev's line is a paraphrase of Pope's line 138:

And Congreve loved, and Swift endured, my lays.

But Pushkin, in *Eugene Onegin*, Eight, II, 5, is thinking not of Pope or La Porte, but of Dmitriev, and I submit that, in an accurate English translation, we should keep the "detractor" and resist the formidable temptation to render Pushkin's line as:

> And Dmitriev, too, endured my lays.

5. *Problems of Flora*

Among fifty college students whom I once happened to ask (in planned illustration of the incredible ignorance concerning natural objects that characterizes young Americans of today) the name of the tree, an American elm, that they could see through the classroom windows, none was able to identify it: some hesitantly suggested it might be an oak, others were silent; one, a girl, said she guessed it was a shade tree. The translator, when tackling botanical names in his author, should try to be more precise.

In *Eugene Onegin*, Six, VII, Pushkin describes his reformed rake Zaretski as having returned to the country and found refuge, or shelter, (укрывшись) under certain plants. The line to be analyzed goes thus:

> 9 Под сень черёмух и акаций

The translation of под (beneath, under) сень (the overhead shelter provided by anything in the way of covert, roof, pend, arch, eaves, "leafy ceil," canopy, bower, metaphorical wing and so forth) presents only a minor difficulty; true, it is an irritating one, because под сень (sing. acc.), под сенью (sing. instr.), and other formulas founded on сень (fem. sing.) and сени (plur.; not to be confused with the well-known word for "hall" or "vestibule"), are metrically very tractable, and therefore too much favored by Russian poets for their translator's comfort. Сень cannot always be rendered in English by any one word. The specious "shade" does not lure the incorruptible literalist for the important reason that its exact Russian equivalent, тень, in phrases similar to those given above is not quite synonymous with сень, and in fact may occur with it in the same passage as a sheepish rhyme. However, the sensuous meaning of сень is so evanescent that in many instances — of which this is one — none should deem it a crime if "beneath" or "under" be used instead of "beneath the shelter" or "in the shelter."

The bower alluded to in the line under discussion is formed by two kinds of shrubs or trees. Do their mere names suggest anything to the Russian reader? We all know that the popular name of a plant may strike the imagination differently in different languages; its stress may be on color in one country, and on structure in another; it may have beautiful classical connotations; it may be redolent of unbelievable Floridas; it may contain a honey drop as a residue of the cumulative romantic sense bestowed upon it by generations of elegiasts; it may be, in floral disguise, a plaque commemorating (like the dahlia) the name of an old botanist or (like the camellia) that of a roving Jesuit back from Luzon. The words черёмух and акаций (both fem. plur. gen.) convey to the Russian mind two flowery masses and what may be termed a stylized blend of aromas, one part of which, as will presently be shown, is artificial. I do not think that it is the pure translator's duty to trouble much about the rendering of associations in his text, but he should explain them in his notes. It is certainly a pity that, say, *l'alidore* of the French with its evocations of love philters and auroral mists should become in England hog's wart (because of the singular form of its flowers), or cotton bud (because of the texture of its young leaves), or Parson's Button (allusion untraceable). But unless a name of that kind might puzzle or mislead the reader by referring to a dozen different plants (and then the Latin specific name should be given), the translator is entitled to use any available term so long as it is exact.

Dictionaries usually translate черёмуха as "bird cherry," which is so vague as to be practically meaningless. Specifically, черёмуха is the "racemose old-world bird cherry," Fr. *putier racémeux, Padus racemosa* Schneider. The Russian word, with its fluffy and dreamy syllables, suits admirably this beautiful tree, distinguished by its long racemes of flowers, giving the whole of it, when in bloom, a gentle pendulous appearance. A common and popular woodland plant in Russia, it is equally at home among the riverside alders and on the pine barren; its creamy-white, musky, May-time bloom is associated in Russian hearts with the poetical emotions of youth. This racemose bird cherry lacks such a specific English designation (it has a few generic ones, all of them either uncouth or homonymous, or both) as would be neither pedantic, nor as irresponsible as the nonsense names which harmful drudges carefully transport from one Russian-English dictionary to another. At one time I followed the usually reliable Dahl Dictionary in calling the tree "mahaleb," which proves to be, however, another plant altogether. Later I coined the term "musk cherry," which renders rather well the sound of черёмуха and the fragrance of its bloom, but unfortunately evokes a taste which is not characteristic of its small, grainy, black fruit. I now formally introduce the simple and euphonious "racemosa" used as a noun and rhyming with "mimosa."

We now turn to its companion, акация, and the question is: should the translator take the name of a plant at its face value (sticking to his dictionary, which says that акация is acacia) or should he find out what the word really means, in its contextual habitat, within the terms of a certain imagined place and in the light of a certain literary device? I advocate following the second course.

While racemosas grow wild throughout the habitat of our novel (northwestern and central Russia), the true acacia does not. The latter is a beautiful and useful genus of tropical mimosaceous trees, of which one, the Australian *A. dealbata* F.v.M., the Silver Wattle of nurserymen, is acclimatized in coastal Caucasia: it used to be sold — after Pushkin's time — as a мимоза by St. Petersburg florists. Neither is the акация of our text the "locust" of one translator, although it is true that to southern Russians белая акация ("white acacia") means only one thing, the sweetly perfumed American *Robinia pseudoacacia* Linn., cultivated in the Ukraine and sung by hundreds of Odessa rhymesters. It is neither the Silver Wattle nor the False Acacia. What then is the акация of our text? It is quite certainly a yellow-flowering *Caragana* species, namely C. *arborescens* Lam., imported from Asia and cultivated in gentlemen's bowers and along garden alleys in Northern Russia. French tutors called it "l'acacia de Sibérie"; little boys would slit open, in a certain way, its dark beanlet and produce a nasty blare by blowing into it between their cupped hands. But what really settles the identity of the plant with absolute certainty is the following consideration. Pushkin's line is a parody of two passages in a poem entitled Беседка Муз (bower of the muses), 1817, by Batyushkov, minor poet and literary pioneer to whose idiom Pushkin owed at least as much has he did to that of Karamzin and Zhukovski. The poem, which is written in free, or fable, iambics, that is, iambics of varied length, begins:

> In the shade of milky racemosas
> and golden-glistening pea trees (акаций)

and closes with:

> carefree as is the child of ever carefree Graces,
> some day he'll come to sigh in the dense shelter of his racemosas
> and pea trees.

The epithet in the second line of the poem suits well the bright flower of *Caragana* and does not suit at all the white blossoms of the False Acacia. Consequently, the correct way to translate *Eugene Onegin*, Six, VII, 9, is:

> beneath the racemosas and pea trees

— leaving other trees to those noble paraphrasts whom Sir John Denham praised three centuries ago, in his address to another worthy, Sir Richard Fanshaw (see Dryden's "Preface concerning Ovid's Epistles"):

> That servile path thou nobly dost decline
> Of tracing word for word and line for line.

6. *Borrowings and imitations*

In introducing Zaretski, Lenski's second, Pushkin describes his disreputable past, and then clinches the stanza (Six, IV) by having him become a placid squire

> and even an honorable man:
> thus does our age correct itself.

> И даже честный человек:
> Так исправляется наш век.

The first of these two lines — as Lerner pointed out twenty years ago — is the echo of a sentence at the end of Voltaire's *Candide ou l'Optimisme* (1759) [4] in reference to Brother Giroflée who "turned out to be a very good worker in wood and even became an honorable man" ("et même devint honnête homme"); but it has not been noticed that Pushkin's *next* line (так исправляется наш век) comes also from Voltaire, namely from an authorial footnote of 1768 to the beginning of Canto Four of *La Guerre Civile de Genève* (which Pushkin seems to have admired so much): "Observez, cher lecteur, combien le siècle se perfectionne." — and this in its turn suggests that век, which can be either "century" or "life span," should rather be taken to mean the former in Pushkin's line.

Evariste Parny ("tender Parny," as Pushkin calls him in Three, XXIX) in the second piece (*La Main*) of his *Tableaux* has the following:

> 5 On ne dit point: "la résistance
> Enflamme et fixe les désirs;
> Reculons l'instant des plaisirs."
> . . . .

9 Ainsi parle un amant trompeur
Et la coquette ainsi raisonne.
La tendre amante s'abandonne
A l'objet qui touche son coeur.

5 One does not say: "resistance
inflames and fixes the desires;
let us defer the moment of delights."
. . . .
9 Thus speaks the lover who deceives
and the coquette thus reasons.
The tender mistress yields
to the object that affects her heart.

In speaking of the forthright Tatiana Larin, Pushkin imitates Parny as follows (Three, XXV, 1–6):

1 Кокетка судит хладнокровно,
Татьяна любит не шутя
И предаётся безусловно
4 Любви как милое дитя.
Не говорит она: отложим —
Любви мы цену тем умножим

We are completely entitled to reflect the imitation and synchronize the two sets of terms, in Parny and Pushkin, by choosing for our translation of Pushkin's lines such words among the English equivalents of кокетка судит, предаётся and отложим as suit best both Parny and Pushkin:

1 The coquette reasons coolly,
Tatiana in dead earnest loves
and unconditionally yields
4 to love, like a sweet child.
She does not say: Let us defer;
thereby we shall augment love's value

The pursuit of reminiscences through an author's work is, of course, a dangerous sport. There is no doubt that in many cases Pushkin picks his flowers on the very brink of sheer plagiarism, but we have often to reckon with similarities due to the presence, backstage, as it were, of a common source, or to inevitable combinations within the comparatively narrow limits of an established genre. There is also plain coincidence. In the odd case of One, XXIII, 4, describing Onegin's metamorphoses in his *cabinet de toilette*:

Одет, раздет, и вновь одет

is dressed, undressed, and dressed again

we may either argue that, given the mock-heroic manner, one element
must lead to another in the same series, or we may maintain that the
quadruple coincidence (stylistic formula, meter, rhythm-cut, and
sound of words) suggests that despite Pushkin's lack of English in
1823, he was actually influenced by line 69 of Samuel Butler's *Hudi-
bras* (First Part, *Canto One*, 1662):

Confute, change hands, and still confute

printed *en regard* in the French rhymed version ("change la thèse
et puis refute") by John Towneley (Paris, 1757), which Pushkin
may have seen in Jombert's edition, London and Paris, 1819.

In describing in Canto Seven, VII, Lenski's neglected tomb by the
roadside in Russian Arcadia, Pushkin expresses the work of weeds
and oblivion by means of two remarkable enjambments:

9 Но ныне. . . памятник унылый
Забыт. К нему привычный след
Заглох. Венка на ветви нет

The translator would dearly have wished to preserve the exact cut
and the alliterations (the long-drawn *ni*, the recurrent rhythm of
the two disyllables in *z*), but must content himself with the following:

9 But now . . . the mournful monument
forgotten is. The wonted trail to it,
weed-choked. No wreath is on the bough

The opening word in line 11 is most accurately translated by the
word "weed-choked" but, strictly speaking, no Russian equivalent of
"weed" actually appears within заглох. This would not matter much
had not the presence of "weed" improved upon a situation which is
quite extraordinary enough as is. I doubt very much that at the time
this was written (between autumn of 1827 and Feb. 19, 1828), Pushkin
had acquired enough English not only to read through an English
poem of almost two thousand lines, but to catch niceties of English
rhythm. However, the fact remains that verses 9–11 in *Eugene
Onegin*, Seven, VII, bear a striking resemblance, both in mood and
modulation, to a passage in Canto Seven of Wordsworth's *The White
Doe of Rylstone* (1807–1808):

1570 Pool, terraces, and walks are sown
with weeds; the bowers are overthrown

. . . .
1575 The lordly mansion of its pride
is stripped; the ravage hath spread wide

I shall probably tone down the заглох to "is choked" in my final text so as not to embellish the coincidence.

7. *Conclusion*

An appreciation of the limpid harmonies with which *Eugene Onegin* brims, of the multiple melodies reverberating through its stanzas, of its precise and luminous images, and of the unique purity of its Russian diction, lies beyond the scope of these utilitarian notes. They do not aim at belittling a giant, but merely seek to provide an honest translator with a better understanding of the text. Some rude prying into Pushkin's workshop is inevitable, nor can one help being surprised at a great man's stealing from lesser men; but a knowledge of the period and place yields an obvious answer to those who would try to draw too strict a line between imitation and emulation. There is also Pushkin's sportive temperament to be reckoned with. To the parallelist as to the moralist he might retort in the manner of a famous epistle by his favorite André Chénier (I translate ten alexandrines, 97–102 and 137–140, into eleven pentameters, mostly unrhymed):

> A bumptious judge, scanning my works, denounces
> All of a sudden, with loud cries, a score
> Of passages, from so and so translated·
> He names their author, and on finding them,
> Admires himself, pleased with his learning.
> > Why
> Does he not come to me? To him I'll show
> A thousand thefts of mine he may not know.
>
> . . . .
> Deeming himself most clever, the rash critic
> Will give a slap to Vergil on my cheek,
> And *this* (I stick to my own rule, you see)
> Montaigne has said — remember? — before me.

Namely, in *Essais*, 1580, Book Second, Chapter Ten, *Des Livres* (Bordeaux Ms, spelling after Armaingaud's edition, 1925): "Je veus qu'ils donent une nasarde a Plutarque sur mon nez et qu'ils s'eschaudent a injurier Seneque en moi."

NOTES

1. "Problems of Translation: *Onegin* in English," *Partisan Review*, XXII (1955), 496–512.

2. Letourneur's initial version is *Hamlet, Prince de Dannemarck* in Volume 5 of Shakespeare's *Oeuvres*, Paris, 1779. In 1823, when writing Two, Pushkin consulted the 1821 edition (Volume 1 of *Oeuvres complètes*, revised by Guizot and Pichot).

3. Gresset, *Vert-vert*, 1734; Parny, *Souvenir*, in *Poésies érotiques*, 1778; Bertin, *Elégie II à Catilie*, 1785; Ducis, *Epître à l'amitié*, 1786.

4. The sentence is completely botched in John Butt's execrable English version of *Candide* in the Penguin series, 1947, unfortunately used in Humanities courses.

SOME REFLECTIONS ON THE DIFFICULTY
OF TRANSLATION

ACHILLES FANG

All a man ever thought would go onto a half sheet of notepaper.
The rest is application and elaboration.

THE PROBLEM of translation may be treated from three angles: adequate comprehension of the translated text, adequate manipulation of the language translated into, and what happens in between. The last question properly belongs to linguistic psychology, of which I know little. The second question has been treated eloquently by Matthew Arnold in the last century (*On Translating Homer*) and by Ezra Pound in the present (*Notes on Elizabethan Classicists* and *Translators of Greek*); I do not see any way of adding to their excellent studies on the subject of the style of translation.[1]

All studies on the problem of translation take it for granted that the translator has comprehended the language and thought of his text. But comprehension is not an easy thing, as we all know through bitter experiences. Especially so in Chinese, a language reputedly invented by the devil to prevent the spread of the Gospel in the Middle Kingdom. Besides, as D. G. Rossetti once wrote, "a translation remains perhaps the most direct form of commentary." Hence it may not be irrelevant to treat the first problem of translation in this paper.

1. Test and Protest

J'estime les Danois et leurs dents de fer.

When a professional phonologist reads 六書音均表 as *Liu shu yin kün piao* in place of *Liu shu yin yün piao* or when the greatest of all Sinologists entitles his *magnum opus Les Mémoires historiques* instead of *Les Mémoires du* (or *d'un*) [*grand*] *historien*, we should remind ourselves that Benjamin Jowett occasionally "mistranslated" δέ. We should not put them in the same class with Rapaud of the Institut F. Brossard who amuses us with his original rendition of *timeo Danaos, et dona ferentes* (see George du Maurier, *The Martian*). The phonologist ("the world's authority on Ancient Far Eastern Art" according to a New York bookdealer) was perhaps intentionally practicing the art of deception beloved of Chinese art-dealers; and the Sinologist probably was following the inaccurate but tradition-hallowed interpretation of the title. It is reasonable to believe that these two eminent scholars sinned with their eyes open; at least they have earned the benefit of a doubt.

On the other hand, when so eminent a Japanese student of Sinology as Professor Shionoya, an *ordinarius* and himself a practicing poet *à la chinois* or at least a versatile versifier, misleads and continues to mislead (in edition after edition) his readers with a totally impossible interpretation of the second line in an almost pellucid poem of Yüan Ch'en's

元稹　遣悲懷.[2]

昔日戲言身後事　今朝都到眼前來
衣裳已施行看盡　針線猶存未忍開
尚想舊情憐婢僕　也曾因夢送錢財
誠知此恨人人有　貧賤夫婦百事哀,

we cannot but raise our eyebrows. The line in question simply means that after his wife's death the poet gave away her dresses one after another (to her friends and relatives) until almost all of them disappeared and that he could not bear to open her sewing basket with its needles and thread simply because he found the reminder painful. MM. Bynner and Kiang render the line thus:

> Almost all your clothes have been given away;
> Your needle work is sealed, I dare not look at it.

The sentiment can be understood by anyone who has, *inter alia*, read the two really sentimental stories of Elizabeth Villiers and Elinor Forester in *Mrs. Leicester's School*. But Professor Shionoya, who seems to be characteristically "deficient in love,"[2] cannot understand such a human sentiment. Instead he paraphrases the line

身ニ衣裳ヲ着タテ, ツブツグト眺メ,
針線ガ尚ホ存シテイテモ, 取去ルニ忍ビナイ.

In a recent English translation of *Tao-te-ching* the well-known translator Edward Erkes seems to have surpassed all his past originalities: instead of taking Ho-shang-kung's glosses as glosses, he reads them as homiletics. For example, the simple sentence 知者不博, 博者不知 (chap. 81) should not puzzle even a tyro provided that he knows how to locate the four characters in his dictionary. Nor should a sophisticated tyro worry himself to death over this couplet, for our translator's oracle is quite explicit:

知者謂知道之士, 不博者守一元也,
博者多見聞, 不知者失要真也.

Furthermore, Ho-shang-kung's commentary quoted in *I-lin* seems to make the point still more explicit:

知道守一，則不必博，多見聞失要真，故不知.

All that the couplet purports to say is that a true philosopher need not be a walking encyclopedia and that a man of encyclopedic learning is not necessarily a true philosopher. After giving the couplet a Chestertonian twist, "The knowing one is no scholar. The scholar is ignorant," our translator turns to his oracle: "The knowing one is the knowing Taoist. The unlearned one comprehends unity at the origin. The scholar sees and hears much, but as he is ignorant, he loses what is important and true." His translation of the *I-lin* quotation is no less original: "Who knows Tao and preserves unity is surely no scholar. As he sees and hears much, he loses what is more important. Therefore he is ignorant." It looks as though the translator could not see the gloss for paraphrase, or the pedant for the preacher.

A Chin dynasty poet wrote a touching poem on "The Desecration of the Han Tombs," in which occurs the line: 毀壞過一抔. A remarkably competent translator renders it as "Of earth they have carried away more than one handful" (second edition: "crumbled" for "carried away") and informs his readers in a footnote, "In the early days of the dynasty a man stole a handful of earth from the imperial tombs, and was executed by the police. The emperor was furious at the lightness of the punishment." (Second edition: "In the early days of the Han dynasty a man who stole one handful of earth from the Imperial Tombs was put to death.") The story refers to *Shih-chi* 102 (or *Han-shu* 50), where it is told that when the chief justice of the empire, Chang Shih-chih, sentenced to death a man who stole a jade ring from the temple of the founder of the Han dynasty, the emperor Wen-ti was furious at the lightness of the sentence and wanted to exterminate the man's entire family, but that Chang Shih-chih stood firm on the text of the criminal code and tried to make the emperor reasonable by asking him what severer sentence remained to mete out to the man who should (Heaven forbid, 萬 一) carry away a handful of earth from the tomb of the later emperor, upon which the emperor had to satisfy himself with confirming the original sentence. As commentators agree, the phrase "to carry away a handful of earth" is a euphemism for "to desecrate the imperial tomb." There is no question of anybody's desecrating the tomb "in the early days" of the Han dynasty.

How, then, do absurdities like these come about? *Lapsus calami?* Deficiency in love? Or (as St. John of the Cross would have said) *un no sé qué?* It is easy to say that there is such a thing as sheer incompetence in comprehending a foreign language and a system of alien and often "subversive" thoughts enmeshed in that language, and to prescribe a strict and sensible regimen in the Sinological techniques to cure such a malady. But the matter goes a bit deeper than that. For the so-called Chinese language is a really froward child, a most recalcitrant thing in the hand of the logical-minded.

The Literary Revolution may be viewed as in part an attempt to eliminate some of its recalcitrance. The original program for that revolution was something far more comprehensive in scope than a mere restoration of the spoken language as the literary medium, for it demanded that all allusions, clichés, parallelism, stock-in-trade emotions, and ancient tradition be thrown overboard; it insisted on grammar, content, and colloquialisms. But the revolution started a bit too late for the students of Chinese literature. Practically every important piece of writing dating before 1916 (and even some subsequent to that date) abounds in allusions, clichés, parallelism, stock-in-trade emotions, and ancient tradition with little grammar and sometimes with less content to speak of. (It is in a way a blessing in disguise that colloquialisms were not the order of the day; which of us do not groan when we try to read Yüan drama, written in the dead colloquial speech of the time?) In fact, "obscurity, erudition, allusiveness, . . ." as a critic in *Partisan Review* describes the modernist poetry of Europe and America, have always characterized Chinese literary style.

T. E. Hulme, the ancestor of Imagism and Amygism, once wrote: "Personally I am of course in favor of the complete destruction of all verse more than twenty years old." If there had been a dozen or more Ch'in-shih-huang-ti (First Emperor of all China, burner of the books), the state of Chinese literature could have been more accessible to Sinological comprehension. But there was only one Ch'in-shih-huang-ti. And, by the nature of things, it is doubtful if more than one could have been tolerated. As Hulme continues, "But that happy event will not, I am afraid, take place until Plato's desire has been realized and a minor poet has become dictator." (Perhaps Ch'in-shih-huang-ti was a minor poet.)

2. Text and Context

Pensiamo perche non sappiamo.

A translator must comprehend the text he is translating in the light of its own context as well as of that of other texts. He cannot be too subtle about this matter; it would be nothing short of folly to translate a passage before he is perfectly satisfied with the text and can explain every word in it. He must, furthermore, look into variant editions and compare the basic text with the fragments and excerpts as quoted elsewhere, such as *T'ai-p'ing Yü-lan*, etc. It is very fortunate that a large number of Chinese texts are duplicated: a huge segment of *Han-shu* is almost, but not quite, identical with *Shih-chi*, which in its turn overlaps with many pre-Ch'in texts; there are also two *T'ang-shu*, two *Wu-tai-shih*, and two *Yüan-shih*. A translator has to compare his text with a parallel passage in other books before he is entitled to feel satisfied with his comprehension.

He must furthermore make a thorough study of all available scholia. True, most of them are rather silly and stuffy; yet a translator will profit much if he assesses them for what they are worth. In short, a translator must comprehend not only his text but also its numerous glosses, actual and possible. If he cannot understand the language of the scholiasts, he would be well advised to postpone his translation until he is competent in this respect.

Take, for example, the sentence:

雖說擇術不正，可知時會使然．

It is translated: "You may say that they didn't go the right way about their business, but you must know that it is really the fault of the times." What the passage means is that the two men who applied their ingenuity to the invention of bagatelles like the opium lamp and the smoking pipe were misguided, hence they deserved to remain in obscurity, and yet it is to be conceded that, had they been citizens of Europe or America, they could have made themselves famous by their inventions. It definitely does not mean that they were ignorant of the value of publicity. The phrase 擇術不正, of course, alludes to *Hsün-tzu* (非相篇):

故相形不如論心，論心不如擇術，
形不勝心，心不勝術，術正而心順，則形相
雖惡，而心術善，無害為君子也．

The meaning of the original text may come out more accurately in: "You may blame them for their misguided intelligence, yet you will have to agree with me that their obscurity was due to a lack of opportunity." This sounds a little *non sequitur*, but this is what was intended.

Another instructive example is the passage

士為知己者死，女為悅己者容，

translated as follows: "A man will die for the one who appreciates him; a woman will beautify herself for the one who pleases her." The text,

found in *Shih-chi* 86, is derived from *Chan-kuo Ts'e* (Chao-ts'e). Ssu-ma
Ch'ien himself uses this sentence in his letter to Jen An, where he alters
死 to 用 (see *Wen-hsüan* 41; the letter is also in *Han-shu* 62, where the
two 者 are omitted). Whether 悅 means "to please me" or "to be
pleased in me" is a minor point, but the translator could have been
a bit more painstaking and accurate. Lü Hsiang's paraphrase
女為愛己貌者而飾其容 (in *Wen-hsüan*) definitely shows that the
translation may be revised: ". . . A woman will beautify herself for the
man who is pleased in her." Why not even "for her lover"?

Of course it is not an easy matter to evaluate glosses and commentaries. Some of the Ch'ing scholars have thrown much light on ancient
texts; hence a student of, say, the *Shih*, must acquaint himself with
Ch'en Huan's contributions. But it is quite likely that the writer of the
text the translator is interested in, and who is quoting the *Shih*, may not
have followed or anticipated Ch'en Huan's interpretations; he may have
been a follower of Chu Hsi. In other words, the translator must decide
which interpretation the writer had in mind when he adopted the particular *Shih* passage.

Another serious task for the translator is to be critical of his text.
The sentence 嘗從觀畫虞舜見娥皇女英 is nonsensical; it cannot
be translated. But a translator has interpreted the passage as: "On one
occasion they were looking at a picture of the emperor Shun gazing at
[his wives] E-huang and Nü-ying." As the text does not make sense, the
translator ought to have emended it before translating. The emendation
should be made on the basis of the original Ts'ao Chih text: either as
嘗從觀畫,過虞舜之像,見娥皇女英 ("On one occasion she was
looking at pictures in his company: they were inspecting the portraits of
the Emperor Shun [and his entourage], when they saw the portrait of
E-huang and Nü-ying") as in *T'ai-p'ing Yü-lan*; or as

嘗從觀畫,過虞舜之廟,見娥皇女英

("On one occasion, etc., when they visited the temple of Shun, they saw
the portraits of E-huang and Nü-ying") as in *I-wen Lei-chü*. (The second
reading seems to be inferior.) At any rate, there is no question of the
good emperor's leering at his wives in public.

The sentence

後漢光武明德馬皇后.美於色,厚於德,帝用嘉之

is translated: "Under the later Han, 'the Empress Ma, [termed] "Illustrious Virtue," consort of Kuang Wu Ti, was as beautiful in face as
she was great in virtue, so that the Emperor took much delight in her.'"

Now the empress Ma was not the consort of Kuang Wu Ti but of his son Ming Ti, hence the character 明 here. The text seems to be derived from an essay of Ts'ao Chih (now existing in excerpts in *T'ai-p'ing Yü-lan* 137 and 750 and *I-wen Lei-chü* 74), where the telltale 光 武 does not occur. (The translator could have looked into Giles's *Biographical Dictionary*, which he seems to be familiar with, under No. 1471, "Ma Hou" 馬 后, where the information is correctly given.) 明 德, then, means "Consort of Ming-ti and canonized 'Virtuous.' " Furthermore, 明 in the canonization is supposed to mean 照 臨 四 方 (i.e., it means "omnilucent," not "illustrious"). Incidentally, "illustrious" seems to be a favorite word with Sinologists: a newcomer thinks he is improving on MM. Bynner and Kiang by translating 不 才 明 主 棄 as "Because I lack talent, the *illustrious* ruler has rejected me." Of course, 明 主 means "a wise ruler," as Bynner and Kiang have it. The phrase always refers to the intelligence of a ruler as in 明 王 in *Shu* ("intelligent kings," Legge's translation, p. 526), and in 明 主 好 同 而 暗 主 好 獨 in *Hsün-tzŭ*.

The problem of context can be best illustrated by an actual example. When James Legge makes Mencius say (*The Works of Mencius*, pp. 321–22), "The great man does not think beforehand of his words that they may be sincere, nor of his actions that they may be resolute;—he simply speaks and does what is right," it is not fair to father on Mencius the intention to absolve the great man from sincerity of words and resoluteness of action. Yet one of the acutest minds in the West can comment: "The opportunism which has been regarded as the chief merit and the chief defect of Confucianism shows clearly here." Does it? What was it that Mencius had in mind when he made "this rather sinister seeming pronouncement"? Opportunist as he may now and then have been in actual life, Mencius was not preaching anything very sinister, for he was merely trying to make more precise what Confucius had said. Once asked by Tzŭ-kung to describe an "officer" (*shih*), Confucius described three types, in the following anticlimactic scale—a man with the sense of shame in him, never failing in his mission for the sovereign; a man praised for filial piety and fraternal love; and "a man who makes point of sincerity in his words and resoluteness in his actions, a truly obstinate little man," 言 必 信, 行 必 果, 硜 硜 然 小 人 哉. Now, Mencius probably was asked to describe a great man (*ta-jen*); and he chose to state the opposite of what Confucius described as "a little man," by inserting the negative *pu* into the two Confucian sentences and adding something positive after them:

大人者言不必信，行不必果，惟義所在. As Ezra Pound once wrote, "Mencius nowhere turns against K'UNG, all of Mencius is implicit in K'ung's doctrine" (see *The Criterion*, July, 1938). The poet himself translates the passage in question as follows:

> not words whereto to be faithful
> nor deeds that they be resolute
> only that bird-hearted equity make timber
> and lay hold of the earth.

There is no compromise in this version (except the compromise with popular etymology in the last two lines). In spite of the fact that Mencius' mind has been analyzed and his book is used in classrooms, it does not seem always to be easy to understand Mencius' text in the light of context.

3. Rhetoric and Sentiment

> Tain't what a man sez, but wot he means that the traducer has got to bring over.

Bernard Berenson, in his *Sketch for a Self-portrait*, has recently thrown down the gauntlet to translators from the Chinese:

> When one comes to German and attempts to translate its abstract and qualitative terms the task is fraught with almost insurmountable difficulties, as the English or French or Italian versions of German poets and philosophers prove amply. Yet, though many of us have a living language group to help us out, who can offer a contemporary satisfactory rendering of *Gemüt?* When it is a question of Greek—Plato, for instance—how convey in any speech of today the exact meaning of σωφροσύνη? Then dare to translate the ancient Chinese and Indian thinkers.

Surely, most of us wince at this challenge, for it is a very serious one. And the reason why such a challenge is so difficult to meet is that we know very little of what might be called the rhetoric and sentiment of the ancient Chinese thinkers. If it is true, as T. S. Eliot says in *The Sacred Wood*, that "an understanding of Elizabethan rhetoric is as essential to the appreciation of Elizabethan literature as an understanding of Victorian sentiment is essential to the appreciation of Victorian literature and George Wyndham," affairs are still more complicated in the case of Chinese writers and thinkers. Where nothing is obsolete or even obsolescent and all writers of reputation are conscious of and groan under the dead weight of the past, it is no easy matter to disentangle true sentiment from false rhetoric, to distinguish between tradition and individuality, to discriminate a sentiment of the heart from mere lip service to respectable rhetorical devices—in short, to place every word in the proper perspective of space and time.

There is a good example illustrating the rhetorical aspect: in the "Canon of Shun" we read

詩言志　謌永言　聲依永　律和聲.

There has been some earnest controversy over the precise meaning of this passage. In spite of the fact that the first two sentences have been bandied about by almost every literary historian or critic, it is a moot point whether to take the words at their face values (if there are such things). Moreover, the matter becomes complicated when each writer appropriates the sentences in his own fashion and makes them put on some new coloring, without being aware (I have the temerity to assert) of their rhetorical nature.

If "psychosinology" (we must thank the author of *Finnegans Wake* for inventing this handy word) is a necessary discipline (how else do we hope to get at each writer's sentiment?), "etymosinology," otherwise known as "the ideogrammatic method," is usually frowned upon. But we will have to apply the methodology of that discredited discipline to evaluate the first two sentences of Shun's definition. We all know that 詩 $_o$si < *siag and 志 tsi° < *ţiag were to all intents and purposes homophonous in ancient phonology; furthermore, the 寺 element of 詩 and the character 志 have an identical component, 之 (degenerated in conventionalized writings to 土); finally, 言, the other component of 詩, is the same as the second character in the first sentence. In other words, the sentence is a very clever but essentially etymological or etymosinological trick. In fact, the *Shih-ming* 釋名, whose characteristic feature is its definition by homophones, defines 詩 as 之也, 志之所之也,.[3] In the second sentence, 謌永言, none of the three characters is homophonous; but we must note that one component of the first character in the phrase stands independently as the third character. To that extent the second sentence is also an etymological definition.

How seriously, then, do we have to take those two statements? Etymology by itself lends neither credit nor discredit to any definition; only when it excludes all other things does it become suspect. A translator faced with a passage like the above must see it in its true light before he attempts to comprehend its import or sentiment. Furthermore, he ought to interpret all subsequent adoptions of such a passage (e.g., in Liu Hsieh's *Wen-hsin Tiao-lung*) in the light of the adopters' inferred understanding of the original passage. A veritable Chinese box indeed.

Years ago G. L. Dickinson wrote, naïvely I am sure, of Chinese poetry: "It is of all poetry I know the most human and the least symbolic or romantic. It contemplates life just as it presents itself, without any veil of ideas, any rhetoric or sentiment." Many of us would agree with most of this statement; it is not for nothing that Dickinson claimed to have been a Chinaman in one of his former incarnations. But "without rhetoric or sentiment"? Of course, Dickinson is here using the two words in slightly different senses from Eliot; perhaps he meant that Chinese poetry is entirely sincere and without cant. And yet there is enough of rhetoric and sentiment—even in Dickinsonian senses—in Chinese poetry and prose to confuse innocent translators.

The second aspect, that of sentiment, may be better treated in connection with a word that has played a paramount role in the history of China and seems to have lost not a particle of its efficacy today. I mean 民 or 人民.

We hear often of the so-called oriental contempt for human life. China may be a part of Orient or, as Dickinson and Harold Acton would insist, may not be one, but the salient feature of Chinese political philosophy has always been its attention to the idea of the people. In fact, 民 has always been identified with *Homo sapiens* and never with *Homo pekinensis* alone. It is a word which never has sunk as low as "vulgar," "plebeian," "popular," "le bas peuple" (下 民 never meant anything of this sort), "peuple" (used as an adjective), "populace" (as in Matthew Arnold's renowned tripartite classification of English society into Barbarians, Philistines, and Populace).

It would be the height of folly to believe that the Chinese have always realized their political ideal. Nor is it relevant to discuss the gap between ideal and action here, for our immediate concern is with the simple words *min* and *jen-min*. The problem for the translator, then, boils down to this: Has he done justice to the full connotation of those words by rendering them as "the people"? Is there any other way of rendering them?

More or less allied with the problem of rhetoric and sentiment is the annoying nature of Chinese literary style in general. In most of the civilized languages the two categories of prose and verse are usually distinguished more or less sharply. Speaking of prose rhythm, George Saintsbury wrote: "The great principle of foot arrangement in prose and of Prose Rhythm, is Variety." With regard to diction and other technical devices, T. E. Hulme thought that "prose [is] a museum where all the old weapons of poetry [are] kept." It is, on the other hand, pretty much of an impossibility to demarcate between the two categories in the Chinese literature of the past. If they have developed as more or less separate entities in the West, they coalesce and merge in

Chinese; in fact, it would not be incorrect to say that the genius of Chinese prose is verse. Take the case of *p'ien-t'i-wen*, "parallel prose." Is it prose or verse? (That some of the things written in this genre are anything but *poetry* is beyond question, but it is not so simple to decide whether parallel prose is *verse* or prose.) And parallelism or symmetry are ingrained in Chinese thinking.

In the West a prosateur who writes blank verse is the butt of critics; Charles Dickens with his "As we struggle on, / nearer and nearer to the sea, from which / this mighty wind was blowing dead on shore, / its force became more and more / terrific, etc.," has served as an object lesson. But a Chinese prosateur is all the more appreciated for the blank verse he might scatter through his prose writing.

The matter becomes still more complicated when we consider the appalling amount of evocation in Chinese prose. It is not only in regard to rhythm and diction that Chinese prose approaches verse but also in the quality known specifically as poetic. When a well-known student of Chinese art translates a verse inscription on a painting as a piece of prose, chopping the lines into bars of two, three, or even eight, nine characters, we cannot simply deplore his incompetence; it must be quite difficult to recognize verse as verse. The same applies to the Japanese musicologist who punctuated a *lü-shih* ("regular verse") as if it were a *tz'u;* probably he also thought it was a piece of prose.

4. Parataxis versus Syntaxis

> For purposes of translation one has to cut various knots, and make arbitrary decisions.

Most Chinese texts can be readily punctuated; moreover, a large number of important texts have been printed with punctuation marks, especially those reprinted in recent years. If a translator cannot correctly put dots and circles in the body of his text, obviously he is not ready for translation; he will have to wait some more years.

A serious problem, however, remains; it is not to be disposed of so lightly. Unless the translator is really competent, he will be at a loss to obtain syntaxis out of the predominantly paratactical structure of Chinese texts. For the so-called punctuation marks in Chinese texts, which any school child of ten can put down, represent nothing much beyond breathing pauses. They are neither grammatical nor logical.

There are, of course, two kinds of parataxis; one in the strict sense of the word, and the other in a loose sense. When Louis MacNeice (*Modern Poetry* [1938]) speaks of Arthur Waley's translation of Ode No. 26:

Tossed is that cypress boat,
Wave-tossed it floats;
My heart is in turmoil, I cannot sleep.

汎彼柏舟, 亦汎其流
耿耿不寐, 如有隱憂

as paratactical, he is using the word in the strict sense. The problem that concerns us here is not poetic devices like this but how to group a series of breath-units (called *chü*) into logically coalescent units. Take the passage: "My humble opinion is this concerning Master Ch'ang, who undertook the practice of art while dwelling amid the shadows of the North, and was truly competent without ever having received the cultural influence of the Middle Kingdom; who could not be moved by force nor beguiled by profit: this was indeed a MAN! How could it have been easy to get hold of him?" It is hard to understand what these sentences mean. Quite possibly the translator did not have access to a syntactically punctuated text, which would read:

愚以為: 常生者擅藝, 居幽朔之間, 不被中國
之聲教, 果能不可以勢動, 復不可以利誘; 則,
斯人也, 豈易得哉.

The translator must have punctuated the text something like the following:

愚以為常生者擅藝, 居幽朔之間; 不被中國
之聲教果能; 不可以勢動, 不可以利誘; 則斯
人也; 豈易得哉.

If the correct syntactical punctuation is followed, the text may be translated: "I would like to observe:—Master Ch'ang, a devotee of art, cannot be moved by force nor beguiled by profit, in spite of the fact that he lives in the Northern Land where Chinese civilization has not penetrated. In other words, this man is a rare phenomenon." (Here the two characters 果能 are only emphatic; they do not mean that the painter was a competent artist. The last four characters 豈易得哉 merely mean "How is it possible that such a man exists?")

A rather instructive example is furnished by a recent translation from the biography of the poet Meng Hao-jan in *Hsin T'ang-shu:* "[Already] in his youth, he loved steadfastness and righteousness, and liked to help people in distress." This should sound strange to anyone who has done any translation: what connection is there between the poet's love of steadfastness and of righteousness and his willingness to help others?

Now, the text has:

少好節義,喜振人患難.

It is possible that the translator was aware of Legge's translation of the Confucian sentence 夫達也者質直而好義, "Now the man of distinction is solid and straightforward, and loves righteousness" (*Analects*, XII, 20). But how does one love steadfastness? Did the poet love that quality in other people? or in himself, or is it that the poet was steadfast himself? If so, steadfastness in what? "Steadfastness and righteousness" for *chieh-i* is, to be sure, far better here than Giles's "chaste and good,—as a widow who does not remarry." Nor do the examples given in *P'ei-wen Yün-fu* (widows who remained steadfast to their late husbands' memory, a girl who took revenge on her father's killer by killing him, men who held fast to the course of life their conscience had dictated to them) fit with the context in question. But Meng Hao-jan (remarkable a personality as he was) was not particularly distinguished for *chieh-i* in the usual sense; the translation strikes a false note.

As the translator himself knows, the passage is derived or rewritten from Wang Shih-yüan's preface to the collected poems of Meng Hao-jan:

救患釋紛,以立義表.

Which sounds very much like Ssu-ma Ch'ien's prefatory remark on his chapter on knight-errants:

救人于厄, 振人不贍 —— 仁者有乎;
人既信, 不倍言 —— 義者有取焉;

except that Ssu ma Ch'ien uses 仁 in place of Wang Shih-yüan's 義.

The writer who penned the *Hsin T'ang-shu* passage must have intended it to be a syntactical, not a paratactical, sentence; that is, he was not enumerating three qualities that distinguished Meng Hao-jan's youth (love of steadfastness, love of righteousness, and readiness to come to men in distress); he rather expected his readers to punctuate the sentence as follows:

少好節義:喜振人患難.

Moreover, he must have used 節 either as a synonym of 義 or as its qualifier or even intensifier; at any rate, he must have thought 少好義 was not rhythmic enough. In other words, all he intended was that Meng Hao-jan was fond of playing the role of a knight-errant, *for* he was ready to come to the help of anyone in distress. The phrase 好節義, then, must mean the same thing as 好義 or 樂義 in the following sentences from *P'ei-wen Yün-fu*:

其 輕 財 好 義 如 此（漢書, 楊 惲 傳）杜 李 良 豪 俠
好 義﹕ 憂 人 之 憂, 樂 人 之 樂（馬 援, 誡 兄 子 書）
輕 財 樂 義﹕急 人 之 急, 憂 人 之 憂（宋 史, 孝 義 傳）．

The phrase 好義 occurs also in the colloquial saying 急公好義. If 義 is translated as "righteousness," the translator must warn the reader that he is using the word in the sense of Hebrew *zedokah*, "justice, righteousness," which stands for "charity," for 義 in the *Hsin T'ang-shu* does not connote the same thing as when the word is joined with 執 or 守, etc.

As a syntactical sentence, the passage should then mean: "As a youth he was generous to other people, always ready to help them when they were in distress."

5. Particles and Principles

> You crush all particles down into close conformity, and walk back and forth on them.

It is fortunate that few Sinologists, except those who are still struggling with their characters, have been victimized by particle specialists. Quite justifiably, they leave their particles to take care of themselves. Particle books are necessary evils: a standard treatise (P'ei Hsüeh-hai), very valuable for the number of illustrative examples, is a delectably concocted *olla podrida* of grammatical and lexicographical equations. And what equations indeed! The final 夫 is first equated with 乎, under which heading instances of its interrogative and interjective usages are marshalled; then it is equated with 也 , 矣, and 焉, the illustrative passages put under each of these equations being all indicative sentences. That is, the particle *fu* seems to spice almost any kind of sentence. The truth of the matter is that it is not the particle which makes a sentence indicative, etc., for the sentence itself is already indicative enough, with or without the additional seasoning.

A parallel instance is furnished by a textbook meant for classroom use, in which 罷, which is more or less a colloquial counterpart of the final 夫, is handled in the same fashion; only that the author, who incidentally does not go into any equation, invents a special category called "idiomatic" into which he puts a phrase like 就是罷, "bien entendu."

Our quarrel with the analytic particlist is that his work, legitimate and often necessary as it is, stops with analysis. We are justified in demanding that such an expert, who does not mind spending his time and energy on such rarefied things, give us some over-all and synthesizing outlook, an outlook that would tell us why a particle behaves as it does and not otherwise. He should call quits with his in-gathering of particles and samples, which has become as *recherché* as Eric Partridge's study of Shakespeare's bawdy, and with his penetrating analysis, as *raffiniert* as in the *Kama Sutra*. He should instead think boldly on the larger plane of his problem.

A tentative suggestion may be offered to such a student. All particles are divided, like Caesar's Gallia, into three tribes: functional particles (e.g., pronominal 其), which should be dealt with as a regular part of speech; decorative particles (like 之 in certain context), ubiquitous in parallel prose and allied genres; and attitudinizing particles, which convey the writer's mood toward the statement to which they are attached. (There is another category of particles, which grammarians call 辭 or 助辭 or 助字, "expletives," out of sheer despair, because they are ignorant of their real functions. But this class may turn out to belong to one of the three categories mentioned above.)

Take the Confucian saying 辭達而已矣. The last *i* is generally accepted as expressing the speaker's modesty (or mock-modesty) because it expresses the conclusion drawn from a supposition, whether expressed or not. In the present case, the protasis is a gentleman (à la Confucius) and his activities; Confucius is here making the statement *tz'u-ta* with his idealized gentleman as the frame of reference or even as the point of departure. The compound *erh-i* (而已) is translated, in the classroom cant, with "and that's all." But from what point of view? The heretical translation, "Problem of style? Get the meaning across and then STOP," seems to prove that the translator took *erh-i* as referring to or continuing the act expressed in the verb *ta*. What Confucius intended to say was probably something like this: "As for your question about the problem of style, there is nothing more for me to say in answer than that you should be able to get your meaning across." Which should have reminded the interrogator of the poor estimate Confucius had of a mere "literary" man, who may be eloquent with the three hundred odes but performs miserably as an ambassador. In short, it is a mistake to read such particles into the words of the statement itself. Attitudinizing particles, then, have to be given a psychological and even a psychoanalytical treatment.

When it comes to decorative particles, a totally different approach is needed: an aesthetic treatment. A convenient parallel is to be found in the practice of calligraphy. As is well known, no calligrapher starts a stroke abruptly; he rather deploys and maneuvers for a while the forces of his brush back and forth, up and down. Then he carries his brush resolutely forward until he reaches a point where the direction is to change; here he does the same thing as in the beginning. Nor does he lift the brush without warning, for he tarries a while before he completes the stroke. Just as there are many ways of executing the initial, medial, and final stages in executing a stroke (see the *Eight Techniques of Yung*, 永字八訣), there are any number of particles for the initial, medial, and final positions in a sentence. Take for example the beginning of Ou-yang Hsiu's essay,

相州晝錦堂記：仕宦而至將相，富貴而歸故
鄉，此人情之所榮，而今昔之所同也.

The three 而 can hardly be called functional. In fact, according to Chu Hsi, Ou-yang Hsiu did not insert the first two *erh* in the original draft; it was probably for rhetorical or decorative reasons that Ou-yang Hsiu inserted them later, for they would make the first sentences less abrupt. The reader has to take a pause when he comes to *erh*, looking backward to the two conventional and hence challenging words and looking forward, with certain anticipation, to what is coming; in a way, Ou-yang Hsiu is playing a cat-and-mouse game with his reader. Thus considered, the two initial *erh* are merely stylistic. It is baffling, therefore, to understand what Dr. Walter Simon means when he asserts that the particle *erh* placed before "the verb of which it is the object" contributes to "greater precision of thought" (cf. *Asia Major*, New Series, II, 1). The two *chih* here are also quite superfluous medial particles. The final 也, of course, belongs to the third category, but it has also a rhetorical use here: by its assertative force it challenges the reader to think, and (if he is so minded) to disagree even; but, if he wants to read on, he has to grant the truth of the statement *pro tem* at least.

Frankly, all these particles could have been excised without damaging an iota of the writer's meaning and attitude; even the functional 此, which subsumes the two preceding sentences, could have been omitted. 仕宦至將相，富貴歸故鄉，人情所榮，今昔所同 (也) could have conveyed everything meant and implied in the original passage; the reader could take recourse to, what John Addington Symonds in his book on blank verse terms, "sense and pauses" in his own fashion. Indeed, the characteristic feature of particles, as far as they are of the second and/or third category, is their dispensability.

This being so, it is wisdom not to translate particles at all rather than to translate wrongly; rather *suppressio veri* than *suggestio falsi*. As long as particlists do not come forth with some synthetic suggestions, the principle of particles can be stated thus: Particles are like pornography; one may study them if one has a taste for them and one ought to know them (just as Tseng-tzǔ maintained the necessity of knowing the art of burglary in order to protect his property), but it is not wise to talk about them publicly.

The *Hsin T'ang-shu* sentence 年 四 十 乃 遊 京 師 is faultlessly rendered in: "At the age of forty, he finally traveled to the capital." But the translator must give himself away in a footnote: "Possibly the particle *nai* 乃 here merely serves to connect the preceding adverbial phrase with the predicate. But I believe it fits the context better to take it in the sense of 'finally,' 'at last.' Literati interested in an official career usually went to the capital when they were about thirty years old." The original *Chiu T'ang-shu*, however, has: 年 四 十 來 遊 京 師, which shows that the *Hsin T'ang-shu* writer altered 來 to 乃. He could equally well have altered it to 而 or 始, or even omitted it altogether. When the translator wrote "finally" he was not translating 乃 but was merely interpolating a felicitous word. One wonders how he would have translated all the 逎 (乃) occurring in the spirited story of Hsiang Yü in *Shih-chi*. (Chavannes didn't.) Would he also translate the twenty 也 in Ou-yang Hsiu's piece 醉 翁 亭 記? (Giles didn't.)

It seems that the Anglican archbishop of Quebec was right when he said, "Logical-minded unimaginative people make great mistakes by studying the texts too intensively. . . . You need to relax—to open your heart—to listen."

6. *Quotation and Allusion*

> I have heard that the finest flower of Chinese education is that which, steeped in the Chinese classics, can convey in three pages of allusive writing, to the right readers, what would otherwise take thirty.
>
> E. E. KELLETT

Allusive style, of course, is not the monopoly of Chinese literature; it is a truly universal aspect of all literatures, past and present. The modernist poetry in the West seems to vie with ancient Chinese literature in this respect. We know that in spite of vociferous denunciation *The Waste Land* has been translated into several languages by men without serious claims to comprehending all the *bêtes noires* of the *Saturday Review of Literature*; and yet they seem to have produced tolerably accurate versions.

Whether because of the supposedly abysmal gulf between the Chinese mind and occidental mentality or for other reasons, Sinological translators seem to stumble very frequently over quotations and allusions. Yet, one cannot but admire the tolerably accurate versions they have produced in spite of the odds. The fact is, it is almost always rewarding to track down the immediate and ultimate sources of allusions and quotations, for more often than not they are glossed or commented on in those sources; hence, a translator works against odds, by despising those sources.

The sentence

記曰,將貽父母令名,必果,將貽父母羞辱,必不果

is rendered: "In the scriptures there is the saying: whoever adds to the honor and renown of his parents will be successful, whoever disgraces his parents will be unsuccessful." What scriptures? Certainly not Exod. 20:12 ("Honor thy father and thy mother . . .")? Had the translator looked into *Li-chi*, "Nei-tse," he would have found that in

父母雖没,將為善,思貽父母令名,必果
將為不善,思貽父母羞辱,必不果

where the key word *kuo* means, as Cheng Hsüan says, 決 ("resolute, unwavering"). "Certe perficiet . . . certe non perficiet" (Couvreur).

It is not difficult to discover the *locus classicus*, but it is, on the other hand, not so easy to be able to recognize a quotation or allusion as such; a second sight or a sixth sense is perhaps needed for this. The most difficult and most important thing for the translator, however, is to be able to evaluate the quoted passage in the context of the text he is translating. It is not enough to refer the reader to the *locus classicus* or quote someone else's translation of the passage. For it often happens that the writer of the text may not have interpreted the passage in question in the same way as the translator thinks, on the best authority, it should be interpreted. Furthermore, it is quite possible that the writer was not a conscientious scholar; he may have quoted the passage indirectly from a secondhand source. A parallel instance is furnished by the later French Symbolists who thought they were true disciples of Edgar Allan Poe, all the while they were misinterpreting him on the basis of a secondhand authority.

Literary history has neglected this process of misinterpretation and misunderstanding. We need to investigate, not the dreary chains of influence where we can show that one writer copied another in literal detail, but the more fascinating chains which link one poet to another he has never read but only read about or heard about, whose ideas vaguely apprehended or even misapprehended serve as catalytic agents for his own development.[4]

To give a concrete example, Lu Chi's *Wen-fu* has the following two lines:

雖區分之在茲,亦禁邪而制放,要辭達而理
舉,故無取乎冗長.

What does Lu Chi mean by 辭達, which is here made parallel to
理舉? In my version in the *Harvard Journal of Asiatic Studies* I rendered
the last line with "Essentially, words must communicate, and reason
must dominate; prolixity and long-windedness are not commendable,"
and referred the reader to Legge's *Analects*, page 305. This bare reference to an existing translation is highly irresponsible, not much more
creditable than the total silence maintained by the three previous translators. From the very fact that the two lines containing the phrase conclude a discussion of the ten genres, it seems beyond doubt that Lu Chi
did not take the Confucian saying 辭達而已矣 in the usual accepta-
tion. The traditional interpretation of this enigmatic saying seems to
have gone into Legge's translation: "In language it is simply required
that it convey the meaning." That is, a gentleman as idealized by Confucius was essentially a *Homo politicus*, whose interest in life should be much
more comprehensive than mere stylistic accomplishment; hence, he has
no time to waste on polishing his literary ability, for all he has to do is to
be able to make others understand him—a sentiment which is so poign-
antly echoed by Hsiang Yü when he said that all he wanted in the art of
letters was the ability to write down his name (書足以記姓名而已).
And this interpretation seems to have been in Yen Fu's mind when he set
up as desiderata of translation 信達雅, "Accuracy, Intelligibility,
Elegance."

It is, however, doubtful if Lu Chi accepted this interpretation in his
context, especially when he rounds out the paragraph (or strophe) with
an injunction against prolixity and long-windedness. It is quite possible
that he intended what Ezra Pound meant when he interpreted the Confucian saying with

> in discourse what matters is
> to get it across *e poi basta*.

If he did, there is no question of Lu Chi's "vaguely apprehending"
the Confucian meaning; a scholar of no mean accomplishment, he must
have wilfully distorted the import of the Sage.

And I like Augustine Birrel. I happened to correct him when he said that the Apocry-
pha was not read in the Church services; and again when he said that Elihu the Jebusite
was one of Job's comforters. He tried to override me in both points, but I called for a
Bible and proved them. He said, glowering very kindly at me: "I will say to you what
Thomas Carlyle once said to a young man who caught him out in a misquotation,
'Young man, you are heading straight for the pit of Hell!' "

Like Robert Graves, the Sinological student has to cite Scripture for
his purpose, unmindful of the consequence.

7. *Grammar and Dictionary*

Lisez, lisez; jetez la grammaire.

GUSTAVE SCHLEGEL

Un dictionnaire peut toujours être amélioré.

CHAVANNES

In recent years a number of vernacular grammarians, some of them determined to live down the allegedly idiosyncratic analogic or anagogic or even bifocal reasoning of the Chinese, have been producing grammatical treatises. And there have been also no small number of Sinologists who, laudably following the dictum *docendo discimus*, do not seem to mind washing their dirty linen in public. When in 1916 Mr. Hu Shih wrote to the editor of the *Hsin Ch'ing-nien* advocating Literary Revolution, he managed to put "Insist on Grammar" as one of the eight points in his program. This is a bit surprising because such a schoolmasterly *Gebot* was not to be found in the Imagist credos which must have inspired that program. But it is not so surprising to see Ch'en Tu-hsiu (the editor of the journal) and Ch'ien Hsüan-t'ung reacting violently against that injunction.

Ch'en Tu-hsiu thought (and Ch'ien Hsüan-t'ung confirmed it) that, as grammar in the usual senses of the word does not exist in Chinese, what Dr. Hu Shih considered to be grammar should be, as had always been, relegated to *Stilistik* (or rhetoric). Probably the writer had in mind Yü Yüeh's *Ku-shu I-i Chü-li* and its continuations. At any rate, it cannot be seriously disputed that books like that have more use for Sinological students than Gabelentz or even Stanislas Julien. Gustave Schlegel was not the best of Sinologists; yet he had a modicum of sound sense when he advised his students to forget their grammar. Indeed, no one has ever learned to read ancient Chinese texts from analytical grammar; a warning example is that of Angelo Zottoli, S.J., who is known for his imposing tomes of *Cursus*. In his Latin grammar written in Chinese the phrases (*chü*) are mostly perfect, but the juxtaposition is nightmarish. It would take a genius to string together those phrases (some in the *Shih-chi* style, some in the *fu* style, some sheer colloquialisms) into coherent sentences. The sooner we forget grammar, the speedier will we recover our sanity.

Another fetish of a group of Sinologists who still think Chinese (classical Chinese) is a "language" in the conventional sense is their firm conviction that a perfect dictionary will smooth their way. Alas, they are whoring after false gods. First, such a dictionary is impossible to make; next, what earthly use is a two-hundred-volume dictionary to anyone? After all is said and done, the meaning is determined from the context; *ergo*, a translator must get a firm grasp of his context in the largest sense of the word, and there no dictionary will avail him. Moreover, a dictionary is no help if the wrong entry is chosen.

It is generally known that Chinese scholars themselves seldom use any dictionary except the *Shuo-wen* and the *Ching-chi Tsuan-ku* (Juan Yüan); certainly, Sinologists can profit from the monumental *Shuo-wen Chieh-tzŭ Ku-lin* and *Shuo-wen T'ung-hsün Ting-sheng* (which incorporates most of the *Ching-chi Tsuan-ku* entries), plus *P'ei-wen Yün-fu*. No self-respecting translator should use Mathews, Giles, Couvreur, etc., after he has studied a year, unless it be to find English synonyms.

As an illustration, take the sentence 作 長 夜 之 樂 of *Han-shu* 100 A/3 *b* (ed. Wang Hsien-ch'ien) or 為 長 夜 之 樂 as in *Lieh-nü Chuan*. What does 樂 mean here? Which of the three dictionary meanings should be accepted? "Music" (*nglŏk / ngåk₀ / yüeh⁴*)? "Joy, dissipation" (*glâk / lâk₀ / lê⁴*)? "To like" (*nglŏg / ngau° / yao⁴*)? A recent translator seems to have accepted the first meaning, for his version makes the sentence "to make the night long with music." He probably did not look into the corresponding passage in *Shih-chi* 3: 為 長 夜 之 飲, "il donna des orgies qui duraient toute la nuit" (Chavannes). Of course there is no reason why Pan Ku should not have meant *music* when he altered 飲 to 樂. But Pan Ku was no puritan, nor had he to reckon with Mrs. Grundy. Hence it is more likely that he used 樂 in the second sense, which comes nearest to 飲. In fact, it must have been used in the sense of 淫 樂 in the phrase 好 酒 淫 樂 occurring a few lines ahead in Pan Ku's own text. What boots a dictionary then? Probably the translator was trying to give a sophisticated translation; witness "to make night long" for 為 長 夜 ("in order to prolong the night"?). If it comes of sophistication it is quite unfortunate, for the sense of the entire sentence is totally altered.

The couplet

微 雲 淡 河 漢, 疏 雨 滴 梧 桐

is rendered by a recent scholar as:

> Delicate clouds dim the Milky Way,
> Drizzling rain drops from the wu-t'ung trees.

The translator seems to have labored on this; witness the alliteration, more or less corresponding to the original scheme. But "drizzling rain drops *from* the wu-t'ung trees" is totally false, for it drops onto the wu-t'ung leaves; the poet could hear the tatoo of raindrops. Of course, no dictionary or grammar can ever hope to take notice of such individual examples.

Needless to say, amateur Sinologists whose obsession with their pet theories is as great as their veneration of dictionaries tend to lose sight of context. Take a translation of the passage which summarizes the gist of dialectical metaphysics of the "Book of Changes":

> When the sun goes, the moon comes;
> When the moon goes, the sun comes.
> Sun and moon alternate; thus light comes
>   into being.
>
> When cold goes, heat comes;
> When heat goes, cold comes.
> Cold and heat alternate, and thus the year
>   completes itself.
>
> The past contracts.
> The future expands.
> Contraction and expansion act upon each other;
>   hereby arises that which furthers.

It is almost unbelievable that the translator took 往者 and 來者 as "the past" and "the future." The third strophe means that the sun, the moon, heat, and cold go because they have to stoop (lit. "bend") before the cyclic law, and come because they are allowed to have their due (lit. "unbend") in the cyclic system. That *che* here serves the function of quotation marks can be seen by anyone who has examined the context. (It is also possible that *che* is a personifier; i.e., *wang-che* may mean "the goer.")

A similar example of the oversophistication is: "When anger, sorrow, joy, pleasure are in being but are not manifested, the mind may be said to be in a state of Equilibrium; when the feelings are stirred and co-operate in due degree the mind may be said to be in a state of Harmony." Which is meant to be a translation of

喜怒哀樂之未發謂之中，發而皆中節謂之和。

As the translation is made to support the synaesthesis theory, there is no doubt that the word "co-operate" is to be understood in a normal sense: the four feelings, after they are stirred one and all, *work together* in an ideally harmonious manner. This is a unique interpretation of the passage. Of course, the original text is vague; and there is nothing to forbid our translator from taking the four feelings as working and acting simultaneously, but anyone who has studied all the competent commentaries on the text will have no doubt whatsoever that the writer of the passage probably intended to leave the matter to the reader's sense of proportion as to whether he should consider one feeling or more than one stirred. He will at any rate have no hesitation in thinking that the stirred feeling or feelings work in harmony with the personality of the man whose feeling or feelings are stirred and, *ipso facto*, with the cosmic scheme itself. The translator is likely to defend his position by referring to the dictionary meaning of 皆 as "all."

8. Traduttore, Traditore

And the end of all our exploring
Will be to arrive where we started
And know the place for the first time.

All the difficulties mentioned in the above can and should be surmounted, sooner or later, by honest and earnest students. But there is a big roadblock still looming large before them: our ignorance of Chinese psychology. What do we know about terms like 性, 情, etc.? And what does 義 really mean? And when shall we come to know more precisely about all these terms?

illa cantat, nos tacemus: quando ver venit meum?
quando fiam uti chelidon ut tacere desinam?

As long as we are ignorant of their meanings, we will have to be cautious about what we do with them; we should certainly abstain from reading our favorite theories into the innocent texts.

Meanwhile I see no reason why we should desist from translating Chinese texts; we cannot expect to enjoy "another lifetime," nor would our translations be perfect if we enjoyed several. But translations made with all conscientiousness are the *sine qua non* of all Chinese scholarship, and the effort to translate heightens one's awareness of his own heritage even as he seeks to understand another.

NOTES

1. The last word on the art of translation was said in 1950 by Marianne Moore, the gifted translator of La Fontaine's *Fables*: "The first requisite of a translation, it seems to me, is that it should not sound like a translation. That similacrum of spontaneity can be a fascinating thing indeed. A master axiom for all writing, I feel, is that of Confucius: 'When you have done justice to the meaning, stop.' That implies restraint, that discipline is essential."

2. Which is what Goethe charged Heine with but is also a term used by Lu Chi (賽愛).

3. Cf. 詩者志之所之也，在心為言，發言為詩 in the "Great Preface" to the *Shih*. Does this mean the same thing as Ezra Pound's definition: "Poetry is a verbal statement of emotional values. A poem is an emotional value verbally stated"?

4. Jacob Isaacs, *The Background of Modern Poetry* (London, 1951), p. 19.

II

APPROACHES TO THE PROBLEM

THE ADDED ARTIFICER

RENATO POGGIOLI

ONE MAY very well wonder about the psychic urge, or cast of mind, that turns a writer into a translator, or makes him behave like one. Is that urge more or less identical with the one leading a painter or sculptor to make a copy? Even if the motive were the same, the outcome would still be different, since a translation is more than a mere study or unpretentious formal exercise. Would it be more correct to assume that the operation of translating does not differ too radically from interpretive performances such as playacting, or, to adopt a more fitting simile, such as the public reading of a poem? In theory the difference may seem slight, but it is far from negligible in practice. The intent in playacting and poetry reading is to give voice and gesture to a verbal composition which, though physically mute and inert on the written or printed page, may speak and "act" eloquently by itself for the inner ear, and imaginary vision, of the "lonely crowd" of its readers. Translating, however, endeavors to give the verbal composition a strange clothing, a changed body, and a novel spirit. Should we then extend the previous analogy to another set of interpretive crafts, and suggest that translating is the literary equivalent of musical direction and execution? After all, like the performing musician, the translator goes to work only when he has another artist's creation before his eyes. The parallel may seem less misleading if we keep in mind that the complex technique of musical execution demands of its practitioners the deciphering and retranscribing of the whole score.

That translation is an interpretive art is a self-evident truth. Yet it is a paradox peculiar to the translator that he is the only interpretive artist working in a medium which is both identical with, and different from, that of the original he sets out to render in his own terms. Except for him, all artistic interpreters may be said to belong to one of the following categories. The first is that of the performing artist, who, whether he is an actor, singer, or instrumentalist, employs as his own vehicle the expressive material forming the aesthetic substance of the original work he is interpreting. The second is made up of all those artists I would like to call decorative, in the figurative sense

of that epithet, and is exemplified by the scene designer, by the composer writing music to accompany a play or a ballet, by the mime or
dancer reshaping words and tunes into facial gestures, bodily acts,
and choreographic figures. Obviously the mime and the dancer who
manipulate the pure stuff of their art, and treat their literary script
or musical score as servants rather than as masters, are not interpreters,
but creators in their own right. Otherwise, the artists of the decorative
class are equivalents of the book illustrator, who is their archetype,
and who, like them, uses a medium other than that which is specific
to the work he is supposed to decorate or illustrate.

Giving the term a restricted and derogatory connotation, one
might designate the artists of the first category as mere "interpreters,"
while the members of the second deserve to be called "translators"
in a general or ideal sense. As for the artist whom we name translator
in the normal and restricted meaning of that term, he is in a class
by himself, since he works in a dual mode, and follows both methods
at once. If we look at him from an abstract and generic perspective,
we see that he molds the same aesthetic material as that of his model,
namely, language. But if we replace that perspective with a more
concrete and specific one, we discover that he elaborates a linguistic
and literary material alien to, or estranged from, that of the text he
translates. In scholastic terms, both original and translation deal with
a single substance, differentiated into two unique, and incommen-
surable, accidents. It is this oddity, or quiddity, that changes the translator from a decorator into a re-creator, that turns him into an author
or a poet, a lesser author or a minor poet, to be sure, but still a genuine
one. From this viewpoint he stands at the opposite pole from the
performing artist, whether musician, singer, or actor: especially from
the last two, since the one dresses himself all too often in the peacock's
feathers, and the other conceals his menial task under the cover of his
professional "hypocrisy," to use a term originally alluding to the hiding of the actor's face under the mask of his role.

Thus the translator is the only interpretive artist who reveals his
modest calling and precious craft under the honest trademark of his
name. By reducing all other interpretive artists to a common denomi-
nator, one can see that when compared to the translator most members of the second group are hardly more than simple transliterators,
while those of the first descend to the level of mere scribes. The truth
of this must not allow us to forget that the nature of the translator's
task denies him an opportunity that lies within the grasp of his more

fortunate rivals. A few of them, like the illustrator who takes his text as a pretext, may become original creators by transcending rather than by transposing their model. What enables them to achieve this feat is the absolute estrangement of their technical modes from those of the original work. The translator cannot be original in the same degree because he works with images and words which, like a grafted branch, or even a transplanted tree, still owe their new life to a seed planted elsewhere by other hands. This is the reason that the translator cannot share with any one of his fellow adapters or remakers the classical definition of *artifex additus artifici*, which suits him alone, even though originally it was not coined for his exclusive benefit.

As in the case of every interpretive artist, the chief task of the translator seems to be the transposing of an alien aesthetic personality into the key of his own. If this is true, then the most relevant question one can ask is whether, when he feels his way toward the foreign text — close contact with which will finally ignite the vital spark — the translator looks at that text in a mirror reflecting the other or the self. It is my contention that, like the original poet, the translator is a Narcissus who in this case chooses to contemplate his own likeness not in the spring of nature but in the pool of art. This may not apply to those translators who flourished in other more traditional cultures, and who took upon themselves the single task of rendering into the living speech of their own nation or people the sacred books of divine revelation and of ancient wisdom. If the translators of the Holy Writ worked only in teams of scholar-priest, searching through the babel of tongues for no other mirror than that reflecting the Word of God, the individual authors of those pre-Renaissance vernacular versions of the classics which took in Italian the significant name of *volgarizzamenti* (a word containing already, at least potentially, the very meaning it would acquire only in our time) acted primarily as servants of culture, as transmitters of a beauty or truth which would be lost without them. Using the dichotomy by which Schiller divided the poetic world of the ancients from that of the moderns, one could define the translators of that old-fashioned type as "naïve," and those of the type we now know as "sentimental." This is another way of saying that the translator of our time is, like all moderns, a highly subjective artist. It seems evident to me that the modern translator, like the modern artist, strives after self-expression, although the self-expression may well be a not too literal expression of the self. The experience he tries to fix within an alien framework may be either psychological or cultural, or both: it may be rooted in history, or even in biography. In brief, the translator, no less than the literary creator, tries to reshape within his work an *Erlebnis* in the Diltheyan sense of the term.

In reality, what Dilthey named *Erlebnis* does not differ too greatly from what more traditional thinkers or more conventional critics are wont to name with the old-fashioned designation of content. Yet, if such a conception is applied to the translator, it seems at first sight that he works without a content of his own. This is the generally accepted hypothesis, so well conveyed by the images describing translating as the decanting of a liquid from one vessel into another, or as the pouring of an old wine into a new bottle. Both metaphors obviously suggest that there is a single content, the original one, supplying the one thing or substance that remains unchanged, or hardly changed, in the translating process. Both similes, within the limits of the hypothesis they express, are apt and proper in more ways than one. Their greatest merit lies in the dialectical complexity of their very images, which thus qualify and modify the hypothesis itself. So the first metaphor implies that during the operation of decanting or pouring, the liquid may be spilled, or a more than a negligible part of the original content may be lost. As for the second metaphor, it may suggest the altogether paradoxical case of an *old* wine breaking a *new* bottle. All this notwithstanding, both metaphors are dangerously misleading: the student of translation can no longer be satisfied with the conventional supposition that what takes place during the operation is but a change of containers, affecting only slightly the decanted content.

It may well be an error to believe that the translator has nothing to offer but an empty vessel which he fills with a liquor he could not distill by himself. One should play, at least tentatively, with the contrary hypothesis; one should even suppose, using a related, if opposite, image, that the translator himself is a living vessel saturated with a formless fluid or sparkling spirit, which he cannot hold any longer in check; that when the spirit is about to fizzle, or the liquid to overflow, he pours it into the most suitable of all the containers available to him, although he neither owns the container nor has he molded it with his own hands. Were this true, one could even claim that translating is like pouring a new wine into an old bottle; and that if the wine fails to burst the bottle, it is only because the new wine required the old bottle as the only form or frame within which it could rest. To accept such a hypothesis one must believe, with the protagonist of *Dr. Zhivago*, the recent novel by the great Russian poet Boris Pasternak (who by the way is also a great translator of Shakespeare), that art is not "an object or aspect of form, but rather a mysterious and hidden component of content." According to such a view, the translator is a literary artist looking outside himself for the form suited to the experience he wishes to express.

This seems to run against the usual presupposition that the translator is not a creator or a poet but merely an artisan or a craftsman of words, by which one means that he himself has nothing to say. Yet one must reject the notion that the translator's is a voice singing tunes that others have composed for him. The view that he is a shallow virtuoso or an empty formalist is fundamentally wrong. There are to be sure translators of this sort, but they are not exemplary ones: even among so-called original authors there are also artists of the same breed. The translator who aims solely at reproducing the web or shell of an alien poem through his own technical skill should be considered an imitator, and treated as if he were an unconscious parodist (not a plagiarist, because to plagiarize means to copy, and the very necessity of re-creating a foreign original into another set of verbal norms prevents the translator from copying, even if he wants to). At any rate what moves the genuine translator is not a mimetic urge, but an elective affinity: the attraction of a content so appealing that he can identify it with a content of his own, thus enabling him to control the latter through a form which, though not inborn, is at least congenial to it.

Such a hypothesis turns translation into a kind of *Gelegenheits-dichtung*, in a sense which is not at too great variance with the Goethean use of that term. Through the shock of a recognition primarily psychic in quality, the translator suddenly finds that a poem newly discovered, or discovered anew, offers him an exemplary solution for his own formal problems, as well as an expressive outlet for his subjective *Erlebnis*. The foreign poem becomes in him a "model," in the sense that this word has recently acquired in the field of scientific theory and inquiry. It is in such a context that we can define translation as a form of literary mimesis, and in such a context alone. If this is true, then translation is, both formally and psychologically, a process of inscape, rather than of escape; and this is why, of all available aesthetic concepts, the best suited to define the activity and the experience of the translator is that of *Einfühlung* or "Empathy," which must not be understood merely as the transference of an emotional content. The foreign poem is not merely an object, but an archetype, which provokes an active spiritual impact. The translator is peculiarly *disponible*, to use an epithet which was very dear to André Gide, a man of letters who paid tribute to translation in words and deeds, and who publicly praised literary influence and the writer's willingness to submit to it.

The *disponibilité* of the translator is primarily formal, precisely because an external formal sanction is the main object of his quest. There is no paradox in maintaining that this leads us to a psychological theory of translation, and even in claiming that such a theory must be a Freudian one. Yet the translator is not an inhibited person; he is rather an inhibited artist, satisfied only when he is able to lay the burning ashes of his heart in a well-wrought urn outside of himself. Or one can say that he succeeds in overcoming his repressions only in his tête-à-tête with a foreign poet; and that he ends by sublimating his inhibitions through the catharsis of an alien form. Translation is up to a point an exorcism, or, if we prefer, the conjuration, through another spirit, of one's Self. Using for our own purpose the title of a famous play of Pirandello, one may say that the translator is a "character in search of an author," in whom he can identify, or at least transpose, a part of himself. Such identification is not an impersonation; it is rather a transference, in the psychoanalytic meaning of the term. The translator is not a masquerader who deceives others as well as himself by acting an alien role, or by aping somebody else: the ultimate mimesis for which he is striving is after all an aesthetic one. He is a character who, in finding an author without, finds also the author within, himself. There may be some sense in the claim that the translator even more than the critic is a poet *manqué*, but this applies not to the translator's achievement, but rather to his pursuit or quest. Nor must we forget that such a quest or pursuit may intermittently attract the original writer also, when he too must search anew for the author in himself.

The process by which an artistic personality is "transposed" into the key of another takes place on such a mysterious plane that critical evaluation must content itself with inarticulate acknowledgments — a nod of approval, an outburst of applause, or some graphic sign of enthusiasm such as the exclamation point the reader traces on the margin of his text. When looking at the raw material which the translator molds and reshapes into a work of his own, however, the critic finds a set of concrete problems that may and must be submitted to detailed analysis and elaborate judgment. Here the terms of comparison are not only the language of the original work and the language of the translated one, but even more the two literary traditions involved. It is difficult, but possible, to establish a critical bridge between them. To a foreign reader any literary composition, even if relatively near in spirit and time, always looks in part or in degree like an exotic product. This impression of exoticism is often due to the very traits that make the work intimate and familiar to the native reader. How should the translator deal with such traits? Should he reduce them to a maximum, or a minimum, degree? Should he attenuate or accentuate the effects implied in details like these? In simple terms, should the translator's diction tend toward under- or over-statement? Or, in a broader literary context, should he lean toward the splendid anonymity, toward the glorious commonplaceness of classical taste, or toward that picturesque emphasis, that sense of local color, that predilection for the characteristic and the unique, which distinguish the romantic outlook? These are some of the questions which the critic of translation must ask of the translator and his work. The translator addresses the same questions to himself, and answers them, both in theory and practice, through a written or unwritten *ars poetica* of his own.

If these are the most pertinent questions, the only ones really worth asking, I wonder whether we can still consider unavoidable the double alternative suggested by the well-known French saying that translations are like women, homely when faithful, and unfaithful when lovely. After all, in every artistic pursuit beauty is the highest kind of fidelity, and ugliness is only another name for disloyalty: there is no literary genre where immorality is less frowned on than translation itself. Its immorality is to be seen only in transgressing the precept of Dante Gabriel Rossetti, according to which no good poem should ever be turned into a bad one. A famous aesthetician maintains that the modes of the ugly are many, and yet easy to classify, while the beautiful has in each case a mode that is at once universal and unique. If this is true, then Novalis was right in claiming that successful translations can be only *verändernde*, or "metamorphic," not literal. The gifted translator is an alchemist who changes a piece of gold into another piece of gold, thus obeying Rossetti's rule in full.

Those who repeat approvingly the old Italian pun making a

traditore of every *traduttore* forget that the translator becomes the traitor only out of necessity and against his will. The good translator errs almost always in good faith; his greatest vice is not falsity, but ignorance, which is one of the blessings of innocence, as well as one of its frailties. Ignorance leads primarily to sins of omission, which are venial ones. Outrageous as the mistakes of a translator may appear, they are faults, not wrongdoings, a fact all too often overlooked by his critics, who in this seem still to follow the old-fashioned practice of pointing out failings and failures, rather than merits and *réussites*. The reviewer of a translation in print who, before recognizing its worth with faint, final praise that sounds like a supercilious dismissal, yields for too long to the nasty self-indulgence of *Schadenfreude*, endlessly and sneeringly listing all the occasions on which the poor translator fumbled and stumbled, is a worse sinner than he. There is no other literary situation where a plea for critical fairness is equally overdue.

The mythology of translation all too often compares the plight of the translator to that of Tantalus and Sisiphus, thus emphasizing the helplessness and powerlessness of his role. Heine made the same point when with a quaint image he defined the translator's attempt to recapture the ravishing and vanishing beauty of his model as "straw-plaiting sunbeams." Heine seemingly forgot that the poet tries to achieve the same miracle, and that he succeeds only rarely in doing so. How many mystics or symbolists have claimed that even original poetry is a form of translation, an attempt to rephrase the heavenly music that many can no longer hear in the noisy chaos of this world! Yet the fact that the translator tries to reproduce at once two pre-established harmonies, one of which has already been shaped into literary form, does not necessarily mean that he must accept the latter as his absolute aesthetic norm. He may well break the pattern he has chosen, before rebuilding it anew. Many critics think otherwise, and this is why they make too much of the difference between translating into verse and translating into prose. (If I use the preposition *into* rather than *from*, it is because the distinction so suggested is the more significant of the two.) Yet translation is not a composition, as the Italians say, on a set of *rime obbligate*; its measure is never given beforehand. The challenge of the original predetermines an infinite number of responses: and one may easily mention numberless instances of the rendering of poetic works into non-metered speech. Even such a master of versecraft as Mallarmé, who believed that verse was the whole of literature, chose to translate Poe's poems into prose. One could also list a few of the rarer occasions when a work originally composed in *sermo solutus* was subjected by some of its translators to the yoke of rhyme, or to the rule of rhythm. To cite a single case, which is also a famous example, Melchiorre Cesarotti transformed the leaden prose of Macpherson's Ossian, through the alchemy of his Italian translation, into a golden blank verse. At any rate, the miracle of translating may differ in degree, but not in kind, when its medium is prose rather than verse. The only differentiation worth making is between a translation undertaken with an artistic intent, provided it achieves the intent it strives for, and a translation which aims at being nothing more than a pedagogical tool: a type that does not exclude the far less educational intent of helping the lazy student unable to translate Horace, Virgil, or Cicero by himself. Functional and utilitarian as this type of translation is, it is effective only in a constant reference to the original, without which it has no independent existence. Artistic translation presupposes however both the ideal presence of the original, and its physical absence. This is the reason the Abbé Galiani recommended that a good translation be read for itself, without comparing it to the original work.

Ars est celare artem: if this principle is but a matter of tactics for any creative artist, it becomes a matter of strategy for the man of letters who cannot call himself an author precisely because he gives his voice to another one. The aesthetic inhibition that leads a *littérateur* to become a translator (either permanently or intermittently) does not easily transform itself into its own opposite, even in the most successful, or unsuccessful, cases. The ethos of the translator is a perfect blend of humility and pride. His two greatest virtues or assets are the reverence he feels toward the author or work he translates, and the sense of his own integrity as an interpreter, which is based on both modesty and self-respect. It is this alliance of independence and honesty that saves him from the temptation of peddling under his own trademark wares manufactured by others, even though he often remolds them after a design that is at least in part his own. There is no literary worker more respectful of the property of his fellow artist, none less willing to infringe on what takes the legal name of copyright. The translator always gives full credit, sometimes even more credit than is due, to the maker of a blueprint that he could not use without considerably changing and adapting it. All these characteristics indicate that the translator is perhaps the only modern artist who acts and behaves as if he were only an artisan, "pure in heart" and "poor in spirit," serving with simple and single-minded devotion a beauty to which he cannot give his name, and yet not unaware of the nobility of his calling, of the dignity of his task.

The critic must never forget that translation is an art in the old sense of the term, a sense which has disappeared in the word "artist," but which is still preserved in the word "artisan." In brief, translation must still be considered a "craft." Thus the practical criticism of translation must deal, even more than in the case of original literary creation, with what the French call *questions de métier*. While the over-all judgment of the value of a translation (which, like all values, is a value *per se*) must be a synthetic judgment, a judgment *a priori*, thus involving no parallel with the original text, the analysis of the technical problems that the translation has faced and solved cannot be made without comparisons and contrasts. The comparisons and contrasts need not turn exclusively on the relation of the translation to the original work. They should extend to its relations with the particular literary traditions to which the original and the translation belong. If we cannot relate a uniquely personal style to another style equally personal and unique, we can and must relate two historical styles, as well as all possible historical variations within each of them. Perhaps there is no literary genre where the comparative method is an apter tool of critical investigation than translation itself. The literary equivalent of the stylistic tendency which in the field of painting takes the name of "mannerism" is after all never so frequent as in the field of translation: and the latter should perhaps be considered as the most typical and perfect manifestation of what Friedrich Schlegel once called *Poesie der Poesie* (although its author wanted to define by that formula the attempt to translate the poetry of the world into the poetry of the word).

Yet, when all is said, the translator is something more than a "mannerist," than a "poet of poetry," than an artisan or juggler of words. Even when he seems attracted only by the novel and the strange, by the foreign and the exotic, by the innovations or experimentations of an alien advance-guard of which he wants to become the representative *in partibus infidelium*, the translator is always a humanist, a worshiper of tradition, a believer in the eternal values of arts and letters. In every translation there is always, even if it is hidden or buried, a vein of classicism. The whole poetics of translation could be reduced to a single tenet, that of *la difficulté vaincue*, which implies on one side the free acceptance, or better the deliberate choice, of a resistant, even refractory material, and on the other the hard-won triumph of the worker, who by the will of his mind and the skill of his hand succeeds in remolding and reshaping that material into the orderly pattern of art. Yet the translator is a classic also in a less formal sense: as I have already said, he is a kind of humanist. Like the humanist, he is at once a learner and a teacher, or a cultivator of *humanitas*, which involves both appraisal and learning, and which nobody has defined so pointedly as Aulus Gellius in a celebrated passage of *The Attic Nights*: "Those who created the Latin tongue and spoke it well never gave *humanitas* the notion inherent in the Greek word *philanthropia*. They gave that word the meaning of what the Greeks call *paideia*, i.e., knowledge of the fine arts." The noble paradox of his craft allows the translator, however, to transcend even this distinction: far from being a mere humanistic pedagogue, he may often become a humanitarian *Aufklärer*, serving even higher causes than "the aesthetic education of the human kind."

All this simply means that the translator's over-all function cannot be defined except through each one of his manifold tasks. Let us not forget that he often willingly pays the tribute which the human mind owes to science by contributing to learning and knowledge as well as to beauty and art. Sometimes the translator must take erudition as his province; often, like Martianus Capella's Mercury, he must marry Philology, who is not always a lovely maid. The variety and multiplicity of the gifts required of him make the great translator as infrequent an apparition as the great critic, who, as everybody knows, is an even rarer bird than the great poet. Yet literature cannot afford to do without good translators; in given situations, it may well need them even more than good authors. Translators are after all the most cosmopolitan among the citizens of the Republic of Letters; their absence from the scene, or their presence in a too limited number, may mean that the literary tradition will rest all too easily within the Chinese wall it has erected around itself. By denying itself a look beyond that wall, a literature is bound to die of slow exhaustion, or, as Goethe said, of self-boredom. Especially in modern times, a national literature reveals its power of renewal and revival through the quality and number of its translators. Sometimes it is able to survive only because of their efforts. We know all too well that a culture survives only by a proper response to the challenge of change, and by its timely refusal to go on aping itself.

MEANING AND TRANSLATION

WILLARD V. QUINE

1. Stimulus meaning

EMPIRICAL meaning is what remains when, given discourse together with all its stimulatory conditions, we peel away the verbiage. It is what the sentences of one language and their firm translations in a completely alien language have in common. So, if we would isolate empirical meaning, a likely position to project ourselves into is that of the linguist who is out to penetrate and translate a hitherto unknown language. Given are the native's unconstrued utterances and the observable circumstances of their occurrence. Wanted are the meanings; or wanted are English translations, for a good way to give a meaning is to say something in the home language that has it.

Translation between languages as close as Frisian and English is aided by resemblance of cognate word forms. Translation between unrelated languages, e.g., Hungarian and English, may be aided by traditional equations that have evolved in step with a shared culture. For light on the nature of meaning we must think rather of *radical* translation, i.e., translation of the language of a hitherto untouched people. Here it is, if anywhere, that austerely empirical meaning detaches itself from the words that have it.

The utterances first and most surely translated in such a case are perforce reports of observations conspicuously shared by the linguist and his informant. A rabbit scurries by, the native says "Gavagai," and our jungle linguist notes down the sentence "Rabbit" (or "Lo, a rabbit") as tentative translation. He will thus at first refrain from putting words into his informant's mouth, if only for lack of words to put. When he can, though, the linguist is going to have to supply native sentences for his informant's approval, despite some risk of slanting the data by suggestion. Otherwise he can do little with native terms that have references in common. For, suppose the native language includes sentences S_1, S_2, and S_3, really translatable respectively as "Animal," "White," and "Rabbit." Stimulus situations always differ, whether relevantly or not; and, just because volunteered responses come singly, the classes of situations under which the native happens to have volunteered S_1, S_2, and S_3, are of course mutually exclusive, despite the hidden actual meanings of the words. How then is the linguist to perceive that the native would have been willing to assent to S_1 in all the situations where he happened to volunteer S_3, and in some but perhaps not all of the situations where he happened to volunteer S_2? Only by taking the initiative and querying combinations of native sentences and stimulus situations so as to narrow down his guesses to his eventual satisfaction.

Therefore picture the linguist asking "Gavagai?" in each of various stimulatory situations, and noting each time whether the native is prompted to assent or dissent or neither. Several assumptions are implicit here as to a linguist's power of intuition. For one thing, he must be able to recognize an informant's assent and dissent independently of any particular language. Moreover, he must be able ordinarily to guess what stimulation his subject is heeding — not nerve by nerve, but in terms at least of rough and ready reference to the environment. Moreover, he must be able to guess whether that stimulation actually prompts the native's assent to or dissent from the accompanying question; he must be able to rule out the chance that the native assents to or dissents from the questioned sentence irrelevantly as a truth or falsehood on its own merits, without regard to the scurrying rabbit which happens to be the conspicuous circumstance of the moment.

The linguist does certainly succeed in these basic tasks of recognition in sufficiently numerous cases, and so can we all, however unconscious we be of our cues and method. The Turks' gestures of assent and dissent are nearly the reverse of ours, but facial expression shows through and sets us right pretty soon. As for what a man is noticing, this of course is commonly discernible from his orientation together with our familiarity with human interests. The third and last point of recognition is harder, but one easily imagines accomplishing it in typical cases: judging, without ulterior knowledge of the language, whether the subject's assent to or dissent from one's sudden question was prompted by the thing that had been under scrutiny at the time. One clue is got by pointing while asking; then, if the object is irrelevant, the answer may be accompanied by a look of puzzlement. Another clue to irrelevance can be that the question, asked without pointing, causes the native abruptly to shift his attention and look abstracted. But enough of conjectural mechanisms; the patent fact is that one does, by whatever unanalyzed intuitions, tend to pick up these minimum attitudinal data without special linguistic aid.

The imagined routine of proposing sentences in situations is suited only to sentences of a special sort: those which, like "Gavagai,"

"Red," "That hurts," "This one's face is dirty," etc., command assent
only afresh in the light of currently observable circumstances. It is a
question of *occasion sentences* as against *standing sentences*. Such are
the sentences with which our jungle linguist must begin, and the ones
for which we may appropriately try to develop a first crude concept
of meaning.

The distinction between occasion sentences and standing sentences
is itself definable in terms of the notion of prompted assent and dissent
which we are supposing available. A sentence is an occasion sentence
for a man if he can sometimes be got to assent to or dissent from it,
but can never be got to unless the asking is accompanied by a prompting stimulation.

Not that there is no such prompted assent and dissent for standing
sentences. A readily imaginable visual stimulation will prompt a
geographically instructed subject, once, to assent to the standing
sentence "There are brick houses on Elm Street." Stimulation implemented by an interferometer once prompted Michelson and Morley
to dissent from the standing sentence "There is ether drift." But these
standing sentences contrast with occasion sentences in that the subject
may repeat his old assent or dissent unprompted by current stimulation, when we ask him again on later occasions; whereas an occasion
sentence commands assent or dissent only as prompted all over again
by current stimulation.

Let us define the *affirmative stimulus meaning* of an occasion
sentence S, for a given speaker, as the class of all the stimulations that
would prompt him to assent to S. We may define the *negative* stimulus meaning of S similarly in terms of dissent. Finally we may define
the *stimulus meaning* of S, simply so-called, as the ordered pair of
the affirmative and negative stimulus meanings of S. We could distinguish degrees of doubtfulness of assent and dissent, say, by re-
action time, and elaborate our definition of stimulus meaning in easily
imagined ways to include this information; but for the sake of fluent
exposition let us forbear.

The several stimulations, which we assemble in classes to form
stimulus meanings, must themselves be taken for present purposes
not as dated particular events but as repeatable event forms. We are
to say not that two stimulations have occurred that were just alike,
but that the same stimulation has *re*curred. To see the necessity of
this attitude consider again the positive stimulus meaning of an
occasion sentence S. It is the class Σ of all those stimulations that

would prompt assent to S. If the stimulations were taken as events rather than event forms, then Σ would have to be a class of events which largely did not and will not happen, but which would prompt assent to S if they were to happen. Whenever Σ contained one realized or unrealized particular event σ, it would have to contain all other unrealized duplicates of σ; and how many are there of *these*? Certainly it is hopeless nonsense to talk thus of unrealized particulars and try to assemble them into classes. Unrealized entities have to be construed as universals, simply because there are no places and dates by which to distinguish between those that are in other respects alike.

It is not necessary for present purposes to decide exactly when to count two events of surface irritation as recurrences of the same stimulation, and when to count them as occurrences of different stimulations. In practice certainly the linguist needs never care about nerve-for-nerve duplications of stimulating events. It remains, as always, sufficient merely to know, e.g., that the subject got a good glimpse of a rabbit. This is sufficient because of one's reasonable expectation of invariance of behavior under any such circumstances.

The affirmative and negative stimulus meanings of a sentence are mutually exclusive. We have supposed the linguist capable of recognizing assent and dissent, and we mean these to be so construed that no one can be said to assent to and dissent from the same occasion sentence on the same occasion. Granted, our subject might be prompted once by a given stimulation σ to assent to S, and later, by a recurrence of σ, to dissent from S; but then we would simply conclude that his meaning for S had changed. We would then reckon σ to his affirmative stimulus meaning of S as of the one date and to his negative stimulus meaning of S as of the other date. At any one given time his positive stimulus meaning of S comprises just the stimulations that *would* prompt him then to assent to S, and correspondingly for the negative stimulus meaning; and we may be sure that these two classes of stimulations are mutually exclusive.

Yet the affirmative and negative stimulus meaning do not determine each other; for the negative stimulus meaning of S does not ordinarily comprise all the stimulations that would not prompt assent to S. In general, therefore, the matching of whole stimulus meanings can be a better basis for translation than the matching merely of affirmative stimulus meanings.

What now of that strong conditional, the "would prompt" in our definition of stimulus meaning? The device is used so unquestioningly in solid old branches of science that to object to its use in a study as shaky as the present one would be a glaring case of misplaced aspiration, a compliment no more deserved than intended. What the strong conditional defines is a disposition, in this case a disposition to assent to or dissent from *S* when variously prompted. The disposition may be presumed to be some subtle structural condition, like an allergy and like solubility; like an allergy, more particularly, in not being understood. Whatever the ontological status of dispositions, or the philosophical status of talk of dispositions, we are familiar enough in a general way with how one sets about guessing, from judicious tests and samples and observed uniformities, whether there is a disposition of a specified sort.

2. *The inscrutability of terms*

Impressed with the interdependence of sentences, one may well wonder whether meanings even of whole sentences (let alone shorter expressions) can reasonably be talked of at all, except relative to the other sentences of an inclusive theory. Such relativity would be awkward, since, conversely, the individual component sentences offer the only way into the theory. Now the notion of stimulus meaning partially resolves the predicament. It isolates a sort of net empirical import of each of various single sentences without regard to the containing theory, even though without loss of what the sentence owes to that containing theory. It is a device, as far as it goes, for exploring the fabric of interlocking sentences a sentence at a time. Some such device is indispensable in broaching an alien culture, and relevant also to an analysis of our own knowledge of the world.

We have started our consideration of meaning with sentences, even if sentences of a special sort and meaning in a strained sense. For words, when not learned as sentences, are learned only derivatively by abstraction from their roles in learned sentences. Still there are, prior to any such abstraction, the one-word sentences; and, as luck would have it, they are (in English) sentences of precisely the special sort already under investigation — occasion sentences like "White" and "Rabbit." Insofar then as the concept of stimulus meaning may be said to constitute in some strained sense a meaning concept for occasion sentences, it would in particular constitute a meaning concept for general terms like "White" and "Rabbit." Let us examine the concept of stimulus meaning for a while in this latter, conveniently limited, domain of application.

To affirm sameness of stimulus meaning on the part of a term for two speakers, or on the part of two terms for one or two speakers, is to affirm a certain sameness of applicability: the stimulations that prompt assent coincide, and likewise those that prompt dissent. Now is this merely to say that the term or terms have the same *extension*, i.e., are true of the same objects, for the speaker or speakers in question? In the case of "Rabbit" and "Gavagai" it may seem so. Actually, in the general case, more is involved. Thus, to adapt an example of Carnap's, imagine a general heathen term for horses and unicorns. Since there are no unicorns, the extension of that inclusive heathen term is that simply of "horses." Yet we would like somehow to say that the term, unlike "horse," *would* be true also of unicorns if there were any. Now our concept of stimulus meaning actually helps to make sense of that wanted further determination with respect to nonexistents. For stimulus meaning is in theory a question of direct surface irritations, not horses and unicorns. Each stimulation that would be occasioned by observing a unicorn is an assortment of nerve-hits, no less real and in principle no less specifiable than those occasioned by observing a horse. Such a stimulation can even be actualized, by papier-mâché trickery. In practice also we can do without deception, using descriptions and hypothetical questions, if we know enough of the language; such devices are indirect ways of guessing at stimulus meaning, even though external to the definition.

For terms like "Horse," "Unicorn," "White," and "Rabbit" — general terms for observable external objects — our concept of stimulus meaning thus seems to provide a moderately strong translation relation that goes beyond mere sameness of extension. But this is not so; the relation falls far short of sameness of extension on other counts. For, consider "Gavagai" again. Who knows but what the objects to which this term applies are not rabbits after all, but mere stages, or brief temporal segments, of rabbits? For in either event the stimulus situations that prompt assent to "Gavagai" would be the same as for "Rabbit." Or perhaps the objects to which "Gavagai" applies are all and sundry undetached parts of rabbits; again the stimulus meaning would register no difference. When from the sameness of stimulus meanings of "Gavagai" and "Rabbit" the linguist leaps to the conclusion that a gavagai is a whole enduring rabbit, he is just taking for granted that the native is enough like us to have a brief general term for rabbits and no brief general term for rabbit stages or parts.

Commonly we can translate something (e.g., "for the sake of") into a given language though nothing in that language corresponds to certain of the component syllables (e.g., to "the" and to "sake"). Just so the occasion sentence "Gavagai" is translatable as saying that a rabbit is there, though no part of "Gavagai" nor anything at all in the native language quite correspond to the term "rabbit." Synonymy of "Gavagai" and "Rabbit" as sentences turns on considerations of prompted assent, which transcend all cultural boundaries; not so synonymy of them as terms. We are right to write "Rabbit," instead of "rabbit," as a signal that we are considering it in relation to what is synonymous with it as a sentence and not in relation to what is synonymous with it as a term.

Does it seem that the imagined indecision between rabbits, stages of rabbits, and integral parts of rabbits should be resoluble by a little supplementary pointing and questioning? Consider, then, how. Point to a rabbit and you have pointed to a stage of a rabbit and to an integral part of a rabbit. Point to an integral part of a rabbit and you have pointed to a rabbit and to a stage of a rabbit. Correspondingly for the third alternative. Nothing not distinguished in stimulus meaning itself will be distinguished by pointing, unless the pointing is accompanied by questions of identity and diversity: "Is this the same gavagai as that? Do we have here one gavagai or two?" Such questioning requires of the linguist a command of the native language far beyond anything that we have as yet seen how to account for. More, it presupposes that the native conceptual scheme is, like ours, one that breaks reality down somehow into a multiplicity of identifiable and discriminable physical things, be they rabbits or stages or parts. For the native attitude might, after all, be very unlike ours. The term "gavagai" might be the proper name of a recurring universal rabbithood; and *still* the occasion sentence "Gavagai" would have the same stimulus meaning as under the other alternatives above suggested. For that matter, the native point of view might be so alien that from it there would be just no semblance of sense in speaking of objects at all, not even of abstract ones like rabbithood. Native channels might be wholly unlike Western talk of this and that, same and different, one and two. Failing some such familiar apparatus, surely the native cannot significantly be said to posit objects. Stuff conceivably, but not things, concrete *or* abstract. And yet, even in the face of this alien ontological attitude, the occasion sentence "Gavagai" could still have the same stimulus meaning as "(Lo, a) rabbit." Occasion sentences and stimulus meanings are general coin, whereas terms, conceived as variously applying to objects in some sense, are a provincial appurtenance of our object-positing kind of culture.

Can we even imagine any basic alternative to our object-positing pattern? Perhaps not; for we would have to imagine it in translation, and translation imposes our pattern. Perhaps the very notion of such radical contrast of cultures is meaningless, except in this purely privative sense: persistent failure to find smooth and convincing native analogues of our own familiar accessories of objective reference, such as the articles, the identity predicate, the plural ending. Only by such failure can we be said to perceive that the native language represents matters in ways not open to our own.

3. Observation sentences

In §§ 1–2 we came to appreciate sameness of stimulus meaning as an in some ways serviceable synonymy relation when limited to occasion sentences. But even when thus limited, stimulus meaning falls short of the requirement implicit in ordinary uncritical talk of meaning. The trouble is that an informant's prompted assent to or dissent from an occasion sentence may depend only partly on the present prompting stimulation and all too largely on his hidden collateral information. In distinguishing between occasion sentences and standing sentences (§ 1), and deferring the latter, we have excluded all cases where the informant's assent or dissent might depend wholly on collateral information, but we have not excluded cases where his assent or dissent depends mainly on collateral information and ever so little on the present prompting stimulation. Thus, the native's assent to "Gavagai" on the occasion of nothing better than an ill-glimpsed movement in the grass can have been due mainly to earlier observation, in the linguist's absence, of rabbit enterprises near the spot. And there are occasion sentences the prompted assent to which will *always* depend so largely on collateral information that their stimulus meanings cannot be treated as their "meanings" by any stretch of the imagination. An example is "Bachelor"; one's assent to it is prompted genuinely enough by the sight of a face, yet it draws mainly on stored information and not at all on the prompting stimulation except as needed for recognizing the bachelor friend concerned. The trouble with "Bachelor" is that its meaning transcends the looks of the prompting faces and concerns matters that can be known only through other channels. Evidently then we must try to single out a subclass of the occasion sentences which will qualify as *observation sentences*, recognizing that what I have called stimulus meaning constitutes a reasonable notion of meaning for such sentences at most. Occasion sentences have been defined (§ 1) as sentences to which there is assent or dissent but only subject to prompting; and what we now ask of observation sentences, more particularly, is that the assent or dissent be prompted always without help of information beyond the prompting stimulation itself.

It is remarkable how sure we are that each assent to "Bachelor," or a native equivalent, would draw on data from the two sources — present stimulation and collateral information. We are not lacking in elaborate if unsystematic insights into the ways of using "Bachelor" or other specific words of our own language. Yet it does not behoove us to be smug about this easy sort of talk of meanings and reasons, for all its productivity; for, with the slightest encouragement, it can involve us in the most hopelessly confused beliefs and meaningless controversies.

Suppose it said that a particular class Σ comprises just those stimulations each of which suffices to prompt assent to an occasion sentence S outright, without benefit of collateral information. Suppose it said that the stimulations comprised in a further class Σ', likewise sufficient to prompt assent to S, owe their efficacy rather to certain widely disseminated collateral information, C. Now couldn't we just as well have said, instead, that on acquiring C men have found it convenient implicitly to change the very *meaning* of S, so that the members of Σ' now suffice outright like members of Σ? I suggest that we may say either; even historical clairvoyance would reveal no distinction, though it reveal all stages in the acquisition of C, since meaning can evolve *pari passu*. The distinction is illusory. What we objectively have is just an evolving adjustment to nature, reflected in an evolving set of dispositions to be prompted by stimulations to assent to or dissent from occasion sentences. These dispositions may be conceded to be impure in the sense of including worldly knowledge, but they contain it in a solution which there is no precipitating.

Observation sentences were to be occasion sentences the assent or dissent to which is prompted always without help of collateral information. The notion of help of collateral information is now seen to be shaky. Actually the notion of observation sentence is less so, because of a stabilizing statistical effect which I can suggest if for a moment I go on speaking uncritically in terms of the shaky notion of collateral information. Now some of the collateral information relevant to an occasion sentence *S* may be widely disseminated, some not. Even that which is widely disseminated may in part be shared by one large group of persons and in part by another, so that few if any persons know it all. Meaning, on the other hand, is social. Even the man who is oddest about a word is likely to have a few companions in deviation.

At any rate the effect is strikingly seen by comparing "Rabbit" with "Bachelor." The stimulus meaning of "Bachelor" will be the same for no two speakers short of Siamese twins. The stimulus meaning of "Rabbit" will be much alike for most speakers; exceptions like the movement in the grass are rare. A working concept that would seem to serve pretty much the purpose of the notion of observation sentence is then simply this: *occasion sentence possessing intersubjective stimulus meaning*.

In order then that an occasion sentence be an observation sentence, is it sufficient that there be *two* people for whom it has the same stimulus meaning? No, as witness those Siamese twins. Must it have the same stimulus meaning for all persons in the linguistic community (however *that* might be defined)? Surely not. Must it have *exactly* the same stimulus meaning for even two? Perhaps not, considering again that movement in the grass. But these questions aim at refinements that would simply be misleading if undertaken. We are concerned here with rough trends of behavior. What matters for the notion of observation sentence here intended is that for significantly many speakers the stimulus meanings deviate significantly little.

In one respect actually the intersubjective variability of the stimulus meaning of sentences like "Bachelor" has been understated. Not only will the stimulus meaning of "Bachelor" for one person differ from that of "Bachelor" for the next person; it will differ from that of any other likely sentence for the next person, in the same language or any other.

The linguist is not free to survey a native stimulus meaning *in extenso* and then to devise *ad hoc* a great complex English sentence whose stimulus meaning, for him, matches the native one by sheer exhaustion of cases. He has rather to extrapolate any native stimulus meaning from samples, guessing at the informant's mentality. If the sentence is as nonobservational as "Bachelor," he simply will not find likely lines of extrapolation. Translation by stimulus meaning will then deliver no wrong result, but simply nothing. This is interesting because what led us to try to define observation sentences was our reflection that they were the subclass of occasion sentences that seemed reasonably translatable by identity of stimulus meaning. Now we see that the limitation of this method of translation to this class of sentences is self-enforcing. When an occasion sentence is of the wrong kind, the informant's stimulus meaning for it will simply not be one that the linguist will feel he can plausibly equate with his own stimulus meaning for any English sentence.

The notion of stimulus meaning was one that required no multiplicity of informants. There is in principle the stimulus meaning of the sentence for the given speaker at the given time of his life (though in guessing at it the linguist may be helped by varying both the time and the speaker). The definition of observation sentence took wider points of reference: it expressly required comparison of various speakers of the same language. Finally the reflection in the foregoing paragraph reassures us that such widening of horizons can actually be done without. Translation of occasion sentences by stimulus meaning will limit itself to observation sentences without our ever having actually to bring the criterion of observation sentence to bear.

The phrase "observation sentence" suggests, for epistemologists or methodologists of science, datum sentences of science. On this score our version is by no means amiss. For our observation sentences as defined are just the occasion sentences on which there is pretty sure to be firm agreement on the part of well-placed observers. Thus they are just the sentences to which a scientist will finally recur when called upon to marshal his data and repeat his observations and experiments for doubting colleagues.

4. Intrasubjective synonymy of occasion sentences

Stimulus meaning remains defined all this while for occasion sentences generally, without regard to observationality. But it bears less resemblance to what might reasonably be called meaning when applied to nonobservation sentences like "Bachelor." Translation of "Soltero" as "Bachelor" manifestly cannot be predicated on identity of stimulus meanings between persons; nor can synonymy of "Bachelor" and "Unmarried man."

Curiously enough, though, the stimulus meanings of "Bachelor" and "Unmarried man" are, despite all this, identical for any one speaker. An individual will at any one time be prompted by the same stimulations to assent to "Bachelor" and to "Unmarried man"; and similarly for dissent. What we find is that, though the concept of stimulus meaning is so very remote from "true meaning" when applied to the inobservational occasion sentences "Bachelor" and "Unmarried man," still synonymy is definable as sameness of stimulus meaning just as faithfully for these sentences as for the choicest observation sentences — as long as we stick to one speaker. For each speaker "Bachelor" and "Unmarried man" are synonymous in a defined sense (viz., alike in stimulus meaning) without having the same meaning in any acceptably defined sense of "meaning" (for stimulus meaning is, in the case of "Bachelor," nothing of the kind). Very well; let us welcome the synonymy and let the meaning go.

The one-speaker restriction presents no obstacle to saying that "Bachelor" and "Unmarried man" are synonymous for the whole community, in the sense of being synonymous for each member. A practical extension even to the two-language case is not far to seek if a bilingual speaker is at hand. "Bachelor" and "Soltero" will be synonymous for him by the intra-individual criterion, viz., sameness of stimulus meaning. Taking him as a sample, we may treat "Bachelor" and "Soltero" as synonymous for the translation purposes of the two whole linguistic communities that he represents. Whether he is a good enough sample would be checked by observing the fluency of his communication in both communities, by comparing other bilinguals, or by observing how well the translations work.

But such use of bilinguals is unavailable to the jungle linguist broaching an untouched culture. For radical translation the only concept thus far at our disposal is sameness of stimulus meaning, and this only for observation sentences.

The kinship and difference between intrasubjective synonymy and radical translation require careful notice. Intrasubjective synonymy, like translation, is quite capable of holding good for a whole community. It is intrasubjective in that the synonyms are joined for each subject by sameness of stimulus meaning for him; but it may still be community-wide in that the synonyms in question are joined by sameness of stimulus meaning for every single subject in the whole community. Obviously intrasubjective synonymy is in principle just as objective, just as discoverable by the outside linguist, as is translation. Our linguist may even find native sentences intrasubjectively synonymous without finding English translations — without, in short, understanding them; for he can find that they have the same stimulus meaning, for the subject, even though there may be no English sentence whose stimulus meaning for himself promises to be the same. Thus, to turn the tables: a Martian could find that "Bachelor" and "Unmarried man" were synonyms without discovering when to assent to either one.

"Bachelor" and "Yes" are two occasion sentences which we may instructively compare. Neither of them is an observation sentence, nor, therefore, translatable by identity of stimulus meaning. The heathen equivalent ("Tak," say) of "Yes" would fare poorly indeed under translation by stimulus meaning. The stimulations which — accompanying the linguist's question "Tak?" — would prompt assent to this queer sentence, even on the part of all natives without exception, are ones which (because exclusively verbal in turn, and couched in the heathen tongue) would never have prompted an unspoiled Anglo-Saxon to assent to "Yes" or anything like it. "Tak" is just what the linguist is fishing for by way of assent to whatever heathen occasion sentence he may be investigating, but it is a poor one, under these methods, to investigate. Indeed we may expect "Tak," or "Yes," like "Bachelor," to have the same stimulus meaning for no two speakers even of the same language; for "Yes" can have the same stimulus meaning only for speakers who agree on every single thing that can be blurted in a specious present. At the same time, sameness of stimulus meaning does define intrasubjective synonymy, not only between "Bachelor" and "Unmarried man" but equally between "Yes" and "Uh huh" or "Quite."

Note that the reservations of §2 regarding coextensiveness of terms still hold. Though the Martian find that "Bachelor" and "Unmarried man" are synonymous occasion sentences, still in so doing he will not establish that "bachelor" and "unmarried man" are coextensive general terms. Either term to the exclusion of the other might, so far as he knows, apply not to men but to their stages or parts or even to an abstract attribute; cf. §2.

Talking of occasion sentences as sentences and not as terms, however, we see that we can do more for synonymy within a language than for radical translation. It appears that sameness of stimulus meaning will serve as a standard of intrasubjective synonymy of occasion sentences without their having to be observation sentences.

Actually we do need this limitation: we should stick to short and simple sentences. Otherwise subjects' mere incapacity to digest long questions can, under our definitions, issue in difference of stimulus meanings between long and short sentences which we should prefer to find synonymous. A stimulation may prompt assent to the short sentence and not to the long one just because of the opacity of the long one; yet we should then like to say not that the subject has shown the meaning of the long sentence to be different, but merely that he has failed to penetrate it.

Certainly the sentences will not have to be kept so short but what some will contain others. One thinks of such containment as happening with help of conjunctions, in the grammarians' sense: "or," "and," "but," "if," "then," "that," etc., governing the contained sentence as clause of the containing sentence. But it can also happen farther down. Very simple sentences may contain substantives and adjectives ("red," "tile," "bachelor," etc.) which qualify also as occasion sentences in their own right, subject to our synonymy concept. So our synonymy concept already applies on an equal footing to sentences some of which recur as parts of others. Some extension of synonymy to longer occasion sentences, containing others as parts, is then possible by the following sort of construction.

Think of $R(S)$ first as an occasion sentence which, though moderately short, still contains an occasion sentence S as part. If now we leave the contained sentence blank, the partially empty result may graphically be referred to as $R(.\ .\ .)$ and called (following Peirce) a *rheme*. A rheme $R(.\ .\ .)$ will be called *regular* if it fulfills this condition: for each S and S', if S and S' are synonymous and $R(S)$ and $R(S')$ are idiomatically acceptable occasion sentences short enough for our synonymy concept, then $R(S)$ and $R(S')$ are synonymous. This concept of regularity makes reasonable sense thus far only for short rhemes, since $R(S)$ and $R(S')$ must, for suitably short S and S', be short enough to come under our existing synonymy concept. However, the concept of regularity now invites extension, in this very natural way: where the rhemes $R_1(.\ .\ .)$ and $R_2(.\ .\ .)$ are both regular, let us speak of the longer rheme $R_1(R_2(.\ .\ .))$ as regular too. In this way we may speak of regularity of longer and longer rhemes without end. Thereupon we can extend the synonymy concept to various long occasion sentences, as follows. Where $R(.\ .\ .)$ is any regular rheme and S and S' are short occasion sentences that are synonymous in the existing unextended sense and $R(S)$ and $R(S')$ are idiomatically acceptable combinations at all, we may by extension call $R(S)$ and $R(S')$ synonymous in turn — even though they be too long for synonymy as first defined. There is no limit now to length, since the regular rheme $R(.\ .\ .)$ may be as long as we please.

5. *Truth functions*

In §§2-3 we accounted for radical translation only of observation sentences, by identification of stimulus meanings. Now there is also a decidedly different domain that lends itself directly to radical translation: that of *truth functions* such as negation, logical conjunction, and alternation. For, suppose as before that assent and dissent are generally recognizable. The sentences put to the native for assent or dissent may now be occasion sentences and standing sentences indifferently. Those that are occasion sentences will of course have to be accompanied by a prompting stimulation, if assent or dissent is to be elicited; the standing sentences, on the other hand, can be put without props. Now by reference to assent and dissent we can state *semantic criteria* for truth functions; i.e., criteria for determining whether a given native idiom is to be construed as expressing the truth function in question. The semantic criterion of negation is that it turns any short sentence to which one will assent into a sentence from which one will dissent, and vice versa. That of conjunction is that it produces compounds to which (so long as the component sentences are short) one is prepared to assent always and only when one is prepared to assent to each component. That of alternation is similar but with the verb "assent" changed twice to "dissent."

The point about short components is merely, as in §4, that when they are long the subject may get mixed up. Identification of a native idiom as negation, or conjunction, or alternation, is not to be ruled out in view of a subject's deviation from our semantic criteria when the deviation is due merely to confusion. Note well that no limit is imposed on the lengths of the component sentences to which negation, conjunction, or alternation may be applied; it is just that the test cases for first spotting such constructions in a strange language are cases with short components.

When we find a native construction to fulfill one or another of these three semantic criteria, we can ask no more toward an understanding of it. Incidentally we can then translate the idiom into English as "not," "and," or "or" as the case may be, but only subject to sundry humdrum provisos; for it is well known that these three English words do not represent negation, conjunction, and alternation exactly and unambiguously.

Any construction for compounding sentences from other sentences is counted in logic as expressing a truth function if it fulfills this condition: the compound has a unique "truth value" (truth or falsity) for each assignment of truth values to the components. Semantic criteria can obviously be stated for all truth functions along the lines already followed for negation, conjunction, and alternation.

One hears talk of prelogical peoples, said deliberately to accept certain simple self-contradictions as true. Doubtless overstating Levy-Bruhl's intentions, let us imagine someone to claim that these natives accept as true a certain sentence of the form "p ka bu p" where "ka" means "and" and "bu" means "not." Now this claim is absurd on the face of it, if translation of "ka" as "and" and "bu" as "not" follows our semantic criteria. And, not to be dogmatic, what criteria will you have? Conversely, to claim on the basis of a better dictionary that the natives *do* share our logic would be to impose our logic and beg the question, if there were really a meaningful question here to beg. But I do urge the better dictionary.

The same point can be illustrated within English, by the question of alternative logics. Is he who propounds heterodox logical laws really contradicting our logic, or is he just putting some familiar old vocables ("and," "or," "not," "all," etc.) to new and irrelevant uses? It makes no sense to say, unless from the point of view of some criteria or other for translating logical particles. Given the above criteria, the answer is clear.

We hear from time to time that the scientist in his famous freedom to resystematize science or fashion new calculi is bound at least to respect the law of contradiction. Now what are we to make of this? We do flee contradiction, for we are after truth. But what of a revision so fundamental as to count contradictions as true? Well, to begin with, it would have to be arranged carefully if all utility is not to be lost. Classical logical laws enable us from any one contradiction to deduce all statements indiscriminately; and such universal affirmation would leave science useless for lack of distinctions. So the revision which counts contradictions as true will have to be accompanied by a revision of other logical laws. Now all this can be done; but, once it is done, how can we say it is what it purported to be? This heroically novel logic falls under the considerations of the preceding paragraph, to be reconstrued perhaps simply as old logic in bad notation.

We *can* meaningfully contemplate changing a law of logic, be it the law of excluded middle or even the law of contradiction. But this is so only because while contemplating the change we continue to translate *identically*: "and" as "and," "or" as "or," etc. Afterward a more devious mode of translation will perhaps be hit upon which will annul the change of law; or perhaps, on the contrary, the change of law will be found to have produced an essentially stronger system, demonstrably not translatable into the old in any way at all. But even in the latter event any actual conflict between the old and the new logic proves illusory, for it comes only of translating identically.

At any rate we have settled a people's logical laws completely, so far as the truth-functional part of logic goes, once we have fixed our translations by the above semantic criteria. In particular the class of the *tautologies* is fixed: the truth-functional compounds that are true by truth-functional structure alone. There is a familiar tabular routine for determining, for sentences in which the truth functions are however immoderately iterated and superimposed, just what assignments of truth values to the ultimate component sentences will make the whole compound true; and the tautologies are the compounds that come out true under all assignments.

It is a commonplace of epistemology (and therefore occasionally contested) that just two very opposite spheres of knowledge enjoy irreducible certainty. One is the knowledge of what is directly present to sense experience, and the other is knowledge of logical truth. It is striking that these, roughly, are the two domains where we have made fairly direct behavioral sense of radical translation. One domain where radical translation seemed straightforward was that of the observation sentences. The other is that of the truth functions; hence also in a sense the tautologies, these being the truths to which only the truth functions matter.

But the truth functions and tautologies are only the simplest of the logical functions and logical truths. Can we perhaps do better? The logical functions that most naturally next suggest themselves are the *categoricals*, traditionally designated A, E, I, and O, and commonly construed in English by the construction "all are" ("All rabbits are timid"), "none are," "some are," "some are not." A semantic criterion for A perhaps suggests itself as follows: the compound commands assent (from a given speaker) if and only if the positive stimulus meaning (for him) of the first component is a subclass of the positive stimulus meaning of the second component. How to vary this for E, I, and O is obvious enough, except that the whole idea is wrong in view of §2. Thus take A. If "hippoid" is a general term intended to apply to all horses and unicorns, then all hippoids are horses (there being no unicorns), but still the positive stimulus meaning of "Hippoid" has stimulus patterns in it, of the sort suited to "Unicorn," that are not in the positive stimulus meaning of "Horse." On this score the suggested semantic criterion is at odds with "All *S* and *P*" in that it goes beyond extension. And it has a yet more serious failing of the opposite kind; for, whereas rabbit stages are not rabbits, we saw in §2 that in point of stimulus meaning there is no distinction.

The difficulty is fundamental. The categoricals depend for their truth on the objects, however external and however inferential, of which the component terms are true; and what those objects are is not uniquely determined by stimulus meanings. Indeed the categoricals, like plural endings and identity, make sense at all only relative to an object-positing kind of conceptual scheme; whereas, as stressed in §2, stimulus meanings can be just the same for persons imbued with such a scheme and for persons as alien to it as you please. Of what we think of as logic, the truth-functional part is the only part the recognition of which, in a foreign language, we seem to be able to pin down to behavioral criteria.

6. *Analytical hypotheses*

How then does our linguist push radical translation beyond the bounds of mere observation sentences and truth functions? In broad outline as follows. He segments heard utterances into conveniently short recurrent parts, and thus compiles a list of native "words." Various of these he hypothetically equates to English words and phrases, in such a way as to reproduce the already established translations of whole observation sentences. Such conjectural equatings of parts may be called *analytical hypotheses* of translation. He will need analytical hypotheses of translation not only for native words but also for native constructions, or ways of assembling words, since the native language would not be assumed to follow English word order. Taken together these analytical hypotheses of translation constitute a jungle-to-English grammar and dictionary, which the linguist then proceeds to apply even to sentences for the translation of which no independent evidence is available.

The analytical hypotheses of translation do not depend for their evidence exclusively upon those prior translations of observation sentences. They can also be tested partly by their conformity to intrasubjective synonymies of occasion sentences, as of §4. For example, if the analytical hypotheses direct us to translate native sentences S_1 and S_2 respectively as "Here is a bachelor" and "Here is an unmarried man," then we shall hope to find also that for each native the stimulus meaning of S_1 is the same as that of S_2.

The analytical hypotheses of translation can be partially tested in the light of the thence derived translations not only of occasion sentences but, sometimes, of standing sentences. Standing sentences differ from occasion sentences only in that assent to them and dissent from them may occur unprompted (cf. § 1), not in that they occur only unprompted. The concept of prompted assent is reasonably applicable to the standing sentence "Some rabbits are black" once, for a given speaker, if we manage to spring the specimen on him before he knows there are black ones. A given speaker's assent to some standing sentences can even be prompted repeatedly; thus his assent can genuinely be prompted anew each year to "The crocuses are out," and anew each day to "The *Times* has come." Standing sentences thus grade off toward occasion sentences, though there still remains a boundary, as defined midway in §1. So the linguist can further appraise his analytical hypotheses of translation by seeing how the thence derivable translations of standing sentences compare with the originals on the score of prompted assent and dissent.

Some slight further testing of the analytical hypotheses of translation is afforded by standing sentences even apart from prompted assent and dissent. If for instance the analytical hypotheses point to some rather platitudinous English standing sentence as translation of a native sentence S, then the linguist will feel reassured if he finds that S likewise commands general and unprompted assent.

The analytical hypotheses of translation would not in practice be held to equational form. There is no need to insist that the native word be equated outright to any one English word or phrase. One may specify certain contexts in which the word is to be translated one way and others in which the word is to be translated in another way. One may overlay the equational form with supplementary semantical instructions *ad libitum*. "Spoiled (*said of an egg*)" is as good a lexicographical definition as "addled," despite the intrusion of stage directions. Translation instructions having to do with grammatical inflections — to take an extreme case — may be depended on to present equations of words and equations of constructions in inextricable combination with much that is not equational. For the purpose is not translation of single words nor translation of single constructions, but translation of coherent discourse. The hypotheses the linguist arrives at, the instructions that he frames, are contributory hypotheses or instructions concerning translation of coherent discourse, and they may be presented in any form, equational or otherwise, that proves clear and convenient.

Nevertheless there is reason to draw particular attention to the simple form of analytical hypothesis which does directly equate a native word or construction to a hypothetical English equivalent. For hypotheses need thinking up, and the typical case of thinking up is the case where the English-bred linguist apprehends a parallelism of function between some component fragment of a translated whole native sentence S and some component word of the English translation of S. Only in some such way can we account for anyone's ever thinking to translate a native locution radically into English as a plural ending, or as the identity predicate "$=$," or as a categorical copula, or as any other part of our domestic apparatus of objective reference; for, as stressed in earlier pages, no scrutiny of stimulus meanings or other behavioral manifestations can even settle whether the native shares our object-positing sort of conceptual scheme at all. It is only by such outright projection of his own linguistic habits that the linguist can find general terms in the native language at all, or, having found them, match them with his own. Stimulus meanings never suffice to determine even what words are terms, if any, much less what terms are coextensive.

The linguist who is serious enough about the jungle language to undertake its definitive dictionary and grammar will not, indeed, proceed quite as we have imagined. He will steep himself in the language, disdainful of English parallels, to the point of speaking it like a native. His learning of it even from the beginning can have been as free of all thought of other languages as you please; it can have been virtually an accelerated counterpart of infantile learning. When at length he does turn his hand to translation, and to producing a jungle-to-English dictionary and grammar, he can do so as a bilingual. His own two personalities thereupon assume the roles which in previous pages were divided between the linguist and his informant. He equates "Gavagai" with "Rabbit" by appreciating a sameness of stimulus meaning of the two sentences for himself. Indeed he can even use sameness of stimulus meaning to translate nonobservational occasion sentences of the type of "Bachelor"; here the intrasubjective situation proves its advantage (cf. § 4). When he brings off other more recondite translations he surely does so by essentially the method of analytical hypotheses, but with the difference that he projects these hypotheses from his prior separate masteries of the two languages, rather than using them in mastering the jungle language. Now though it is such bilingual translation that does most justice to the jungle language, reflection upon it reveals least about the nature of meaning; for the bilingual translator works by an intrasubjective communing of a split personality, and we make operational sense of his method only as we externalize it. So let us think still in terms of our more primitive schematism of the jungle-to-English project, which counts the native informant in as a live collaborator rather than letting the linguist first ingest him.

7. *A handful of meaning*

The linguist's finished jungle-to-English manual is to be appraised as a manual of sentence-to-sentence translation. Whatever be the details of its expository devices of word translation and syntactical paradigm, its net accomplishment is an infinite *semantic correlation* of sentences: the implicit specification of an English sentence for every one of the infinitely many possible jungle sentences. The English sentence for a given jungle one need not be unique, but it is to be unique to within any acceptable standard of intrasubjective synonymy among English sentences; and conversely. Though the thinking up and setting forth of such a semantic correlation of sentences depend on analyses into component words, the supporting evidence remains entirely at the level of sentences. It consists in sundry conformities on the score of stimulus meaning, intrasubjective synonymies, and other points of prompted and unprompted assent and dissent, as noted in §6.

Whereas the semantic correlation exhausts the native sentences, its supporting evidence determines no such widespread translation. Countless alternative over-all semantic correlations, therefore, are equally compatible with that evidence. If the linguist arrives at his one over-all correlation among many without feeling that his choice was excessively arbitrary, this is because he himself is limited in the correlations that he can manage. For he is not, in his finitude, free to assign English sentences to the infinitude of jungle ones in just any way whatever that will fit his supporting evidence; he has to assign them in some way that is manageably systematic with respect to a manageably limited set of repeatable speech segments. The word-by-word approach is indispensable to the linguist in specifying his semantic correlation and even in thinking it up.

Not only does the linguist's working segmentation limit the possibilities of any eventual semantic correlation. It even contributes to defining, for him, the ends of translation. For he will put a premium on structural parallels: on correspondence between the parts of the native sentence, as he segments it, and the parts of the English translation. Other things being equal, the more literal translation is seen as more literally a translation.[1] Technically a tendency to literal translation is assured anyway, since the very purpose of segmentation is to make long translations constructible from short correspondences; but then one goes farther and makes of this tendency an objective — and an objective that even varies in detail with the practical segmentation adopted.

It is by his analytical hypotheses that our jungle linguist implicitly states (and indeed arrives at) the grand synthetic hypothesis which is his over-all semantic correlation of sentences. His supporting evidence, such as it is, for the semantic correlation is his supporting evidence also for his analytical hypotheses. Chronologically, the analytical hypotheses come before all that evidence is in; then such of the evidence as ensues is experienced as pragmatic corroboration of a working dictionary. But in any event the translation of a vast range of native sentences, though covered by the semantic correlation, can never be corroborated or supported at all except cantilever fashion: it is simply what comes out of the analytical hypotheses when they are applied beyond the zone that supports them. That those unverifiable translations proceed without mishap must not be taken as pragmatic evidence of good lexicography, for mishap is impossible.

We must then recognize that the analytical hypotheses of translation and the grand synthetic one that they add up to are only in an incomplete sense hypotheses. Contrast the case of translation of "Gavagai" as "Lo, a rabbit" by sameness of stimulus meaning. This is a genuine hypothesis from sample observations, though possibly wrong. "Gavagai" and "Lo, a rabbit" have stimulus meanings for the two speakers, and these are the same or different, whether we guess right or not. On the other hand no sense is made of sameness of meaning of the words that are equated in the typical analytical hypothesis. The point is not that we cannot be sure whether the analytical hypothesis is right, but that there is not even, as there was in the case of "Gavagai," an objective matter to be right or wrong about.

Complete radical translation does go on, and analytical hypotheses are indispensable. Nor are they capricious; on the contrary we have just been seeing, in outline, how they are supported. May we not then say that in those very ways of thinking up and supporting the analytical hypotheses a sense *is* after all given to sameness of meaning of the expressions which those hypotheses equate? No. We could claim this only if no two conflicting sets of analytical hypotheses were capable of being supported equally strongly by all theoretically accessible evidence (including simplicity considerations).

This indefinability of synonymy by reference to the methodology of analytical hypotheses is formally the same as the indefinability of truth by reference to scientific method. Also the consequences are parallel. Just as we may meaningfully speak of the truth of a sentence only within the terms of some theory or conceptual scheme, so on the whole we may meaningfully speak of interlinguistic synonymy of words and phrases only within the terms of some particular system of analytical hypotheses.

The method of analytical hypotheses is a way of catapulting oneself into the native language by the momentum of the home language. It is a way of grafting exotic shoots on to the old familiar bush until only the exotic meets the eye. Native sentences not neutrally meaningful are thereby tentatively translated into home sentences on the basis, in effect, of seeming analogy of roles within the languages. These relations of analogy cannot themselves be looked upon as the meanings, for they are not unique. And anyway the analogies weaken as we move out toward the theoretical sentences, farthest from observation. Thus who would undertake to translate "Neutrinos lack mass" into the jungle language? If anyone does, we may expect him to coin new native words or distort the usage of old ones. We may expect him to plead in extenuation that the natives lack the requisite concepts; also that they know too little physics. And he is right, but another way of describing the matter is as follows. Analytical hypotheses at best are devices whereby, indirectly, we bring out analogies between sentences that have yielded to translation and sentences that have not, and so extend the working limits of translation; and "Neutrinos lack mass" is way out where the effects of such analytical hypotheses as we manage to devise are too fuzzy to do much good.

Containment in the Low German continuum facilitated translation of Frisian into English (§1), and containment in a continuum of cultural evolution facilitated translation of Hungarian into English. These continuities, by facilitating translation, encourage an illusion of subject matter: an illusion that our so readily intertranslatable sentences are diverse verbal embodiments of some intercultural proposition or meaning, when they are better seen as the merest variants of one and the same intracultural verbalism. Only the discontinuity of radical translation tries our meanings: really sets them over against their verbal embodiments, or more typically, finds nothing there.

Observation sentences peel nicely; their meanings, stimulus meanings, emerge absolute and free of all residual verbal taint. Theoretical sentences such as "Neutrinos lack mass," or the law of entropy, or the constancy of the speed of light, are at the other extreme. For such sentences no hint of the stimulatory conditions of assent or dissent can be dreamed of that does not include verbal stimulation from within the language. Sentences of this extreme latter sort, and other sentences likewise that lie intermediate between the two extremes, lack linguistically neutral meaning.

It would be trivial to say that we cannot know the meaning of a foreign sentence except as we are prepared to offer a translation in our own language. I am saying more: that it is only relative to an in large part arbitrary manual of translation that most foreign sentences may be said to share the meaning of English sentences, and then only in a very parochial sense of meaning, viz., use-in-English. Stimulus meanings of observation sentences aside, most talk of meaning requires tacit reference to a home language in much the way that talk of truth involves tacit reference to one's own system of the world, the best that one can muster at the time.

There being (apart from stimulus meanings) so little in the way of neutral meanings relevant to radical translation, there is no telling how much of one's success with analytical hypotheses is due to real kinship of outlook on the part of the natives and ourselves, and how much of it is due to linguistic ingenuity or lucky coincidence. I am not sure that it even makes sense to ask. We may alternately wonder at the inscrutability of the native mind and wonder at how very much like us the native is, where in the one case we have merely muffed the best translation and in the other case we have done a more thorough job of reading our own provincial modes into the native's speech.

Usener, Cassirer, Sapir, and latterly B. L. Whorf have stressed that deep differences of language carry with them ultimate differences in the way one thinks, or looks upon the world. I should prefer not to put the matter in such a way as to suggest that certain philosophical propositions are affirmed in the one culture and denied in the other. What is really involved is difficulty or indeterminacy of correlation. It is just that there is less basis of comparison — less sense in saying what is good translation and what is bad — the farther we get away from sentences with visibly direct conditioning to nonverbal stimuli and the farther we get off home ground.

NOTES

[This essay is an adaptation of part of a work still in progress, *Term and Object*, for the financial support of which I have the Institute for Advanced Study and the Rockefeller Foundation to thank. In the spring of 1957 I presented most of this essay as a lecture at the University of Pennsylvania, Columbia University, and Princeton University; and members of those audiences have helped me with their discussion. I used parts also at the fourth Colloque Philosophique de Royaumont, April 1958, in an address that will appear in the proceedings of the colloquium as "Le myth de la signification."]

1. Hence also Carnap's concept of structural synonymy. See his *Meaning and Necessity* (Chicago, 1947), §§ 14–16.

SEVEN AGAMEMNONS

REUBEN A. BROWER

THIS STUDY starts from a remark which a great teacher of Greek[1]
was fond of repeating to his classes. "A translation," he would say,
"is like a stewed strawberry." Everyone familiar with translations
and stewed strawberries will appreciate the perfect justice of this
criticism. Certainly everyone who has read a Greek play and a translation of a Greek play realizes bitterly what a transformation has
taken place in the "stewing." There is of course no escaping such
transformations; every time we read a foreign or an English text, we
remake what we read. Avowed translations are merely the most accessible and disturbing evidence of what happens when we read any
text, particularly a text by an earlier author, whether foreign or
English. Translations forcibly remind us of the obvious fact that
when we read, we read from a particular point in space and time.

When a writer sets out to translate — say, the *Agamemnon* —
what happens? Much, naturally, that we can never hope to analyze.
But what we can see quite clearly is that he makes the poetry of the
past into poetry of his particular present. Translations are the most
obvious examples of works which, in Valéry's words, are "as it were
created by their public." The average reader of a translation in English wants to find the kind of experience which has become identified
with "poetry" in his reading of English literature. The translator
who wishes to be read must in some degree satisfy this want.

The conditions of translating make this almost inevitable, for the
translator in seeking to preserve a kind of anonymity, in seeking to
eliminate himself — to let his author speak — often finds that the
voice which actually speaks is that of his own contemporaries. This
twofold character of anonymity and "contemporaneousness" can
be illustrated from famous translations in which several writers have
taken part. A reader quite familiar with Dryden will find it impossible to distinguish Dryden's own translations of Juvenal from those
of his helpers. What reader of Pope's Homer could confidently separate — on internal evidence alone — the passages by Pope from those
supplied by Broome and Fenton? A reader unacquainted with the

work of Lang, Leaf, and Myers might not believe that three different writers could attain the same degree of unctuous infelicity. If we should define the poetry of Pope or of Dryden from their translations alone, we should find we were omitting most of what distinguishes them from their contemporaries. The prose in which Lang and his associates have immortalized Homer is a mosaic of contemporary poeticisms.

When we say of all these translators that they gave their readers what they expected in poetry, what do we mean by "expect" and "poetry"? We mean that readers assume that they will have the kind of experience which they enjoy in reading poems originally written in their own language. "Kind of experience" is of course an experience through words. The readers of translations look to find words used as other poets use them. They demand, in Johnson's phrase, "those poetical elegancies which distinguish poetry from prose." Though the eighteenth-century audience was more certain what "elegancies" were, the twentieth-century audience has some similar expectations, such as a greater frequency in the use of metaphor than in prose, a predilection for terms which are *not* recognizably the "elegancies" of the Romantics, an approximation to the vocabulary and rhythm of speech, a preference for the act, the immediate sense impression, to the abstraction, and so on.

But we are not to suppose that these expectations are merely rhetorical, that the intelligent reader separates the use from the meaning. Nor are the meanings which satisfy the reader in search of poetry merely "poetic." It is true that there are always stock poetic meanings which become consecrated as "poetic" in each literary era, for instance, the meanings of the "lonely lake" in the nineteenth century, of the "heroic" in the eighteenth century, or of "melancholy" in the late sixteenth and the seventeenth centuries. And readers have never found it hard to convince themselves that these "poetic" meanings satisfy a special "poetic faculty." But even these meanings are never merely "poetic" or "literary" or whatever word we wish to use to label such set reactions to a set vocabulary. The stock "heroic" meaning of the eighteenth century corresponded to something more than the recurrent attitudes evoked by scores of neo-classical epics; it also equaled a certain misreading of ancient history and a code of aristocratic behavior which was in some degree an actuality of contemporary social life. When an eighteenth-century reader found Pope speaking of the women of Troy as "dames," he found at once many kinds of satisfaction. The word belonged to what he recognized as the language of verse; it suggested to him the "high heroic" vein; and it reminded him agreeably of the society to which he belonged while satisfying that society's standard of decorum. Therefore, as we can see from this brief sketch, when we say that a translator gives his readers the kind of experience they expect in poetry, we are saying a good deal. He offers a series of satisfactions no one of which (with the possible exception of meter) is confined to poetry. But taken together they may be said to form a definition of poetry for a group of contemporary readers.

Translations — exactly because of the peculiar conditions of their manufacture — are of special interest to a critic of poetry; for they show him in the baldest form the assumptions about poetry shared by readers and poets. To paraphrase Collingwood, every poem is an unconscious answer to the question: "What is a poem?" But the question is never the same question, any more than the question "What is a man?" is the same question when asked in 1200 or 1600 or 1900. Recently, while reading some translations of Aeschylus' *Agamemnon*, it struck me that the study of translations, especially from a literature produced by a civilization very different from our own, was one of the simplest ways of showing what is expected at various times in answer to the question of "What is poetry?" In the following essay on six translations from the *Agamemnon*, I want to give an example of a method and suggest its usefulness when applied in studying translations of an ancient author which have been made over a long period of time. For instance, a study of English translations of Homer along with the writings of contemporary literary theorists should show us vividly the continuous evolution among English readers of their definition of poetry and their historical picture of ancient Greece.

To show how the implied definitions of "poetry" vary in this set of translations from Aeschylus, we must begin with our reading of the Greek text. Of the *Agamemnon* as an absolute, a fifth-century absolute, we have no knowledge. We can only read Aeschylus in the context of our knowledge of the fifth century, which is a very different thing. I am going to begin with a recent translation of the two passages to be studied, using the Greek text to correct and amplify this version, in order to make quite clear the readings which will serve as a basis for comparison. Later we shall look at this translation, too, as an exhibit of assumptions about poetry. The first passage to

be considered is from the herald's speech to the leader of the chorus
in answer to an inquiry about Menelaus. The herald replies, telling
of the storm which scattered the ships soon after they left Troy.[2]

> For they swore together, those inveterate enemies,
> Fire and sea, and proved their alliance, destroying
> The unhappy troops of Argos.
> In night arose ill-waved evil,
> Ships on each other the blast from Thrace
> Crashed colliding, which butting with horns in the violence
> Of big wind and rattle of rain were gone
> To nothing, whirled all ways by a wicked shepherd.
> But when there came up the shining light of the sun
> We saw the Aegean sea flowering with corpses
> Of Greek men and their ships' wreckage.
> But for us, our ship was not damaged,
> Whether someone snatched it away or begged it off,
> Some god, not a man, handling the tiller;
> And Saving Fortune was willing to sit upon our ship
> So that neither at anchor we took the tilt of waves
> Nor ran to splinters on the crag-bound coast.
> But then having thus escaped death on the sea,
> In the white day, not trusting our fortune,
> We pastured this new trouble upon our thoughts,
> The fleet being battered, the sailors weary,
> And now if any of *them* still draw breath,
> They are thinking no doubt of us as being lost
> And we are thinking of them as being lost.
> May the best happen. As for Menelaus
> The first guess and most likely is a disaster.
> But still — if any ray of sun detects him
> Alive, with living eyes, by the plan of Zeus
> Not yet resolved to annul the race completely,
> There is some hope then that he will return home.

   The noisiness of the images and the shocking character of some of
the metaphors here are not surprising to a reader of Aeschylus in
Greek. By a Sophoclean standard this storm narrative is *démesuré*.
The language is at some points remote from — and at others, close
to — the norm of conversational prose as we find it in Xenophon and
Plato. Over against a "sea flowering with corpses," we can set
"proved their alliance" — which in Greek as in English suggests
military and political contexts — and the everyday interjection "May
the best happen," which is not a solemn prayer but just "Let's hope

that it will all turn out for the best." The speaker here is given the language not merely of an impersonal voice from the stage, but of a blunt herald who had answered the chorus' first question flatly with "I tell no lies."

If we look at the Greek, we shall see that this translation needs some explaining and correcting. "Ill-waved," though literal enough, loses the associations of fated disaster which the compounds have in Greek. As Verrall observes, δυσκύμαντα ("ill-waved") is a word which merges meanings of swelling, labor, and storm. "Butting with horns" is an image comparing the crashing ships to a flock, which is continued in "Whirled all ways by a wicked shepherd." The storm is like a bad shepherd (bad at his herding, not morally evil), who drives (spins) the flock in circles. The "flowering sea" image is less surrealist in effect if we see in it, as Verrall does, a last glimpse of the flock metaphor: a faint reference to a field in flower after a rain. "Saving Fortune" is both simply "our good luck which saved us" and a half-deified, half-personified power, nearer to "chance" than to *Fortuna*. The medieval "tilt" is not matched in Aeschylus. Aeschylus speaks quite plainly of the ship's being filled with water from the waves. "White day" has even more of a sudden "blanket-of-light" effect in the Greek, since it comes right after "death on the sea" ("sea-Hades"), with its associations of blackness and night.

"We pastured this new trouble." The bucolic character of this idiom sets a typical problem for the poet-translator. The question is how much of the literal meaning survives in the metaphor. The verb in its more common use in Greek means "to tend cattle." Perhaps, though it seems unlikely, Aeschylus' phrase was no more suggestive to Greek readers of "tending cows" than "brooding" is suggestive to English readers of "setting hens." The present translation seems to me very good, just because the verb was not commonly used in the sense of "tending thoughts," i.e., "pondering," "going over them." The only instance cited by Liddell and Scott is from the *Eumenides*. Liddell and Scott do cite examples of the verb in the sense of "cheat," "beguile" (with hopes) and wrongly include the present passage under this meaning. But Aeschylus is not saying here that "trouble is beguiled." "Trouble is looked over," "given range in thought," as appears from the lines which follow. Some of the other surprising metaphors in the passage remind us that we are not to suppress the literal level of the meaning for fear of incongruity.

There is only one place where this translation differs on a point of narrative fact from the others we shall use:

> As for Menelaus
> The best guess and most likely is a disaster.

The translation is apparently based on two emendations both of which should probably be rejected: μογεῖν for μολεῖν and δ'οὖν for γοῦν. The original readings are best supported by Wilamowitz. Verrall defends μολεῖν (but not γοῦν) for less acceptable reasons.[3] Without the emendations, the translation runs: "Except that Menelaus will come home, if, at least, any ray. . . ." For the purposes of our comparison a textual difference of this type matters remarkably little, since the differences in translation we are discussing are due to other causes.

The next passage to be used is from the chorus on Helen:

> So I would say there came
> To the city of Troy
> A notion of windless calm,
> Delicate adornment of riches,
> Soft shooting of the eyes and flower
> Of desire that stings the fancy.

It would be hard to improve on this translation. "Notion" gives suggestions of an impersonal abstraction which are very near to those of the Greek term. The only clearly inadequate term is "the fancy." The Greek word rendered by "fancy" is θυμός, the part of man affected by strong emotion. We no longer think of emotions as having a single, definite location in an organ (as implied in the Greek term); but we must here revert to that archaic view and translate "desire that stings the heart." "The fancy," which is a nineteenth-century "faculty," is not archaic enough.

Helen is one of Aeschylus' symbols for the pride which brings ruin. Later in the same chorus he contrasts this *hybris* with *díke* ("rightness," "justice") in lines which show the Aeschylean blend of personalized image and generalization:

> But Honest Dealing is clear
> Shining in smoky homes,
> Honours the god-fearing life.
> Mansions gilded by filth of hands she leaves,
> Turns her eyes elsewhere, visits the innocent house,
> Not respecting the power
> Of wealth mis-stamped with approval,
> But guides all to the goal.

Díke is rendered "Honest Dealing," a translation which may shock readers who put Justice invariably for *díke*, cheerfully assuming that *díke* is always *díke*. This translation attempts to give the meaning defined by Aeschylus' context. Aeschylus has been saying that not mere wealth, but wrong-doing brings ruin to a house. In the quoted strophe he defines *díke* by its opposite: gaining great wealth by wrong methods ("filth of hands") and hence enjoying wealth which does not deserve to be honored. The metaphor means that such wealth is like counterfeit coins, stamped with a value they do not possess. We should note that Aeschylus does not say that Honest Dealing is found among the poor because they are poor. Honest Dealing honors the man who acts as he ought to, making his money by fair means. Honest Dealing does not turn away from rich men, but from men who get their wealth dishonestly.

In comparing this basic text with various versions and in comparing the versions with each other, it is necessary to keep in mind what we are doing. We are trying to see what the comparison tells us about the translator's definition of "poetry." This definition will be one shared by his contemporaries. But we do not expect to formulate a complete definition of poetry for each of the historical periods from which the translations come. We are trying to demonstrate a method of using translations, not to reach general formulas, but to increase our particularized awareness of the assumptions about poetry involved in the words poets use.

If a reader turns to an eighteenth-century translation of the shipwreck passage, he will suffer a curious "shock of recognition":

> The pow'rs, before most hostile, now conspir'd,
> Fire and the sea, in ruin reconcil'd:
> And in a night of tempest wild from Thrace
> In all their fury rush'd the howling winds;
> Tost by the forceful blasts ship against ship
> In hideous conflict dash'd, or disappear'd
> Driv'n at the boist'rous whirlwind's dreadful will.
> But when the sun's fair light return'd, we see
> Bodies of Grecians, and the wreck of ships
> Float on the chaf'd foam of th' Aegean sea.
> Us and our ship some God, the pow'r of man
> Were all too weak, holding the helm preserv'd
> Unhurt, or interceding for our safety;
> And Fortune the deliverer steer'd our course
> To shun the waves, that near the harbour's mouth

> Boil high, or break upon the rocky shore.
> Escap'd th' ingulfing sea, yet scarce secure
> Of our escape, through the fair day we view
> With sighs the recent sufferings of the host,
> Cov'ring the sea with wrecks. If any breathe
> This vital air, they deem us lost, as we
> Think the same ruin theirs. Fair fall th' event!
> But first and chief expect the Spartan king
> T' arrive: if yet one ray of yon' bright sun
> Beholds him living, through the care of Jove,
> Who wills not to destroy that royal race,
> Well may we hope to joy in his return.

The reader has been here before, but the landmarks have been re-decorated. The first difference he notes is a uniformity of tone which is in sharp contrast with the variety of the original as seen in our basic version. It is a *royal* herald who speaks. He uses an idiom which belongs to the high converse of courts: "pow'rs conspir'd," "inter-ceding for our safety," "the royal race," etc. This is tragedy "in Scepter'd Pall." When the herald speaks of good luck, he expresses himself in words suitable to a Roman augur: "Fair fall th' event!" It is easy to see what the readers of this translation assumed as the proper level of tragic discourse.

This level is preserved even though as a result the storm — the subject of the oration — almost disappears. The omissions are more than curious: no mention of the bad waves, the rain (or spray), or the rattle of falling drops. The special character of Aeschylus' ac-count of the storm is lost because the flock-shepherd metaphor is by-passed: for "butting with horns" there is "in hideous conflict dash'd"; for "whirled all ways by a wicked shepherd," we find "Driv'n at the boist'rous whirlwind's dreadful will." The dignity of tone is thus preserved; and there is no awkward mixing of sheep and holy alliances. The difference, not merely one of omission, but of substitu-tion, is that Aeschylus' metaphors have been run through a generaliz-ing machine which produces goods guaranteed to be free from incon-venient particulars. This process, obvious enough in the use of "hid-eous conflict" for "butting with horns," appears even in the rehan-dling of a very common metaphor:

> For they swore together, those inveterate enemies,
> Fire and sea, and proved their alliance, destroying
> The unhappy troops of Argos.

These acts, evidently too technical and too particular, are represented by:

> The pow'rs, before most hostile, now conspir'd,
> Fire and the sea, in ruin reconcil'd.

These metaphors offer more than a generalized version of the original; they explain and rationalize; they tell the audience what Aeschylus "really" meant. The most obvious example of this is the version of

> We saw the Aegean sea flowering with corpses
> Of Greek men and their ships' wreckage

which appears as:

> we see
> Bodies of Grecians, and the wreck of ships
> Float on the chaf'd foam of th' Aegean sea.

How Aeschylus came by this macabre talk of a sea blossoming with corpses is now clear: the foam tossed up by the stormy waves suggests floating plants or flowers. The reader is given the "facts" alone; the metaphor is simply omitted.

This combination of artful rationalizing with perfect elegance of tone effects a rather remarkable sea-change in the picture of Helen:

> To Ilion's tow'rs in wanton state
>   With speed she wings her easy way;
> Soft gales obedient round her wait,
>   And pant on the delighted sea.
>   Attendant on her side
> The richest ornaments of splendid pride:
>   The darts, whose golden points inspire,
> Shot from her eyes, the flames of soft desire;
>   The youthful bloom of rosy love,
> That fills with ecstasy the willing soul;
> With duteous zeal obey her sweet control.

We are not to suppose that Helen was "literally" referred to as "a notion of windless calm" or "delicate adornment of riches." The calm is the sea's; the ornaments adorn the lady (or are near her, or are ladies-in-waiting?). Again, the rationalizing directs us to the "real" facts. As in the "whirlwind's dreadful will" we were given a standard personification in place of Aeschylus' odd metaphor, so here we are offered the familiar tropes of pastoral poetry. The passage supplies a certain kind of eighteenth-century reader with the language of polite love, as that language was rendered in verse. Dr. Johnson, who was surely not a reader of this type, has a remark on Dryden which suits the author of this translation perfectly: "With the simple and elemental passions, as they spring separate in the mind, he seems not much acquainted." The words of our translator refer us mainly to the sensations which such language has aroused in similar poems and do not require us to go back of this ready-made literary response. The writer seems to have no experience — and so no language — which is any sort of equivalent for Aeschylus as we read him.

But his success in translating is very different when he renders the chorus on Justice.

> But Justice bids her ray divine
> E'en on the low-roof'd cottage shine;
> And beams her glories on the life,
> That knows not fraud, nor ruffian strife.
> The gorgeous glare of gold, obtain'd
> By foul polluted hands, disdain'd
> She leaves, and with averted eyes
> To humbler, holier mansions flies;
> And looking through the times to come
> Assigns each deed its righteous doom.

His language shows that he *is* "much acquainted" with certain forms of moral experience. The result is not simply "Aeschylus"; but at least the words make us re-think some of Aeschylus' thoughts (as we have defined them in our basic version). The language here does not offer us an irrelevant diversion.

That this re-thinking has its peculiarities is evident from "bids her ray divine E'en on the low-roof'd cottage shine," and from "ruffian strife" and "humbler, holier mansions." The "low-roof'd cottage," lighted by a "ray divine" has a picturesque charm not found in Aeschylus' "smoky homes." For Aeschylus, Justice, Honest Dealing, can be seen as clearly in the smoke-stained house as in the golden mansion; she honors the just man without shedding a more kindly light over his house. Aeschylus has no adjective at all corresponding to "humbler." In the eighteenth-century version, the inference, "humbler," therefore "holier," implies that Justice has a partiality for the poor — for the decent poor. Justice, who belongs to the aristocracy, does not give her blessing to "ruffian strife," to undecorous or revolutionary behavior. Here, as in the narrative, the dignified level of the discourse is more than a matter of style: it corresponds to the social status and values shared by translator and reader. But here as elsewhere in our analysis, we see how responsive the translator was to social and literary standards completely alien to Aeschylus. The sum of these responses composes a peculiar definition of the proper satisfactions of poetry.

To appreciate its peculiarity let us see what poetry looks like in an Elizabethan translation:

Then first a wynd with pipling puffes our launcing ships did dryve,
Which glyded downe upon our sayles the water beyng calme
With breath of westerne wynd so myld scant moved any walme. . . .
The evening first did burnish bright, and paynt with starres the sky, . . .
When cracking, ratling, rumbling noyse, rusht down with thundring sway
From top of hills, which greatter sturre doth threaten and bewraye.
With bellowings, and yellinges lowde, the shores do grunt and grone,
The craggy clyves and roaring rocks do howle in hollow stone,
The bubling waters swelles upreard before the wrastling wynd,
When sodaynly the lowring light of Mone is hid and blynd.
The glymsing starres do goe to glade, the surging seas are tost
Even to the skyes among the clowdes the light of heaven is lost
More nightes in one compacted are with shadow dim and **blacke,**
One shadow upon another doth more darknes heape and packe,
And every sparke of light consum'd the waves and skyes do meete,
The ruffling windes range on the seas, through every coast they flit. . . .
But when the Gods (besought of us) began the rage to stay,
And Phoebus golden beames began a freshe to render lyght,
The dolefull day discried all the domage done by nyght.

This is not a translation of Aeschylus, but a translation of Seneca's adaptation. But to begin with, let us regard it as an Elizabethan reading of Greek tragedy, to see what the comparison tells us about the writer's definition of poetry. Later, we shall make a very brief comparison with the Senecan original to show where the Elizabethan writer's assumptions coincide with those of Seneca and his audience.

A reader of the narrative portion of this version will certainly not be inclined to speak of "restraint" or "generalizing quality." The essence of poetry here seems to be what Gray called "circumstance"; and "circumstance" at times means using two words where one will do. Of "circumstance" in a better sense there are some nice instances: "pipling puffes" (the soft whistling of a light breeze), "launching ships" (setting out to sea), the "glymsing starres" (glittering), the "ruffling windes." These phrases belong to speakers who know something about the sea; note, for instance, the observation in the last phrase of the wind spreading out across the water, curling up the waves. Aeschylus' language shows similar trueness of eye and ear; and Aeschylus, like the Elizabethan translator, heaps up images to create a super-storm. But the heaping in Aeschylus stops short of repetition. In reading the Elizabethan version it would be hard to say what "cracking" adds to our knowledge of the storm which isn't covered by "ratling"; or how "thundring sway" adds to "rumbling noyse"; and not even a medieval scholiast would try to tell us the difference between a "grunting" and a "groning" shore, or between "threaten" and "bewraye" or "heape" and "packe." The fury in these and similar words is not meteorological, but consonantal and alliterative. The "meaning" is in large part the immediate excitement of matched r's and g's, of assonance, and pairs of rhymed phrases. The smell of the open sea is blended with the smell of the lamp, of much reading in old and new verse.

More curious is the mixture of "literary" and "colloquial," of "high" and "low," to use eighteenth-century terms. This variety, which we noted also in the vocabulary of Aeschylus, appeared more incongruous and comic to readers of the eighteenth and nineteenth centuries than it does to us. For one thing we are more aware that the measure of colloquial quality in any text more than thirty years old is terribly uncertain. From citations in the Oxford Dictionary under "pipling" and "go to glade," it is very hard to decide whether either of these terms was for a contemporary primarily "colloquial" or primarily "literary." On the other hand, we can probably assume that words for such common acts as "grunt," "groan," and "yell," did not have literary associations. The real fact is that our eighteenth- and nineteenth-century categories did not exist for early Elizabethan writers (nor for Aeschylus). They were not so conscious of mixing "kinds" of words; they were using all the language as their needs required. We have to adjust ourselves to accepting seriously a translation in which "grunt" and "groan," "yellings" and "bellowings" are among the ways of talking in the narrative of tragic drama. And this plain speaking does not exclude a good deal of literary artifice. Similar statements might be made for Aeschylus, who, being unacquainted with modern handbooks, felt no obligation to write "classical" poetry and who accordingly put into the herald's speech some very rare compounds and surprising metaphors. But the Elizabethan writer offers more of everything; his readers wanted "the works" in

poetry; and he gave it. In addition to the abundance of circumstantial
detail and varied rhythmic devices, there are conventional literary
tags — such as "burnish," "paynt," and "Phoebus golden beames" —
the accumulation of hyperboles, and witty elaboration, such as appears in the "two-nights-in-one" paradox.

This translator did not always set out so rich a table, as a passage
from a chorus will show:

> What Fortune doth advaunce and hysteth up on hye,
> Shee sets it up to fall agayne more greevously.
> The thinges of midle sort, and of a meane degree,
> Endure above the rest and longest dayes do see:
> The man of meane estate most happy is of all,
> Who pleased with the lot that doth to him befall,
> Doth sayle on silent shore with calme and quiet tide,
> And dreads with bruised barge on swelling Seas to ryde:
> Nor launcing to the depe where bottom none is found,
> May with his rudder search, and reach the shallow ground.

The vocabulary and idiom here are nearer to the Jonsonian standard
of "such words as men do use," although the constant use of doublets
and of alliteration belongs to the same literary strain which appears
in the narrative. The middling quality of language and idea here has
a literary ancestry too; it is Horatian and Roman. Nothing marks
more clearly the line between the Aeschylean and the "classic" view
of tragic fate than this smug Horatianism. Aeschylus does not recom-
mend the "meane estate" because it is safe; he does not in fact re-
commend the mean estate; he is on the side of right action, in palaces
or smoky houses. And the view of tragedy as simply the action of an
arbitrary goddess of Fortune who raises men only to let them fall is
very close to the older, simpler doctrine of *hybris* which Aeschylus
corrects. These doctrines of the good life and the cause of tragedy,
however un-Greek and commonplace, must be included in our full
definition of poetry as it was unconsciously formulated by the Elizabethan translator and his audience.

Before reaching this point in the analysis every reader of Seneca
has been itching to point out that we have been discussing a translation and that the last-mentioned like many other features of our definition is as much Senecan as Elizabethan. As this statement may be
easily reversed, there is less cause for alarm. Since we are not tracing
sources but are mainly interested in English translations for what
they tell us about contemporary definitions of poetry, we need only
point out the more obvious coincidences between the Senecan and

Elizabethan definitions. This can be done by comparison of Seneca's Latin with both the Greek original and the English version. We find that Seneca, like the Elizabethan poet, believes in giving a *full* account of the events:

> Nox prima caelum sparserat stellis, iacent
> deserta vento vela. tum murmur grave,
> maiora minitans, collibus summis cadit
> tractuque longo litus ac petrae gemunt;
> agitata ventis unda venturis tumet—
> cum subito luna conditur, stellae latent,
> in astra pontus tollitur, caelum perit.
> nec una nox est; densa tenebras obruit
> caligo et omni luce subducta fretum
> caelumque miscet.

The darkness of the night is systematically "covered," as compared with Aeschylus' brief "in the night." Of course the English writer outdoes Seneca in sheer repetition; and he adds the picture-epithets whose precision we have already noted. Poetry for the Senecan reader as for the Elizabethan is nothing if not literary: note, for example, the amazing amount of alliteration and the insistent hyperboles (*in astra pontus tollitur; caelum perit; fretum caelumque miscet*). Though Seneca is not the sole source of the alliteration in the Elizabethan version, he may have given an added classical sanction to the device. In Seneca we find the witty paradox which the Elizabethan poet clumsily imitates: *nec una nox est.* If we turn to the original of the chorus (lines 101-107), we shall find as in the translation the reduction of Agamemnon's tragedy to the play of Fortune; and we shall see the substitution of Horatian *mediocritas* for Aeschylus' moral rightness. But these attitudes are so diffused in Elizabethan literature as to be no more Senecan than Marlowian. The rhetorical devices which are common to Seneca and the translator are equally characteristic of many Elizabethan writers. The point to be stressed here is that poetry as it appeared in our analysis of the Elizabethan passages has on some sides a strong likeness to poetry as it was purveyed in the Silver Age.

The translation which follows is as far as possible from the literary conventions of the Elizabethan and Senecan translations:

> For they swore league, being arch-foes before that,
> Fire and the sea: and plighted troth approved they,
> Destroying the unhappy Argeian army.
> At night began the bad-wave-outbreak evils;

For, ships against each other Threkian breezes
Shattered: and these, butted at in a fury
By storm and typhoon, with surge rain-resounding,—
Off they went, vanished, thro' a bad herd's whirling.
And, when returned the brilliant light of Helios,
We view the Aigaian sea on flower with corpses
Of men Achaian and with naval ravage.
But us indeed, and ship, unhurt i' the hull too,
Either some one out-stole us or out-prayed us—
Some god—no man it was the tiller touching.
And Fortune, saviour, willing on our ship sat.
So as it neither had in harbor wave-surge
Nor ran aground against a shore all rocky.
And then, the water Hades having fled from
In the white day, not trusting to our fortune,
We chewed the cud in thoughts—this novel sorrow
O' the army laboring and badly pounded.
And now—of them if anyone is breathing—
They talk of us as having perished: why not?
And we—that they the same fate have, imagine.
May it be for the best! Meneleos, then,
Foremost and specially to come, expect thou!
If (that is) any ray o' the sun reports him
Living and seeing too—by Zeus' contrivings,
Not yet disposed to quite destroy the lineage—
Some hope is he shall come again to household.

This is a bluff and hearty, straight-from-the-shoulder, one-hundred per-cent-Greek translation. (The date of publication is 1877.) No critic would be rash enough to suppose that a definition of poetry based on this version would hold for any large audience in the late nineteenth century. Nor will any reader suppose that this writer was seeking a translator's anonymity. Browning was never more Browning than when as here he was being intensely "Greek." His version represents an attempt to defy the first condition of all translating: the necessity for the translator to find within his own language and civilization some equivalents for what he has experienced through the language of the original.

The rather disastrous results of this defiance of the translator's law do not require much demonstration. One ironic result is that the English version is at times more difficult than the Greek. "Bad-wave-outbreak evils" hardly brings an English reader any nearer to grasping the manifold connotations of δυσκύμαντα. He needs a second translation to discover that "out-stole us or out-prayed us" means that some power (like a thief) snatched the ship from sinking or begged higher gods to save it. The reader finally reaches the limit in this kind of reverse-English with "We chewed the cud in thought." Pasturing leads to ruminating; and ruminating, to this!

Happily Browning had better qualities, some of which appear even in this translation: his hatred of poeticism and his desire to bring into poetry the language and rhythm of speech. Poetry, as it might be defined from this version, does not exclude such words as "butted" and "corpses." And among the monstrosities of literalism come lines that exactly reproduce the conversational tone of corresponding lines in Aeschylus:

> They talk of us as having perished: why not?

Browning does not shun the particularity in metaphor and observation which we find in Aeschylus and in the Elizabethan translation:

> . . . . these, butted at in a fury
> By storm and typhoon, with surge rain-resounding,—
> Off they went, vanished, . . .

All of these better qualities appear in the astonishingly good translation of the Helen chorus:

> At first, then, to the city of Ilion went
> A soul, as I might say, of windless calm—
> Wealth's quiet ornament,
> An eye's dart bearing balm,
> Love's spirit-biting flower.

"Balm" is the only concession to nineteenth-century prettiness, an incidental reminder that Browning was writing to an audience not entirely of his own creation. But in resisting such prettiness as he does elsewhere in this translation, Browning *was* "creating an audience," if by "creating" we mean anticipating the wants of readers not satisfied with popular Tennysonian poetry.

If we include in a definition of poetry the satisfaction of larger interests (such as those represented in the social and moral standards we spoke of at the beginning of this essay), we shall see that Browning's translation is in one respect what the mass of nineteenth-century readers wanted. It is a good example of Henry Adams' remark that "the whole of British literature in the nineteenth century was antiquarianism or anecdotage." Browning's translation is the nightmarish product of the nineteenth-century dream of reproducing the past "as it actually was." It is a Lay of Ancient Greece with the benefit of modern archaeology. The result, ironically, reminds us not of Greece but of Browning, who, as J. J. Chapman says, "established himself and his carpet-bag in comfortable lodgings on the Akropolis — which he spells with a *k* to show his intimate acquaintance with recent research."

After the "scientific forthrightness" of this 1877 translation, it is a shock to turn to a translation of 1920 and find that Browning's revolution had made almost no impression on the definition of poetry held by a large part of the literary public: (That this was a large audience is obvious from the wide sales of the author's translations).

> Two enemies most ancient, Fire and Sea,
> A sudden friendship swore, and proved their plight
> By war on us poor sailors through that night
> Of misery, when the horror of the wave
> Towered over us, and winds from Strymon drave
> Hull against hull, till good ships, by the horn
> Of the mad whirlwind gored and overborne,
> One here, one there, 'mid rain and blinding spray,
> Like sheep by a devil herded, passed away.
> And when the blessèd Sun upraised his head,
> We saw the Aegean waste a-foam with dead,
> Dead men, dead ships, and spars disasterful.
> Howbeit for us, our one unwounded hull
> Out of that wrath was stolen or begged free
> By some good spirit—sure no man was he!—
> Who guided clear our helm; and on till now
> Hath Saviour Fortune throned her on the prow,
> No surge to mar our moorlng, and no floor
> Of rock to tear us when we made for shore.
> Till, fled from that sea-hell, with the clear sun
> Above us and all trust in fortune gone,
> We drove like sheep about our brain the thoughts
> Of that lost army, broken and scourged with knouts
> Of evil. And, methinks, if there is breath
> In them, they talk of us as gone to death—
> How else?—and so say we of them! For thee,
> Since Menelaüs thy first care must be,
> If by some word of Zeus, who wills not yet
> To leave the old house for ever desolate,
> Some ray of sunlight on a far-off sea
> Lights him, yet green and living . . . we may see
> His ship some day in the harbour!

We can get at the peculiarities of "poetry" here by noting the increments which the meaning has received as compared with that of our basic version. First, there is the addition of what we may crudely call the "sad-mad" meanings. There is, for example, the increased pathos of "us poor sailors" as compared with "unhappy [*i.e.*, unlucky] troops." "That night of misery" is offered for "in night." The "ships' wreckage" becomes in this version "spars disasterful." The "lineage" (the house of Atreus) is here "the old house" (!). The scene is horrible: "the horror of the wave;" and so it is easy to slip into a kind of dramatic dementia. Not the "big wind," but a "mad whirlwind" is blowing. With diabolical madness, too: "like sheep by a devil herded." Surprisingly enough, this mad dance of ships gets into the minds of the sailors:

> We drove like sheep about our brain the thoughts
> Of that lost army, . . .

In the conclusion of the narrative madness disappears, and in its place appears a familiar note of wistfulness, of dreams of "old unhappy, far-off things":

> To leave the old house for ever desolate,
> Some ray of sunlight on a far-off sea . . .

The matter-of-fact supposition of the herald of Aeschylus has become sad reminiscence of

> Perilous seas, in faery lands forlorn.

The most surprising increment is what we might call the Biblical-Christian. In addition to the pseudo-archaic, "scriptural" idiom — drave, howbeit, throned her, wrath, hath, methinks — there is a collection of terms from which one could reconstruct much of the Christian myth: devil, blessed Sun, Saviour, hell, evil. The result is a rather sacrilegious miracle: the reader has the pleasant illusion of reading an old pagan author while indulging in all the familiar and approved emotions of Christianity. This "poetry" may be regarded as one of the cruder responses to Arnold's suggestion that poetry might offer the satisfactions of religion, that Christian religious literature might be read as poetry.

The full effect of this caricature of high-seriousness is seen in the lines on Justice:

> But Justice shineth in a house low-wrought
> With smoke-stained wall,
> And honoureth him who filleth his own lot;

But the unclean hand upon the golden stair
With eyes averse she flieth, seeking where
    Things innocent are; and, recking not the power
Of wealth by man misgloried, guideth all
    To her own destined hour.

More curious than the Biblical piety of this strain is the obscurity;
for the moral, which is all-important, is not clear in detail at two
points: "who filleth his own lot" and "wealth by man misgloried."
There may be some justification for the first on the grounds of a
kind of literalness; but the literal meaning conceals from an English
reader the point — that Justice honors the man who acts rightly.
It would be hard to discover without a text or another translation
that "misgloried" has some such meaning as "mis-stamped with approval."

The vagueness of "misgloried" for Aeschylus' peculiar counter-
feiting metaphor is not untypical of this translation. Though much
is added in the way of language which evokes a whole set of pathetic,
strange, and pious-Christian feelings, much is taken away in the elimination of the sense particulars of Aeschylus' metaphors. The "sea
flowering with corpses" has become

    . . . the Aegean waste a-foam with dead,
    Dead men, dead ships, and spars disasterful.

This dead, dead sea — so potent in its suggestion — is not the bright
fresh sea-field of the morning after the storm, incongruously alive
and blooming with bodies of drowned men. The shock of Aeschylus'
connection has disappeared in favor of an appropriate sadness. The
super-charge of emotion produced by the vague metaphors of this
translation comes with full force in the chorus on Helen:

    And how shall I call the thing that came
        At the first hour to Ilion city?
    Call it a dream of peace untold,
    A secret joy in a mist of gold,
    A woman's eye that was soft, like flame,
        A flower which ate a man's heart with pity.

The "windless calm" is a "dream of peace untold." Religiose, ineffable peace is — as so often — confused with the secrecy of passion,
flame-like, and yet tender. This love is the nineteenth-century poet's
stock-in-trade, corresponding to the elegant love of the eighteenth-
century poets. Both are irrelevant to Aeschylus, who is describing

a "lively Idea" of Helen, an image balanced between Helen as "Calm Beauty" and Erinys and Helen as a woman who loved Paris. In looking over our analysis of this translation, it is not difficult to draw an outline picture of what a large part of the literary public during the early years of this century expected in "poetry." "Poetry" is emotion, if by emotion we mean an area of sad, strange, religiose, and dreamy-erotic feelings; and poetry is "high" language — the language of Shakespeare and the Bible.

If we now look back to our basic translation, we shall be struck at once with the revolution which has taken place in the last thirty years. But to state exactly the assumptions about poetry which are involved in this contemporary version is not simple. One of the comforts of communicating with a contemporary lies in the fact that we do not have to state all that we assume. So it is easier to say in the present case what poetry is not than what it is. Poetry in this version (by MacNeice) [4] is not a recognizably poetic vocabulary; it is not confined to a particular area of feelings; it is not strictly confined to accepted metrical patterns. But these negatives carry positive implications. If we recall our original analysis of Aeschylus' metaphors and images, we can see that this translator enjoys a similar freedom in using the language of ordinary occupations and of less pleasant human experiences. In order and idiom alike, the herald's speech is nearer to a conversational norm than any of the other versions excepting a few lines of Browning's. Like Aeschylus he freely "abuses" language when necessary. He will also speak plainly, even if the result is clumsy and repetitious:

> And now if any of *them* still draw breath,
> They are thinking no doubt of us as being lost
> And we are thinking of them as being lost.

But the freedom results in an uncertainty as to tone which we never feel in reading Aeschylus. In the actual reading of Aeschylus, as of Homer, we do not encounter the problem of "high" and "low" which disturbed the eighteenth-century translators. There is variety in language, as there was in heroic behavior; and the variety corresponds to the heroic form of society. As W. P. Ker has pointed out, "this aristocracy differs from that of later and more specialised forms of civilization. . . . The art and pursuits of a gentleman in the heroic age are different from those of the churl, but not so far different as to keep them in different spheres. There is a community of prosaic interests. The great man is a good judge of cattle; he sails his own ship." [5]

The eighteenth-century translator, as we saw, solved his difficulty by elimination, by rejecting words and actions which would be at variance with the contemporary code of aristocratic behavior. The result was a uniformity of tone which the modern translator cannot achieve, for one reason because he has no corresponding assurance as to what constitutes aristocratic manners. He can only be honest in a blundering democratic way.

But this honesty pays some dividends. The reader's attention is directed primarily to what is going on, to what is happening. "Poetry," when so practiced, is concerned with the act, not the pure emotion. Like Aeschylus—we almost might say, like any writer who knows how language works—MacNeice defines the effect of the storm through telling what happens rather than by making an impossible attempt to "convey the emotion *directly*." By contrast, Murray, who translated the passages we have just been discussing, arouses plenty of feelings through obviously emotive language; but the feelings are, on inspection, largely irrelevant. Nor does MacNeice (any more than Aeschylus) give us those generalized summaries of the action and reflections on its meaning which we find in the eighteenth-century translator, Robert Potter. MacNeice is not *descriptive* in the manner of Potter's version, which is a-bloom with adjectives ("tempest wild," "forceful blasts," "hideous conflict," "dreadful will," "wanton state," "easy way," "rosy love," etc.). The reader — perhaps because of mere frequency—knows that so many adjectives cannot mean much; they are signals for a very tepid response compared with Murray's "sad, mad," and "far-off" expressions. But certainly the almost complete diversion of poetry, as in Murray, from the act to an exciting and even irrelevant penumbra begins historically with the eighteenth-century "describers." And a return to the "act" from the "feeling" is a good omen for the translation of Greek poets, especially of Aeschylus, whose six-footed epithets are hardly adjectives (in the sense of the term illustrated above), but whole action-sentences which must be read with a sharp sense of the meaning of the separate roots: "desire that-eats-the-heart."

In the original discussion of MacNeice's translation we noted a good example of the modern translator's preference for the act to the abstraction: the translation of *díke* as "Honest Dealing." This phrase is an indication that in still another way this translation gives us "twentieth-century poetry." Justice is "social Justice." And though the category did not exist in fifth-century Athens, Aeschylus does seem in this passage to stress something like social justice in the sense of getting money without wronging other men. But "dealing" and "deals" carry the connotations of our world of "business" and "labor relations." Even more revealing than the use of such language is the avoidance of the traditional term. The possible "legal" or "moral" or "religious" varieties of justice are carefully excluded; whereas Aeschylus' term was more inclusive, not observing such sharp distinctions. A contemporary writer feels some inhibition against using these all-embracing abstractions which are the traditional value labels. He is less certain of what they stand for; and if he is honest, he must redefine them for himself and his contemporaries.

We have been indicating that MacNeice's translation, like the others, reflects the definition of proper poetic practice which was prevalent at the time it was written. We are of course less able to isolate modes of feeling and speaking which are so much a part of us. But the moral, as in the earlier translations, is essentially the same: the translation of poetry of the past is a translation into the poetry of the translator and his readers. The value to be drawn from noting this rather obvious truth is only in the analysis which it suggests; and the analysis will lead to a more particularized awareness of the definitions of poetry involved in the language-uses of the translators. Such analysis can also remind us of the kind of discounting necessary when we are reading any translation and of the sequel, that reading one translation means an obligation to read many and not merely those of our contemporaries. But the main interest here, as I pointed out at the beginning, is to show the usefulness of translations for ascertaining the various answers at various points in history to the questions "What is poetry?" and "What is a poem?"

NOTES

1. Harry de Forest Smith, teacher of Greek at Amherst College, 1901–1939.

2. For the Greek text see *Agamemnon*, ll. 650–680, *Aeschyli Tragoediae*, ed. A. Sidgwick (Oxford, 1902). For the Greek text of the next two passages quoted in translation, see ll. 737–743 and 772–781.

3. For another reading see G. Murray, ed., *Aeschyli* (Oxford, 1938), *ad loc.*

4. Translations used, in order of quotation: Louis MacNeice, *The Agamemnon of Aeschylus* (London, 1936), 35–36, 38, 39. Robert Potter (1721–1804),

The Works of the British Poets, ed. Robert Walsh, Jun. (Boston, 1823), I, 43, 46, 47. The translation of Aeschylus was first published in 1777. John Studley, *Seneca his Tenne Tragedies*, ed. Thomas Newton anno 1581, The Tudor Translations (London, 1927), II, 118–123, 105. Seneca, *Seneca's Tragedies*, with an English translation by Frank Justus Miller, The Loeb Classical Library (London, 1907), II, pp. 40–42, ll. 465–474. Robert Browning, *Agamemnon, La Saisiaz, Dramatic Idyls, and Jocoseria* (Boston, 1884), 47–48, 50–51. Gilbert Murray, *The Agamemnon of Aeschylus* (New York, 1920), 28–29, 33, 32.

5. W. P. Ker, *Epic and Romance* (London, 1922), 7.

TRANSLATION: THE AUGUSTAN MODE

DOUGLAS KNIGHT

ANY CONCERN with the Augustan idea of translation involves us immediately in a depth and detail of interest which is quite foreign to our own time. Even so, we shall understand the Augustan zeal for translation best if we see it in the light of those qualities which at any time underlie a successful job of making a work of literary art available in a language other than its original. Translation which is concerned only to serve the purposes of a dictionary will not pose such demands, of course, nor will the translation of works of information. But if we are concerned with complex writing, then the translator should possess four major attributes if he is to succeed.

First, he should himself be an artist — at least enough of one to yearn for a living expression of the work to which he has committed his energy. He should want his own achievement to be something, in addition to its power of pointing or gesture toward another work. And he should even feel that the best single compliment he can pay his original is to have its translated version come alive.

Second, he should be a scholar and linguist. This does not mean that he should be a world authority on the work he is translating, but it certainly does mean that he should be alert to a consistent and coherent version of its major statements, attitudes, insights, and artistic means. (If he is determined to present *the* meaning to his own world, of course, he will never complete any work of translation.) His friends and scholarly acquaintances can teach him much, but he must be able to put their interpretations together as a single order. This calls for assimilated knowledge, not for a pastiche of footnotes or a parade of learning. It may not call for great knowledge, but it certainly demands a mastery within more limited knowledge.

To make this artistic and scholarly competence available, however, two other conditions are called for. The translator should have the interests and insight of an educated but unspecialized reader. He cannot translate effectively without some genuine grasp of the reason for translation. This "reason" is a deeply felt need and desire to range into areas of new insight; and without such a desire, such a sense of not standing quite in the presence of the work he is trying to interpret, a translator will not speak to his world. He may produce a superb private version of the poem or play, but he will not produce anything capable of opening the door for another mind.

A second condition in order to make scholarly and artistic competence available is implied in the first — the need for a translator to be profoundly a member of his own world, engaging it at some point, not from the sanctuary of his scholarly work but from the immediate occasions of his own life in his own time. He must be alive to the struggles and dilemmas of his culture, or his work will lack the urgency which good translation needs in order to compensate for the many kinds of loss which take place between original and version.

I have considered this problem briefly as one of the translator rather than the work, not because I doubt the primacy of the latter, but because the special distinction of Augustan translation rests on the four conditions I have just outlined. One can deduce from them, of course, a theory of translation as work which is alive artistically in the two contexts of its original world view and the world view which calls forth its reincarnation. But to understand the Augustan mode, and in particular that of Pope, we need to recognize why the fact of translation is so appealing to the eighteenth-century audience, and why the climate for it is so perfect.

The Augustans, it should be clear, are forced to an awareness of themselves which few ages have accepted so candidly. They have a far more specific and accurate knowledge, for example, of the great work in the Greco-Roman tradition than even the best-educated of the Elizabethans possess. But the very fact of that knowledge stands for them as a constant commentary on themselves. Chapman interprets and translates Homer in exaltation of his own world, in recognition of its dreams and ambitions, but with an amiable disregard for its delusions about itself. The very distance which Pope feels between Homer and himself is a defense against such delusion; it serves both to "exalt" Homer in what Pope considers to be his true character, and to "place" Pope's own time as one which cannot easily or wisely confuse itself with Homer's. It is this sense of distinction and difference which marks the Augustans, and tells us indirectly how critical they are of themselves, how determined not to wander in fancy's maze. Their learning and poetic skill can work comfortably together in the production of British pastoral; but when serious British epic is involved reality keeps breaking in. Only the third-rate and insensitive fancy they can produce it; the best of the Augustans know the pretensions of the true heroic world and the limitations of their own far too clearly to confuse the two.

This double awareness almost demands a serious interest in translation as a means of exploring and reconciling such disparate views of reality. Certain other conditions of Augustan life lend added force to the interest, and make translation a natural kind of discourse as it cannot be for us. The genuine and general interest in learning, for example, centers in a common body of texts and in the attempt, at least, to discover a common group of attitudes toward them as well as convictions about them. Learning for us is often the pursuit of separate and individual paths; we make our learned reputations from those kinds of knowledge which are held in common only by very small groups. For the Augustans this kind of learning is suspect — the preserve of a Scriblerus or a Laputan, with nothing but folly for its fruit. The learned world and the educated world should be the same, and as a result any translator should be writing for his peers, and with the knowledge that they will judge from his grounds. He will not translate to make a poem available in his own language for those who cannot read the original, but rather to express a kind of insight which many of his audience can interpret in the composite matrix of their world and that of the original. He will have no embarrassment about rendering hexameters by means of heroic couplets, because no reader would expect one to be an easy equivalent for the other. And he knows that his audience will ask the same question he has asked himself; how does this idiom of my own time reflect, interpret, apprehend an original work which all of us recognize from the outset as profoundly different from anything we can produce as a version of it?

This sense of common ground between the artist-translator and his audience puts one great responsibility on him, of course. While he must be true to the demanding complexity of his own artistic insight, he must always be so in relation to the interest and support of his readers. Pope made a good deal of money from his translations of Homer, but to say that he wrote in order to make money is to falsify his position. He wrote in order to communicate with a substantial audience, and he would judge himself a failure if he merely mystified them, bored them, or condescended to them. The translations were to be a point where he, they, and Homer could all meet.

This concern is borne out, of course, by the modes of Augustan poetry other than translation. Only a community of artists deeply in touch with the daily life of their own time would be so preoccupied with satire, or with the relation among the various arts, or with the clubs whose purpose is to bring many professions and kinds of insight together. Behind any of these groups or interests stands the desire to master the common bases of life, to grasp the variety and differences they share with one another, to mediate among them. The purposes of translation as I have already described them are also purposes of educated life in general for the Augustans, and their constant interest in translation and imitation thus grows, like our preoccupation with experimental science, from the kinds of understanding they feel themselves most in need of and most competent to embrace.

One result of this coincidence between the desirable theoretical context for translation and the major concerns of the Augustans is a more complex use of the artistic and philosophic possibilities of translation than one would expect or perhaps quite imagine. This use has three major aspects, all of which are strikingly evident in Pope's work but are typical of Dryden or Gay as well.

The first could be put most briefly as a desire to explore central qualities of insight and conviction, even though they may not be easily or simply viable for one's own time and one's own artistic life. The gulf between Pope's world and Homer's is only equaled by the depth of Pope's fascination with Homer as the artist who beyond all others brought into being the major and continuing pattern of heroic insight. This insight, and above all its direct, constant evocation of the centrally violent qualities of pride, love, ambition, and folly, is not superficially relevant to Pope's own world. And yet one or many of these qualities shimmer behind every human action that has substance to it; what is impossible in Pope's "normal" world or ours is the confronting, the direct experience, the extremes of bright and dark, the simplicity of dealing always with final realities. As a result the challenge of Homer to Pope is the double one of apprehending this directness and of somehow bringing it to bear on the infinite nuances and indirections of a conventionally sophisticated world.

It is important to recognize how deep Pope's loyalty to Homer runs here. It would have been easy to versify Homer, and we can see from Pope's correspondence how great the temptation often was to do exactly that and no more. But the manuscripts of the Homer translations show instead an agonizingly meticulous job of interpretation, of study, and of independent creation. The notes, like the translation itself, clearly mirror a concern with Homer that occupied several of Pope's mature years and called forth the gravest kind of discipline,

that of subordinating his own artistic insight to the demands and
world view, not only of a far greater artist but one who was different
from himself in many crucial ways. To sustain this attitude was really
to put himself between two worlds in the only truly effective
way — by immersing himself in the "other" world and acting imag-
inatively as though it were the central one. The discipline of Latin
studies for Milton or Thomist metaphysics for Dante are for Pope
his seven years' encounter with Homer.

One cannot discuss this encounter, of course, as though it were
merely an absorption and obliteration of one's interests in his own
world. It is a bifocal event and looks toward the artist's immediate
world by virtue of the very intensity with which it commands him
to reach out toward another. For a second major use of translation
by the Augustans is the light it throws on current convictions —
and perhaps equally on current self-deceptions. Translation serves as
a corrective to that provinciality of mind which would take as gospel
anything an age seems satisfied with. It is the meeting place of tradition on the one hand and satire on the other — tradition as the living
presence of the past, the relevance of the different, and satire in its
character as the double-faced, the two-edged view of certain certain-
ties. The validity of translation lies in its provision of the necessary
foil for immediate experience.

Because of these two kinds of preoccupation with immediacy —
Homer's, in which the immediate events are always final ones, and
Pope's own, in which immediate events are daily, proximate, partial
ones — Pope inevitably commits himself through the mode of translation to the twofold obligation of any major artist — that of reckon-
ing with the recognizable surfaces of the world on the one hand, and
on the other, showing how the inescapably permanent shines beneath those surfaces. These ends can be realized in many ways, of
course; but it is deeply significant that Pope's way of doing so leads
him to the writing of an absolutely major translation as well as the
mastery of an essential attitude for his own "original" work.

As these two preoccupations work together, they result in
poetic consequences which Pope could not have formulated or even
imagined as he set to work on the Homer. There is a sequential meaning to the various values of translation for him: first, a willingness to
take the alien attitude seriously; second, an ability to bring it into
living relation with all the accepted and unquestioned attitudes of
his own world; and third, the flowering of a poetic maturity not

possible without both these earlier steps. Though the three may occur simultaneously, we can see in a hundred of Pope's notes to the Homer how his meditation on a passage was the necessary first step to translating it — and not just the meditation of looking through the dictionary, but that of functioning as the true critic in sharply loving interpretation of the original. We can see him recapitulate again and again in the Homer the course taken by his interpretive study and direct craftsmanship. This is particularly evident in the manuscripts, of course, where everything from the choice of an adjective to the sequences of a paragraph is clearly the product of a developing understanding of Homer, and reflected in the labor spent on annotation as well as in the building of the verse.

The result, of course, is poetry that has astonishingly coherent life as a version of Homer. The coherence shows itself in three major ways. First, it is evident in a sustained, consistent tone in the poem as a whole. In striking contrast to Chapman's work, for example, Pope gives us a constant sense of motion through the poem, a constant speed and headway which provide a quality comparable to that achieved by Homer's use of formulaic combinations and repetitions. The astonishing range and length of an *Iliad* or a *Paradise Lost* call for some such binding and sustaining power. It is a major triumph of Pope's achievement that he provides it by couplets which have all too often been regarded as self-contained units. They are not that, of course; they are coherent divisions of major paragraphs, providing by their own order a swiftness of motion through large masses of narrative. In his use of them Pope is paying homage to the rapidity and "fire" which he regards as Homer's major poetic qualities.

The homage issues equally in a second great quality of Pope's own poetry — a constant local life and excitement, to protect against the tedium of reading thousands of lines which, in dull heroic writing, may tend toward some grand design but bore the reader to sleep long before he finds out what it is. Pope does not settle for respectable dullness, but gives us instead a death where "the head yet speaking muttered as it fell," a moonlit night which "tips with silver every mountain's head," a love-scene where amorous Paris "rushed to the bed, impatient for the joy." Throughout there is this trembling of local life, never intrusive, never stopping the onward motion of events, but always present to assert the fact of vigor and excitement in every minute event — a fact which is the greatest difference between artistic and normal experience.

These two achievements, great as they are, could not be sustained in a poem of twenty thousand lines, however, unless they furthered and were furthered by some overriding interpretive coherence. Size in a poem must also mean stature, and Pope faces his most difficult job in devising a version of the *Iliad* which will give some recognition to Homer's insight, though within the idiom of a world of totally different preoccupations, ways of life, and superficial values.

He does so in three chief ways. First, he heightens and interprets certain perpetually relevant concerns of the poem — the attributes of the state, for example, or the problems of leadership and the position of the king. Without the easy modernization which can so quickly turn into parody, there is still the ring of currency about speeches like those of Agamemnon in Book I of the *Iliad*:

> Thy years are awful, and thy words are wise.
> But that imperious, that unconquer'd soul,
> No laws can limit, no respect controul.
> Before his pride must his superiours fall,
> His word the law, and he the lord of all?
> Him must our hosts, our chiefs, ourself obey?
> What king can bear a rival in his sway?
> Grant that the Gods his matchless force have
>   giv'n;
> Has foul reproach a privilege from heav'n?

At a somewhat different level of character, though not of importance, the speeches of figures like Eumaeus are treated as wisdom's window on the world. They epitomize a kind of insight about the central action of the poem, and they are presented with a simplicity and aphoristic brilliance that calls our attention to the permanent wisdom of the simple and the humble:

> Take with free welcome what our hands pre-
>   pare,
> Such foods as falls to simple servants share;
> The best our lords consume; those thoughtless
>   peers,
> Rich without bounty, guilty without fears!
> Yet sure the Gods their impious acts detest,
> And honour justice and the righteous breast.
> Pirates and conquerors, of harden'd mind,
> The foes of peace, and scourges of mankind,
> To whom offending men are made a prey
> When Jove in vengeance gives a land away;

Ev'n these, when of their ill-got spoils possess'd,
Find sure tormentors in the guilty breast;
Some voice of God close whisp'ring from within,
"Wretch! this is villany, and this is sin."

A second chief means of sustaining coherence and immediacy in his version of Homer is Pope's attention to the life of the natural world around and beyond man. Homer's similes are, of course, remarkable for their grasp of the texture and detail of nature, constantly used in the poem both as exemplar and foil for the passions and fragilities of men. In the course of the poem they build up a context for the action, a sense of those qualities that are permanent or recurrent in the natural universe and a steady reminder to man of his bondage to that universe as well as his differences from it. The high finish of Pope's treatment of these puts behind them a great pressure of poetic authority:

First of the foe, great Hector march'd along,
With terrour cloath'd, and more than mortal
    strong.
As the bold hound, that gives the lion chace,
With beating bosom, and with eager pace,
Hangs on his haunch, or fastens on his heels,
Guards as he turns, and circles as he wheels:
Thus oft' the Grecians turn'd, but still they
    flew;
Thus following Hector still the hindmost slew.
When flying they had pass'd the trench pro-
    found,
And many a chief lay gasping on the ground;
Before the ships a desp'rate stand they made,
And fir'd the troops, and call'd the Gods to aid.

The poetry insists that such a world is one we inhabit, and so the gap between the Homeric figures and ourselves is diminished. They and we are included in one concourse of natural forces.

Pope's first two means of establishing his version of Homer depend, then, on an immediate poetic evocation of the most insistent aspects of the *Iliad* and *Odyssey*, those which point most clearly to the permanent present of his work. But Pope depends also on another and rather different kind of continuity as a means for making Homer available in an Augustan context. The tradition of heroic poetry, and in particular the work of Virgil and Milton, is a constant voice in the translations. Zeus becomes a Jove and almost a Judeo-Christian god; the heroic situation becomes one of finite, human participation in the final and divine order of things; and the chief poetic absorption is with this dynamic participation of man's freedom in his fate. Traditions and developments of insight which are the major achievement of the *Aeneid* and *Paradise Lost*, yet at the same time a major bond between them and the *Iliad* and *Odyssey*, are for Pope a means of reinterpretation, a road to the past which is equally a road to the present. Homer may legitimately be seen in the light of Virgil and Milton because of the debt they owe him; for Pope (who is in debt to them all) the proper homage to Homer, and the living justice he deserves, are expressed by exploring and transmuting his major kinds of order without doing violence to them.

Yet even this development, remarkable as it is, is not quite all. The full meaning of Pope's homage to Homer (or, to put it another way, the full meaning of translation for him and his time) is only apparent in his best "original" work. There Homer stands as one great dimension of poetic richness, a richness which we see not only in allusiveness of context, but in the incisive presentation of character and the vigorous economy of argument. The stability and range, not only of Pope's poetic world but of the Augustan world around it, are established in part by their "possession" of the great heroic poets — an achievement impossible without the living knowledge, the living poetry of Dryden's *Aeneid* or Pope's *Iliad* and *Odyssey*.

VERSIONS, INTERPRETATIONS, AND PERFORMANCES

JOHN HOLLANDER

"Do you know languages? What's the French for fiddle-de-dee?"
"Fiddle-de-dee's not English," Alice replied gravely.
"Who ever said it was?" said the Red Queen.
Alice thought she saw a way out of the difficulty, this time.
"If you'll tell me what language 'fiddle-de-dee' is, I'll tell you the
French for it!" she exclaimed triumphantly.
But the Red Queen drew herself up rather stiffly and said
"Queens never make bargains."

I

THE DOMAIN of logic is a kind of paradise in which it is easy to be
right. No harder, at any rate, than to be wrong; and from the tangle
of problems that confronts the literary theorist, the regions of formal-
ized discourse are extremely tantalizing. For if the operations of
logicians can reveal no new facts about the world, they remain always
within the neat borders of certainty. There is perhaps no field of
criticism that lies closer to this walled garden than the area of literary
translation. It is only here that *correctness* seems today to matter so
much, both as a condition in itself and in its relationship to whatever
else about translations seems worthy of praise or blame. One often
feels how fine it would be if correctness were all, and if it were to
operate as nicely as logical truth. Substitution, for example, involves
the putting of one logical symbol or expression for another, *salva
veritate*; and it is perhaps with a kind of wishful thinking that we
often tend to consider the simplest kind of translation of ordinary
discourse as something like putting one linguistic entity for another,
preserving some value of the original, and enabling us to determine
the correctness of the whole process by some mechanical means.

But practical experience tells us that no such thing happens. Even
if one has agreed to accept a whole list of word-for-word identities
between two languages, he must abandon his list almost immediately
upon confronting the same words in different syntactic arrangements.
He will discover a hierarchy of exceptional cases, starting with a
specialized use of a word, and continuing on up through the idiom,
the tone, or the style of a particular group of speakers. Thus, even in
the language of everyday statement, the translation of a particular

utterance is subject to a hierarchy of objections such as "misleading" or "it doesn't quite catch the (tone, flavor, spirit, shade) of the original," applied at the level of the word, the phrase, and so forth. Further still from the paradise of certainty, however, lies the domain in which judgments are made concerning the literary texts, which, we tend to feel today, resist even paraphrase into different words of their original tongues with an eternal and necessary obstinacy.

It might be remarked here that no translation can ever be "correct" in quite the same way as an answer to a simple question like "How old are you?" or "Is it Tuesday?" On the other hand, questions like "How do you feel?" have answers which, if at all, seem to be "correct" or "incorrect" in a very different sense. And if translations of a given statement can be correct or incorrect only in *their* special sense, perhaps the whole notion of such a standard is inappropriate here. And perhaps it is in very different ways that we do actually evaluate such translations. Although the precise delineation of such a special sense of "correct" seems more of a technical problem in philosophy than a literary one, one is tempted to examine the question a little more closely. Every literary document that purports to be a translation from an original in some other language makes a kind of contract to be correct, but it is traditional to regard any such contract, if filled to the letter, with a bit of contempt and suspicion.

To avoid confronting the notion of correctness as such, however, is to turn toward other problems. There are two traditional concepts of critical thought which, in period disguise or modern dress, eventually intrude themselves into most discussions of the problems of translation. The first of these is in the general process of being discredited today, although, it must be added, only at the expense of affirming the second. The traditional categorical dissociation of form and content is seldom maintained seriously as the opposition of "judgement" and "fancy" (Hobbes) or "instruction" and "adornment." But we shall see that something very like these poles seems to turn up during the process of translation. It has been in the name of another principle, of what might be called "literary organism," that the form-content dichotomy is usually erased. This view maintains that the "content" or "meaning" of a literary work is in some mysterious way always something more than merely the sum of the meanings of its parts. On the face of it, distinction between form and content is blurred on the grounds that, whatever "content" is taken to mean, purely formal elements can be shown to possess it. This is quite a sensible objection; it springs, however, from a relatively weak principle. For either the "organic whole" position (1) makes sense, but in no way distinguishes literary statements from ordinary ones, or (2) maintains nothing at all but the fact that, with respect to the problem of "meaning" or "content," utterances of any kind are habitually segmented into the wrong sorts of parts.

But it is the specter of the "organic" view which crops up so often in discussions of translation, and it surely lurks behind all the old saws like the comparison of translations and mistresses that can never be both faithful and beautiful. A customary, common-sense type of analysis, I suppose, would put the whole problem in terms of meanings, somewhat as follows: statements of all kinds have meanings. To translate a sentence from one language to another is somehow to discover its meaning and then to construct a sentence in the new, or target language that possesses the same meaning. Now with regard to literary translations, such an account would tend to force one into one of two undesirable directions. In the first place, decisions as to the meaning of the original text must consider such matters as tone and rhetorical level, readings of imagery, the schematic and associative use of sound-patterns — in short, the significance of "form" in the original work, all of the elements of which must then be somehow figured-forth in the target language. In other words, one is tempted here to assert the "form-content" dichotomy against all usual better judgment. But the other alternative would be to cleave to the view of the organic whole, and probably end up by asserting that translation is impossible under any circumstances. In either case, there is a tendency to imply that meanings, because we say that they can be discovered or grasped, are actually things of some kind or another, or else that they are like Aristotelian souls, giving form to the linguistic utterances that embody them.

Even if we adopt a more sophisticated view of the nature of meanings, however, analyzing them into "dispositions" (following C. L. Stevenson and other philosophers), the futility of the above account remains evident. What one has actually done is to fracture any act of translation into two successive sub-translations, the first putting the original text into some queer sort of language of meanings, and the second retranslating into the final form. Any attempt to clarify what is going on in the process by applying the method in successive stages will result in an infinite regress.

It may very well be the case that to try to talk about translations without talking about the meanings of words and sentences and images and poems (and perhaps without talking about the effects of sound-patterns and verse forms and the resonances set up between words that sound alike), is impossible. It may be the case that by ruling out "meanings" or "content" one is utterly dissolving one's subject matter. But it seems much more likely that discussions of what is satisfactory or unsatisfactory about renderings of literary works in other languages have as their subject nothing more than how people react to the literary works themselves, and what they expect of them.

Another point intrudes itself here. Most of the accumulated lore on the subject seems to reinforce the view that there are barely grounds even for grudging praise of any literary rendering at all. Remarks such as the old Italian pun on "translator" and "traitor," or St. Jerome's abuse of the translations of Scripture prior to his own (*"Non versiones, sed eversiones"*) are rather over-polemical, I think, and, as such, beside the point. Unusual also is Voltaire's comment concerning Virgil, addressed to the lady who wished to compare him with Pope: *"Vous le connaissez par les traductions: mais les poëtes ne se traduisent point. Peut-on traduire de la musique?"* [1] This seems to prefigure the views of a later century, in associating with music not the beauty, or decoration, but a strange sort of ineffable, incomprehensible, and (hence?) untranslatable core of pure poetry. The general tenor of translation lore is less extreme than this, however. It confines its skepticism to observations of a necessary incompatibility between accuracy and all other desiderata; its only praise occurs in the traditional remarks about the occasional utility of crutches, although usually coupled with the insinuation that no one should ever be lame. Now for any assessment of the utility of crutches, their relative comfort, their state of adjustment, and so forth, we usually require the testimony of those who are compelled to use them. But the awkward fact remains that the only acknowledged judges of a particular translation must necessarily be drawn from the class of those who have no need of it. As a result of this, translation-criticism gets to be a bandying about of *expertise* among producers, as it were, rather than among consumers.

Writers of the past few decades have been steeped in this tradition. As translators, they have been unusually self-conscious in their predicament. Theirs has been an eclectic age, tirelessly committed to exhuming the artifacts of the literary and artistic past, and yet intent on maintaining a synoptic view of the present. Such an age depends upon a jealous and uneasy friendship with literary translation as almost no other age has, all the while purporting to remain under few illusions as to the fidelity of the comrade in question. The problem of translating poetry has been taken somehow as the model for all translating problems, both because of particular pitfalls and a general hopelessness; at the same time, however, much poetry (in English, at any rate) has sprung from, or even consisted in, translations from writing in other languages. The styles worked out in connection with certain particular renderings have proved influential as poetic styles in themselves. And finally, translation has come to the brink of identification with the process of literary invention as such, with respect both to the practice, and to the role of the practitioner (the job of the poet outlined in T. S. Eliot's "Tradition and the Individual Talent" is strangely like that of an Ideal Translator).

It has been just this age which has begun to employ such quaint devices as literary mistranslation, and to consider their virtues. The deliberate use of the prosaically "incorrect" renderings of particular passages and phrases has come to stand for an assertion of commitment to some sort of poetic truth, to a world in which a kind of literary correctness might flourish. There might be remarked the almost nervous readjustment of names and phrases such as are represented by C. K. Scott Moncrieff's rendering of "Fabrizio" for the Christian name of the hero of *La Chartreuse de Parme*. Far more perilous was his juggling of Proust's titles for the sake of euphony, or even for an allusion (with regard to *The Sweet Cheat Gone* in particular, it is doubtful whether very many readers would recognize the last line of a poem by Walter de la Mare that had appeared less than a decade before). There are occasional cases, however, where such juggling, usually confined to the relative noncommittal safety of titles, produces a peculiarly just result. It might be useful to consider for a moment an example of such fortunate audacity, represented very nicely by a translation of Edouard Dujardin's *Les Lauriers sont coupés*. That fragile little work, first published in 1887, employed interior monologue throughout in an almost programmatic fashion; it suffered extreme neglect during much of its author's life, finally emerging into some small eminence upon the publication of *Ulysses* and Joyce's subsequent testimony to the effect that he had indeed read Dujardin's book as early as 1901. Mr. Stuart Gilbert's translation, undertaken for New Directions in 1938, was thus emblazoned from its very inception with a certain documentary value. In view of this, a certain amount of fastidiousness was to have been expected, and it is quite surprising to note for the first time the title of the English version: *We'll to the Woods No More*. But that phrase is taken from the epigraph to A. E. Housman's *Last Poems*,

> We'll to the woods no more,
> The laurels all are cut

itself a translation of Théodore de Banville's

> Nous n'irons plus au bois, les lauriers sont coupés.

The effect here of quoting Housman's first line, instead of the more "correct" second one, can hardly be said to depend on the greater familiarity of the allusion; it operates quite beyond allusion itself. For any reader unfamiliar with the Housman version would nevertheless react to the two lines in very different ways, and the first of them, elliptically archaic, carries with it much more of the flavor of a half-remembered song than does the second. It is just the slightly recondite nostalgia of such an echo which escapes the unduly prosaic quality of "The laurels all are cut," while avoiding equally well, on the other hand, the trite sentiment of a possibly more "lyrical" rendering ("The laurels are cut down," for example).

Although this substitution may have been a mere whim of the moment on the part of the translator, its effect is undeniably elegant. But other examples of queer or *précieux* mistranslation abound in which a rather different effect is gained. Ezra Pound's *The Seafarer* makes fairly consistent use throughout of the device of cognate-substitution, rendering *"bitre brēost ceare gebiden haebbe"* ("I have endured intense heartache") as "Bitter breast cares have I abided," or *"ealle onmēdlan eorthan rīces"* ("all the shows of the kingdom of this world") as "all arrogance of earthen riches." An editor partial to Pound's virtues as translator, Mr. Hugh Kenner, attempts to argue for the last case on rather ingenious grounds (although he seems not to have construed *"rīces"* properly as a genitive singular). But I think that Mr. Kenner has missed the point of the over-all method employed in *The Seafarer*, where the use of a Modern English word of German derivation over a perhaps more precise one of Latin or French descent is made schematic. Moreover, any word is rendered, if possible, by its cognate in Modern English, sometimes quite arbitrarily so, or even quasi-mistakenly: "keel" for *"cēol"* ("keelboat") suggests wrongly that there is a synecdoche in the original. And yet this is the sort of thing that Pound everywhere seeks to avoid, and is so quick to point out elsewhere in his own and others' translations. Going from one dialect of a language to another one that is either historically or geographically or even sociologically removed raises particular problems of its own, of course. It may be that there is always the temptation to try to blur the distinction between the two, to carve a new "dialect" out of the larger expanse of the inclusive language. To a certain extent, this may have been the intention in the case of *The Seafarer*; there may very well have been an additional desire to call attention to the alliterative scheme and the compressed syntax of the original by making a very queer sort of English to point it up. Certainly the result is archaistic in the extreme, and so grammatically opaque as to be bothersome. Take, for example, Pound's

> Burgher knows not —
> He the prosperous man — what some perform
> Where wandering them widest draweth.

This is given for something very much like "The retainer, the wealthy warrior, knows not what the others suffer, whom the paths of exile have led furthest away." To add that the opacity comes from the density resulting from using the same number of lines as are contained in the original is to imply that the value of the line-for-line quality is considerable. In this case, Pound undoubtedly staked a great deal upon that value, and might have countered the objection to the difficult syntax with a remark he frequently makes elsewhere, that Anglo-Saxon verse did not have to compete with the precision and clarity of prose in the same way in which modern verse must confront the kind of writing typified by Flaubert, for example. But I think that other contingencies were making their demands here as well. The more general of these may have been a desire to leave exposed in the finished product the actual process of composition of the new version, to show up some of the etymological sinews, and to confront the reader with a bit of work in process. Too inaccurate to serve even as a gloss, *The Seafarer* attempts to combine some of the virtues of a finished poem and a crib. Its real accomplishment seems to me to be twofold. In the first place, it maintains considerable intensity through its preservation of the condensed structure of the Anglo-Saxon; it never falls into a tone of elegiac prolixity manifested by all-too-many prose renderings of the original. Second, Pound's translation points up some of the basic devices of Anglo-Saxon verse and carries them over into Modern English, if not tit for tat at each occurrence, then often one for another, and always with sufficient regularity to make them understood as conventions. One of these devices not always seen as such is the word cluster that appears so often in the first half of normal (unexpanded) lines, where two alliterating words bracket an unstressed preposition or function word (Sievers' rhythmic type A): "*hāt ymb hēortan*" ("hot about the heart"); "*bitter in brēosthord*," etc. The syntactical patterns with which nouns, verbs, and adjectives may be associated are widely varied, but the force of the association is undeniable, and the device itself might be better said to function as a trope than as a formula, or perhaps as merely a metrical schema. Pound's *Seafarer* contrives to employ these clusters ("bide above brine"; "weathered the winter"; "corn of the coldest"; "fields to fairness") even when the text calls for something entirely different; one might call this an extension of the cognate-substitution method so as to include cognate tropes as well. As far as the kennings themselves are concerned, the treatment is somewhat less systematic. There are nevertheless many points at which a "dead" circumlocution, already idiomatic in Anglo-Saxon, is reinvested with a metaphoric value. Sometimes this extends to mistranslation based on etymology. For example,

> For thon mē hātran sind
> Dryhtnes drēamas   thonne this dēade līf,
> læne on londe:

"So my lord's joys are warmer to me than this dead life, impermanent on earth," becomes "seeing that anyhow/My lord deems to me this dead life/On loan and on land." "On loan and on land" etymologizes back to "*lǣn*" ("loan" or "grant") the text's adjective "*lǣne*" ("transitory," "frail," perhaps because once "temporarily granted"). This is the sort of reading that Robert Graves has so relentlessly pilloried in an attack on Pound's Propertius translation, but its use here, I think, is a rather different matter. One might be tempted, perhaps, to call the whole thing a case of a fortunate howler, were it not for the fact that the whole translation seems to be based on such howlers. And in a way, the history of semantic change in the life cycle of any language can be naïvely arrayed so as to resemble nothing so much as a string of howlers, successive mistranslations by each generation of the speech of an earlier one.

I have spent so much time on Pound's *Seafarer* because I think that it exemplifies an attitude towards the translation of poetry which has gained considerable power over most modern views on the subject. Pound himself outlined this position in two extremely lucid paragraphs at the very end of his *Cavalcanti* (1934):

> In the long run the translator is in all probability impotent to do *all* the work for the linguistically lazy reader. He can show where the treasure lies, he can guide the reader in the choice of what tongue is to be studied, and he can very materially assist the hurried student who has a smattering of a language and the energy to read the original text alongside the metrical gloze.
>
> This refers to "interpretive translation." The "other sort." I mean in cases where the "translator" is definitely making a new poem, falls simply in the domain of original writing, or if it does not it must be censured according to equal standards, and praised with some sort of just deduction, assessable only in the particular case.[2]

"Interpretive translation" would thus seem to be the sort of thing that *The Seafarer* is aiming at. In the case of both this and the "other sort," however, the older notions of the ideal woman, true and fair, or of the essential nude "meaning" of the original entirely reclothed in a new tongue, or even of the old familiar crutch, are clearly avoided. "To show where the treasure lies" seems to be the essential point of this heuristic kind of translation, in which the new rendering would appear to function more as a process of teaching than as a finished — as Pound would have it, almost a crafted — object. It is often true, particularly within the corpus of Pound's own work, that the distinction between the two types of translation tends to break down somewhat. Where the " 'translator' is definitely making a new poem," he may be teaching, pointing out obscured significances, annotating and commenting, especially in an age when poems have been variously and conflictingly modeled on ornaments, useful instruments of thought, polemical excursions, as well as on this kind of heuristic process (cf. Mallarmé: *"Donner un sens plus pur aux mots de la tribu"* and Eliot: "To purify the dialect of the tribe," in *Little Gidding*). But I think that the conception of the "interpretive translation" is a crucial one for any modern consideration of the subject. It is certainly a notion that any modern rendering of a work considered a "classic" is sure to confront.

In one form or another, the notion has had currency for some time. I believe that it is almost a truism among philosophers that a translation of a text that one knows very well in the original may nevertheless provide extremely useful insights into the philosophic problems treated there. Particular mention is often made of the translation

by Norman Kemp Smith of Kant's *Critique of Pure Reason*, and of
its use by German students who, although in full command of the
original, nevertheless wish to neutralize certain stylistic elements of
the original that they deem insignificant with respect to their philosophic concerns. Any translation might thus, for a student of philosophy, do the work of an "interpretive" one by showing him something in an argument that he had not previously seen, as looking
through a mirror at an unfinished painting lets one perceive relationships that habitual observation had tended to obscure. But the
literary sort of "interpretive translation" differs from this in being
more like a peculiarly constructed sort of distorting mirror, or a
carefully chosen ratio of enlargement or reduction, aimed always at
selecting particular features of the original for emphasis, or even for
being rendered visible at all. It is certainly possible to judge the effectiveness of any individual "interpretive" version, to assess the degree to which it succeeds in bringing the selected features into focus.
The difficulty comes about in assessing the desirability of the particular elements that are chosen for didactic prominence. "To show
where the treasure lies" is surely to point out the hiding place of
something. But there can just as surely always be debate as to the
value of the quarry. This is especially true in a free, and even chao-
tic, aesthetic economy like our own, and even more so in the case of
those treasures that seem to pale and cheapen upon being rooted out
and exposed to the light, or, like some super-mimosa, wither at the
ethereal touch of mere ostension.

It would thus seem that one's arguments for or against a particular
translation of this sort might be very much like one's arguments for
or against a particular critical treatment, or way of "teaching a book"
(in the sense that most American teachers of literature would understand it), or even an edition. Such arguments, of course, can lead
back into endless analytic corridors in chase of ultimate desiderata.
However, this is not the sort of quest to be embarked on here. It
should only be remarked that any particular interpretation of a literary work that might lie at the bottom of such a translation is very
like any particular literary object in general, in that the kind of arguments marshaled in support or in dispraise of it will ultimately have to
come down to discussions of what should be, or else to peculiar kinds
of definitions of what is. That is, to point to part of a text and say,
"This is where the treasure lies," is a statement of fact. Once one
knows what the treasure is, and has one's eye guided properly by the

intellectual finger of the translator, one may affirm or deny the factual basis of such a statement. But to declare that, in a particular poem, "The treasure is thus and so and I am going to show you how to find it" is not to assert a statement of fact so much as to set up a kind of condition, a *donnée*, almost a postulate which can be assented to or not without risking the compromising rearrangements of one's view of the world entailed by denying a fact. One alternative treatment of this difficult situation involves the assertion only that the treasure *ought* to be thus and so, that thus and so *ought* to be treasured. But the language and climate of criticism have seldom tolerated such skeptical guardedness, and the more usual escape, once the difficulty is (if ever) acknowledged, is a withdrawal to a persuasive definition.[3] In such a case, the "treasure" would be held to *mean* thus and so; it would be maintained that they were equivalent by definition, and that the interpretation which brought thus and so to light was in some way uniquely proper. Now it is just such persuasive definitions that form the basis of so much ethical and aesthetic judgment and that proliferate so rapidly during the formulation of critical principles. It is only with a certain audacity that one can frame a literary work itself even, insisting on calling it a proper example of a genre, and defending its peculiarities by invoking persuasive definitions of the genre, or even of the word "proper" itself. This same audacity extends to the framing of interpretive translations, where a persuasive assertion of the rightness of the interpretation corresponds to proscribing the boundaries of the genre, while at the same time purporting to be describing something very like natural barriers.

The idea of an "interpretive translation," then, would seem to lead us directly back into problems of literary theory generally, wherein knowledge and belief, description and judgment run through and amongst each other and seldom seem usefully or practicably separable. It seems almost impossible to escape this predicament in the case of any theory of literary translation, or of any prescription or method purporting to find the proper equivalent in one language of a literary entity in another one. It has been previously shown that this results from the peculiar nature of the original literary entity itself. It would probably be generally agreed that two poems (sonnets by Shakespeare and Ella Wheeler Wilcox, for example) should not be so translated into French that the new versions would sound too much alike. But short of this no general formula for preserving the essence of any poem, or *sort* of poem, seems remotely possible.

It might also be shown that, difficulties of locating the "essence" of the original literary work aside, grave problems are engendered by the very notion of "into French" or "in English." The first of these is a spectacular, if somewhat infrequent, kind of crux. As a limiting case for any conventional set of rules for determining the proper equivalents in another language for words, phrases, images, formal conventions even, we might remark on the occurrence of an enclave of quotation of the target language itself in the passage to be translated. A famous example of this is in Mallarmé's *Brise Marine*:

> Je partirai! Steamer balançant ta mâture,
> Lève l'ancre pour une exotique nature!

These lines create a problem because of "Steamer." To translate them, leaving the word unchanged, perhaps adding only a footnote to the effect that the word is in English in the original is to admit a kind of defeat. One might instead want to use a French word with about the same frequency and area of occurrence in English as "steamer" has in French: *"paquebot"* would do better than *"vapeur"* on these grounds perhaps. Other examples of this may be found among the poems of Verlaine; in the group *Aquarelles* from *Romances sans Paroles*, the significance of the English titles cannot be disregarded. Of course, when the target language enclave is merely a proper name, or a designation or allusion as conventional as a proper name, no such problem occurs. (*"Londres"* or "London," in a French poem, could most usually both be rendered as "London" without too much objection from any quarter.)

Direct quotation, however, presents other difficulties. We might object to the way they were confronted by the late Ernst Robert Curtius in his translation of *The Waste Land*.[4] He seems to have evolved no over-all plan for dealing with specific quotations in many languages, resonating with varying degrees of familiarity. Often, quotations from English authors are left untranslated; for example:

> („Those are pearls that were his eyes" Sehen Sie!)

or the lines from Webster at the end of Part I, or, with brilliant success in a passage hard to resist quoting entire:

> Sie weilt beim Spiegel einen Augenblick,
> Bemerkt kaum, dass ihr Freund nicht gegenwärtig,
> Und denkt nur halbbewusst nochmals zurück:
> „Das wär' erledigt; gut, dass es nun fertig."
> When lovely woman stoops to folly — schon

> Geht sie in ihrem Zimmer hin und her,
> Legt eine Platte auf das Grammophon,
> Und fühlt, ob die Frisur in Ordnung wär'.

This is, on the whole, what might be expected. On the other hand, the opening line of Part II, the quotation from *Antony and Cleopatra*, is given in translation: „*Der Sessel drin sie sass, ein Strahlenthron.*" And elsewhere, Shakespeare (*Ich dachte an den Schiffbruch meines königlichen Bruders*), and troped Marvell (*Aber hinter mir hör ich von Zeit zu Zeit*), are treated as if they were simply Eliot's own lines. The fortunate existence of a kind of international jazz style in the twenties allowed for the tone of "*Doch/O o o o dieser Fetzen Shakespeare — /Ist so elegant,/So intelligent.*" In general, it would seem that this entirely *ad hoc* method based each decision on an assessment of the relative familiarity (if any) of the allusions to Curtius' German-speaking audience.[5] His choices to translate or to leave in the original any English quotation were probably something like Eliot's, in deciding where, and how much, to annotate the poem itself.

Aside from the problem of enclaves of quotation, however, there are other, less trivial problems engendered by our use of the phrase "in English." The name and boundaries of any one language designate a whole class of linguistic systems; dialects, usage levels, technical vocabularies, all compete for the same stock of words, and this competition tends to result in considerable semantic confusion. It is very often true, for example, that a description of some bit of speech or writing as being "in English" is as unsatisfactory as "in America" might be in answer to a census-taker's request for one's previous address. As far as literary texts are concerned, extremely delicate distinctions are continually drawn by critics with the same unquestioned right as the census-taker would claim to his insistence on specific demographic details. Now to treat any particular text as a literary one is already to say that it is "in a certain kind of English." The particular "kind" would in this case usually be called a style or rhetorical type, and would perhaps be distinguished from different senses of "kind of English," such as a regional dialect or even a technical vocabulary. The point here, however, is that such apparently "metalinguistic" considerations as *style* nevertheless involve the drawing of linguistic boundaries just as apparently more fundamental ones do, such as *dialect* and *language*. The boundaries themselves, of course, are more like those drawn for a croquet court on a lawn than like those of the lawn itself. But they have the same relation to how people speak and write as the court-markers to the terrain, as well as having the same relations to the purposes of one's linguistic or literary or social inquiry as these same court boundaries have to the game of croquet itself. When one is far enough away from the lawn (inside the house, say), the distinction between "on the back lawn" and "on the croquet court" may become so trivial as to be annoying. But the boundaries of the court retain their importance for those interested in the course of the game.

I think that in some ways linguistic boundaries are like those of a playing field of some kind which, in the heat of the game, tend to affect the players as if they were natural barriers like ravines and lakes and thickets. But to look at the game from outside it is to see all the more clearly the shining white of the painted lines. Thus, the net between English and French is high and tight enough to permit us to refer to "the other side" without being more specific, and "translating" seems only as hard as throwing a ball over it into the other court (provided that one "knows French," i.e., in this case can use and co-ordinate his eye and arm). This even seems to be the sort of attitude one takes towards simultaneous interpreting. But translating a poem seems to be a different sort of game entirely, in which one is required to get the ball into the right box on the other side of the court, even though the area across the net may be laid out differently, cross-hatched with different combinations of white lines, from our own.

Saying that a poem or play or novel is "in English," then, is seldom saying the same thing (though we are often tempted to think it is) as that a sentence is "in English." To test the latter assertion, we have the relative certainty of grammatical rules which define an English *sentence* as opposed to a French one. But we have no such quasi-mechanical process for defining an English *poem*, other than that its structure might be like those of English sentences. We should probably not wish, on the other hand, to commit ourselves to the view that we call a poem "English" or "in English" in the same half-humorous sense that we might say "Now *that's* a French notion" or "What an English thought!" (where we would be almost punning on "That thought would surely only occur to a Frenchman" and "That seems somehow most right when put in French"). A poem is much more like a sentence than it is like a thought anyway; so that the real difficulty seems to lie in the fact that sometimes we think of "putting a poem into English" as meaning merely turning its French sentences into English sentences, while at other times we demand that it mean making something that is "in English" in the same sense that the original is "in French," in the same *kind* of English, in the same *sort* of kind of English.

The first of these alternatives sounds attractive in that it admits of mechanical operation. It corresponds to the alternative of fidelity in the old saws. The second one is unusually deceptive. It was often felt before the last forty years or so, for example, that "poetic English" was a proper sort of kind of language, and that "poetic French" ought to be translated into it. Although framed in far less crude a form, such is the conceptual basis of Matthew Arnold's prescriptions about style in *On Translating Homer*. The rapidity of "movement," simplicity of "ideas," plainness of "words and style," and nobility of "manner" which Arnold insists are the significant attributes of Homer's language are not presented as being linguistically analyzable. They are only defined ostensively in passages by writers already presumed to exhibit them; we might say that they were formulated as natural predicates (whether actually aesthetic or more properly ethical might perhaps be debated), as descriptive notions which were justifiably clear and clearly justifiable in their status as qualities of language, although never once admitting of the sort of analysis that natural predicates do.

As I have indicated before, this discussion is not the place for an analysis of the justifiability of value terms used descriptively, of nonnatural predicates masking as natural ones, in aesthetic discourse. My only point is that this sort of thing invariably occurs; as far as translations are concerned, it leads to confusion as to what is to be expected of them, as to the sort of work they can actually do. We have seen, I think, how several different approaches to the problem of what literary translation "really is" seem to result from the various conventional ways that have been developed to talk about it; and further, how these approaches tend variously to lead back, in one way or another, to the problem of what a poem or a play or a novel "really is." Now the pulse of this problem is always throbbing along beneath the surface of all literary activity, creative, analytic, or prescriptive. It is only of undue concern for the translation question because of the kind of answer that the question is commonly supposed to receive. Whereas the ultimate questions about literary objects and their relationship to linguistic objects are almost always suspended or begged, matters of translation seem to force them onto the surface of concern.

I should like, therefore, to suggest one other way of talking about the process of translation, in order to try to escape some of the difficulties heretofore encountered, while at the same time avoiding the unwelcome questions about literary and linguistic ontology. Perhaps, by the use of such an interpretation, some light might be shed on the way in which translations are received and assessed, without trying to determine what it is proper, or even possible, to expect of them.

II

When we speak of a translation as a *version*, we tend to emphasize the unique properties of the particular rendering in question. The word "translation" designates the process as well as the result, while "version" is applied to processes only in its senses of "rotating," "turning," or "transforming." Our frequent use of "version" to mean "a special form or variant of something" (O.E.D. sense 2b), or more particularly "an account resting upon limited authority or embodying a particular point of view" (O.E.D. sense 2), actually represents a historically later meaning, derived from "translated rendering" (O.E. D. sense 1). But I think that the later usage keeps a firm grasp on the earlier one, and that we may tend to ask different things of a text when we think of it as a "version" than when we think of it as a "translation."

I should like to contrast this common usage with a specific distinction, almost obsolete in English but still maintained in French, between *version* and *thème*. It differentiates rather nicely between putting something foreign into the mother tongue (*version*), and doing composition in a language foreign to one (*thème*), usually Latin or Greek. For the schoolboy who might have most cause to invoke the distinction, the processes are very different ones, the first seeming to lead from something narrow and limited into something broad and full of possibility, the second apparently moving from the open to the closed. The *thème*, because it usually involves a dead language and rigid linguistic and stylistic models for saying almost anything, seems more like a game with fixed counters. The *version*, however, allows of a greater range of "right" or "correct" solutions: it is here, perhaps, that "feelings" might possibly enter into decisions as to how to "get it right," or as to which alternative rendering finally to select. There is also the implication, however faint, that the *version* is one's own, while the *thème* must be made to approximate a set or ideal passage.

But this distinction has interesting resemblances to a distinction we have been trying to confront all along, and *thème* and *version* seem to be distinguished in many of the same ways that we would distinguish translating ordinary speech and a literary text, respectively. It is also possible to liken the *thème* to "translation" and to its English cognate. In "version" the sense of the "limited authority" or "particular point of view" always manages to make itself felt in one way or another, and to qualify the nature of the relationship of the rendering to the original. We do indeed speak of a poor, bad, or inadequate translation; far less often do we speak of a bad or inadequate *version* without being more specific (we might, that is, mention "the bad Smith version of *Tartuffe*" as opposed to "the delightful Jones one" in a kind of putative way, but here, I think, "version" would have been used in a way absolutely synonymous with "translation"). It is usually assumed from the start that, keeping an original text in mind, there is going to be *something* queer about a version of it, whether a French version, or a shortened one, or a version leaning strongly toward the views of Professor von Braun, or even a garbled version. But we assume that a translation of, say, *Hamlet* into French is somehow going to try to be *Hamlet* as well as it can, that the fact that it is in French is not going to be something queer about it. Or, at any rate, this is what we hope, or even expect; and when we find out that it is indeed extremely queer to find *Hamlet* in French, we can never quite decide which combination of attributes of French, the translator, and the very idea of translating *Hamlet* at all it is that we wish to blame.

Consequently, lurking behind the notion of "a French version of *Hamlet*" (what was announced, perhaps, in the advertisement [6] quoted in the Library Scene in *Ulysses*: "HAMLET/ ou/ LE DISTRAIT/ Pièce de Shakespeare") is something very like our use of the word in such sentences as "Well, that's *your* version of it," or "We'll have to wait for Charles' version before we can decide," where "version" is often colloquially replaced by "story." We think of an "official version" as perhaps being not quite trustworthy, but as being so in a kind of dependable or predictable fashion. However, we never seem to speak of the "*right* version," the "*correct* version" any more than we could think of the "*only* version." There is thus an overtone of "narration" or "description" even that accompanies this "soft" usage of "version." And although it is somewhat odd to think of a translation as a description or narration, there are circumstances under which this seems more proper. Consider, for example, the relationship between translation and paraphrase. "Organic" views of the integrity of the literary object tend to anathematize both of them for similar reasons. Scholars and critics in general tend to speak in a half-mocking way of "the heresy of paraphrase," partially because they know that there is something wrong with it, and partially because they know that they must employ paraphrase fairly regularly throughout the course of their work. On the other hand, translation and paraphrase are at once curiously alike and dissimilar with respect to their ease of execution. For it often seems as if translation in some absolute sense were as theoretically impossible as some kind of uniquely proper, "total" paraphrase. We sometimes feel, conversely, as if translation might be easier to achieve; as if the poem we are working with has not eaten a hole into the target language in a way that it has into its own; as if there were more room, in a new language, to cast about for words out of which to make the poem, while, as far as the original language is concerned, that poem has already used what it needs, and the paraphrase may be just out of luck.

Both translation and paraphrase, however, are regularly employed in answer to requests for descriptions of literary works. And, as descriptions, both of them function rather well, serving acceptably on the occasions at which they are asked to perform. In answer to the question "What was it like?" asked of a play he had seen, one's informant might give a narrative account of what was going on on the stage (a paraphrase from one genre to another), or of what was happening in the theatre as a whole (to the audience as well), or of what was happening in the theatrical-literary world generally (what sort of literary *event* had taken place). He might have to translate actual parts of the play (if it happened to have been in French), or he might give an English account of it (in no sense would anyone object to his not *describing* it in French). But in general, an informant's account of what a play or poem or novel was like would remain quite pliable and subject to *ad hoc* revision.

Now whenever we accept or reject a version of a statement or text, we do so in full recognition of its particular bias or "limited authority," and never make the fact of the existence of such a bias a point of attack against it. One might, of course, ask why such a particular version was needed or desirable in the first place, whether, even though well done, it was worth the effort involved, and so on. The grounds on which we would want to base our praise or blame of a version would involve the success with which a particular version first specified its bias and then proceeded to represent that bias in its rendering. These criteria persist, I think, through other situations in which we use the word: what we would ask of three different "versions" of what had happened in an automobile accident, for example, would be that each one, each witness' recital of "what happened" should adequately represent his particular viewpoint. When, after hearing all of the accounts, we might choose to say that some were closer to what actually happened than others were, we are, after all, choosing among the viewpoints themselves. But this would be a far different matter from rejecting, on the spot, a garbled, or inconsistent, or endless, or hysterical, or insufficient, or stammered account (an implausible one would have to be rejected later, for its viewpoint). In all these cases, the success of the *representation* of the viewpoint would be under the initial scrutiny, and the accounts would be judged as x-biased or y-biased or z-biased versions. Only later would x, y, and z themselves come up for discussion. There is also the sense in which we speak of a version of a joke, or of a folk-song, or of a performance of a musical work (where, in all of these cases, we expect each recital to vary, to be a *version*). Here, too, the success of the recital must be distinguished from the desirability of the bias, even though the latter may operate much more strongly on our feelings than will the former. The version of a folk-song or myth one has learned in childhood, "the way we played it at home" (where some peripheral rule of a game has been varied), like one's own preferred variant of a name ("ketchup," "catsup," "catchup") is always somehow as much fonder as it is more familiar.

But a poem is a kind of Phoenix. Literary works are always unique, canonical, sole, and they seem to guard their official status jealously. To talk of a translation or a paraphrase as a version in the sense we have been outlining seems somehow wrong, somehow as if one were betraying the privileged status of the real, right translation, or the proper, unbiased paraphrase which muddling about with words would lead one to find, rather than cause one to make. Indeed, it may be a necessary condition of what we call literature itself that any work have this property of self-contained uniqueness; perhaps it is just this quality whose gradual appearance we await in tracing the growth of a "literary" from a "pre-literary" period in the history of any language. When songs and stories and dances come to be written down, and when the ways in which other such things have been written down and preserved are known and, in one way or another, acknowledged, this quality of authority for the text begins to emerge. When a literary object becomes less and less a *performance*, or the record of a performance, and acquires more and more of the value and status of *knowledge*, its tolerance for versions of itself grows smaller and smaller.

There nevertheless remains one case in which the proliferation of versions is an accepted business, and in which the sovereign unique- ness of "originals" is more open to transformation than in most others. The relationship of the text of a play to any particular performance of it is much more that of a version to an original than is any particular instance (say, any inscription, or a private or public reading) of a poem. It might be argued that it matters very much, with respect to particular poems or novels, in what sort of inscription one first makes their acquaintance; that there is an iconology of publication involving typography and conventions of all aspects of format, affecting the attitudes of readers in ways unknown to them, even in apparently straightforward, unspectacular cases. But even so we would resist the notion that this sort of thing could make any particular inscription of a poem or novel constitute a new version of it. But in the case of a play, we have something much closer to a folk-song, or a myth, or a musical score, in that any particular instance of it will constitute a version. For an instance of a play is a production of it, in the same way that an instance of a poem during an "oral, pre-literary" period in the history of a culture is a particular recital or performance of it. And even though we might want to speak of the canonical production of any play, of the one best suited to realizing the text, and so forth, there always seems to be room for the same sort of debate as to which one this might be, or as to how to find it, that there might be about the "interpretation" of a poem as it was discussed previously. Perhaps we might flatly decide, for example, that the "original" production, supervised, if possible, by the author to some degree, or at least framed in the theatrical milieu "for which," we usually say, "he was writing," is to be the canonical one; but we would find all too often in the his- tory of Western drama that the plays in which we might take the greatest literary interest could not be automatically assigned canonical performances on the basis of their original productions alone. Consider for a moment the "theater" in which a play is produced — I now use the term, somewhat as Francis Fergusson employs it in *The Idea of a Theater*, to refer to a social institution, a whole set of conditions, habits, attitudes, feelings, expectations, and acquaintances, with modes of conventional speech and gesture on the part of an audience, as well as to the set of dramaturgical practices operating against them. Such a "theater" stands to any play written for it and produced within it very much as a musical score stands to its own musical culture. In this latter case, as the history of musical notation so clearly shows, any musical composition is framed in a "language" that already exists; is made up of fragments of general practice; for, as we see in older and foreign notation systems, much is "left out" of the inscription, there are many musical *données* of all kinds to which no reference is made, but whose existence and familiarity to the musician are taken for granted, and whose "absence" from the score plagues only the musicologists of later generations. Any interpretations of the notation which are made within a different musical milieu, like productions of plays that are framed in later, different "theaters," will tend to vary radically from the original one, the "intended" one. But all too often we know that the author's (or composer's) "ideal" or "intended" production (or performance) was not, in fact, the original one to which he was treated. And all too often we want to say in memorable cases that the author's "conception of the work pushed back the boundaries of his milieu," or that "the work itself indicated its creator's dissatisfaction with the existing conventions," and so forth. But then for us to try to force the canonical interpretation back into the work itself (where, we might say, it "lies implicit"), or back into the author's or composer's intentions, involves us in tendentious discussions of interpretation. And musical "interpretations" tend always to make bids for a generality and timelessness in their authority which "productions" or "performances" seldom do.

In the actual case of virtuoso recitals of solo musical compositions, or of orchestral conducting, of course, it is common to speak of an "authoritative" performance, but it is probably much more a question of a canonical "interpretation," both in the way we have been using it and in the sense in which it is commonly applied to a musical performance. An "authoritative" musical interpretation is seldom one which attempts to reconstruct (save in the case of a contemporary work) the precise musical milieu of the work's original creation. Perhaps we feel that the performer is in some way specially equipped, through long acquaintance with the work in question, with the composer, with the history of interpretive styles, to carry an authority as an interpreter which would extend, without question, to any particular recital he might give. There are also the extreme cases in which the particular point of departure is an archaeological one, like the recent tradition of performances of pre-classic music on the proper instruments, or attempts to reconstruct an Elizabethan stage performance, but here we are dealing with something more like a museum exhibit, or a historian's reconstruction of "what actually happened." This will be especially true in those cases where the archaeological diggings have been most successful, and where the demonstration has been most faithful to the historical facts thereby uncovered, never compromising for a moment with contemporary standards and never once acknowledging the theater or musical milieu of its own day, even to the extent of trying to avoid boredom, uncomprehension or outrage on the part of its modern audience.

Productions, then, like performances, usually aspire to the status of versions rather than to that of final interpretations. And even though a particular production may be defended as if it were a canonical version (like the case of the "authoritative performance"), the defender can usually be made to retract his statement to some degree simply by being shown the proper array of other instances. He may then only claim that his preferred version realizes what "he can see in the text," or, better, what we today would "want to make of the text." What often happens, of course, is that there occurs a cross-fertilization of any particular theater by the literary world contemporary with it, and claims of generality and universality find their way into the rhetoric of the theater's justification of its nature, a justification which only the literary world would demand in the first place. In England, the Restoration Stage evolved a literary aesthetic strong enough to allow it to tamper seriously with the texts themselves of the plays of past theaters which it wished to produce. Only part of this sort of re-writing seems to have been justifiable as a result of the demands of the stage conventions themselves.

A "production," of course, I have understood all along as the total constellation of visual and aural elements from out of which the words of the text will emerge before an audience. The *mise en scène* and all of its various parts, the costumes, the gestures, movements, postures and danced arrangements of the actors' physiques, the sounds of their speech rhythms and intonations, the music if any — in short, every sensible aspect of the event of the production which the particular theater might in any way prescribe as having to be different from the everyday styles of the culture about it. The various elements of a particular production may or may not be co-ordinated in various ways; indeed, it might be shown that the styles of different theaters are distinguished not only by their differing production conventions, but also by the relative degree of co-ordination of the various elements. Some theaters provide for more flexibility of *mise en scène* than do others; some demand a novel spectacle for each play, others, that the standard scene be utilized continually. Different theaters, to continue the personification, have different sensibilities, and tend to admit varying numbers of different elements into the realm of the production to be placed under the control of the writer, director, or producer.

It is in the general case of a play conceived in one theater being produced within the practices of another that the relevance of theatrical productions to literary versions, translations, and interpretations begins to emerge. To recast a play in the ways of a theatrical world for which it was never made may, of course, involve translation of the actual text from one language to another, or from the language of one theater to that of another. It may entail, that is, some sort of linguistic transformation within any one of the hierarchy of senses of "a language" discussed before, from virtual rewriting (as the Restoration remade Shakespeare and Jonson and Beaumont and Fletcher) through editing, cutting, and the like, to dialectal substitutions and matters of handling allusions and references unfamiliar to the audience. All of these are matters of translation in the most usual sense, but their treatment enters into the formation of the bias of the version as a whole at the same level as that of many other elements. So that while we may liken a production of this kind, taken as a whole, to a translation-version, we might want to point out that any actual translation involved would be only one of a number of transformations that would be occurring in the process of taking the play out of one theater and putting it into another.

In this sort of situation, it will also be noticed, to frame the bias of the version, to outline at the very beginning the attitude that the current theater is going to take toward the original one, is often to solve the problem of many individual decisions about particular elements. Matters of actual translation may, of course, be included within these, and even the paradox-generating occurrences of quotation of the target language seem to find solutions within the setting of the over-all production. Such a case as the "Alabama" song in the Bert Brecht-Kurt Weill *Aufstieg und Fall der Stadt Mahagonny*, composed entirely in an implausible, Berlin-accented English, would seem to pose an insoluble difficulty. How, when preparing a version for a New York theater in 1957, for example, would one render —

> O Moon of Alabama
> We now must say good-bye
> We've lost our good old mama
> And must have whisky
> O, you know why!

all those inane non-sequiturs, the first and third lines of the chorus quoted rhyming only in German, the whole half-doting, half-mocking attitude toward the American English of Tin Pan Alley? Only in some consistent viewpoint in which to see the whole original text, some particular plane of polarization through which the English production would turn the original, could the decision be made to leave this alone, or mock some other popular musical style in some other language, or turn the tables and evoke the "nostalgia" of sophisticated New York audiences in the 1950's for a German interpretation of the 1920's they never knew by putting the "Alabama" song back into a parody Berlin jazz, or whatever. Often, in cases like this, a particular decision about one small element of the production will seem to crystallize the bias or viewpoint around it; sometimes, on the other hand, it will take a comparatively major decision to fix the other ones. It is becoming an accepted "experiment," for example, to do Chekhov plays in a Southern American setting, on the grounds that the American language has more room for a rhetoric of self-dramatization in its warmer regions than anywhere else; once the decision about dialect is made, however, the setting, the translation of all the cultural facts and references, even the substitution of emancipated slave for emancipated serf becomes almost mechanical.

Some original productions, such as those of the Baroque theater, tend by and large to be treated today with a quasi-archaeological respect, perhaps because of the model of style-preservation set by the *Comédie Française*. But productions of Shakespeare are continually confronted with the problem of what bias to assume, what sort of version to be. Sometimes, in the case of the Greek and Roman plays, the apparently simple matter of costuming can serve as the pivotal question more readily than it usually does. In the case of Shakespeare, of course, the very notions of some of the plays themselves have almost attained the status of disembodied myths, and any particular production of them may be tangling with these myths, as well as with the texts. It was thus possible some eight years ago for two famous modern dancers to choose to represent two Shakespeare plays behind the proscenia of their peculiarly wordless theaters. The difference between their approaches, however, bore considerable resemblance to a distinction I have been trying to refine throughout this discussion.

Martha Graham in 1950 presented for the first time in New York a dance called *The Eye of Anguish*, purporting to represent *King Lear*. It employed a rather characterless modern score, a *mise en scène*, and a repertory of dance movement (Miss Graham's characteristic one) which in no way seemed integral, united, or co-ordinated; and it seemed obvious that Miss Graham in no sense intended to take any other view toward the text of *Lear* than an interpretive one of a rather shadowy kind. To quote from her program note: "The dance follows both the outward sequence of the story and the inner sequence of the phantasma of Lear's mind"; her theater was essentially an expressionistic one, and her intentions with respect to representing the contents of Lear's mind aimed at those of the "authoritative dance" of *Lear*. What she chose to base her choreography upon, at any rate, was some apparently privileged view of the text which enabled her to visualize, and then render kinetic what she called in her subtitle "*The Purgatorial History of King Lear.*"

For many reasons, Miss Graham's dance invited comparison with a dance called *The Moor's Pavane*, choreographed by José Limón during the previous year. To say that Mr. Limón's dance was even based on *Othello* in the same sense in which *Eye of Anguish* might be said to have been based on *King Lear* would be misleading. In the first place, Mr. Limón's dance never tried to achieve quite the status of a *poem* in a weird sort of *symboliste* sense as does almost every one of Miss Graham's dances. In the second place, *The Moor's Pavane* attempted to represent not *the Othello*, not an account of the play's or the character's inner workings, but instead a particular version of *Othello*, a particular theater's production, in fact. Toward this end the whole dance was directed: a Baroque *Othello*, almost as it might have been rewritten by Dryden and perhaps not quite so distasteful to Rymer. Unlike Miss Graham's production, all the elements of *The Moor's Pavane* were more or less unified. The score was taken from Purcell's music for Mrs. Aphra Behn's *Abdelazar, or The Moor's Revenge*, the costumes were seventeenth century, the choreography, for four dancers (presumably Othello, Desdemona, Iago, and Emilia), was evolved from formal court-dance patterns to which it kept returning, the dancers grouping and regrouping to punctuate the more mimetic sections. The "action" of the dance, too, kept always to the formal, stylized elements — the handkerchief, for example, and the carefully limited "expressive" role of the movement.

Now while Mr. Limón could not be said to have aimed for any essential quality of *Othello*, it was something much like an essence of *King Lear* that Miss Graham would probably admit to trying to grasp. Her dance was in many ways much more "literary" than *The Moor's Pavane* perhaps just because of its interpretive purpose, its unwillingness to seize upon some formulation of a bias that might be adequately represented choreographically. Both of these danced productions were dreadfully crippled, in one sense, as a mere result of their being kinetic and non-linguistic. But it is a crippling very much like this that might be observed in the case of modern representations of Greek plays, for example, where a spoken text is all that we have to make do with. In adapting Greek plays to our theater, it is a literary sort of view which predominates, and the "play" (in our sense of the word) is carved out of the text (itself a relic of a whole theater) in the same way in which a "poem" (in a post-symbolistic sense) is carved out of the text of a Shakespeare play by recent critics in the tradition of G. Wilson Knight. To "translate" the Greek play without one hand tied behind our back we should perhaps have to involve more of the resources of our various theaters than we normally do, perhaps to engage somehow some of the musical and ritual elements of our life that only seep into the peripheries of our theaters, such as bull and prize rings. It is the modern French theater which most successfully handles the problem of "translating" Greek plays, perhaps, by continually rewriting them, by managing to reinterpret neo-classicism for itself in every new generation.

But in general, the question of translation for a theater is always part and parcel of the general problem of production version. And perhaps the distinction between a literary and a more properly performatory approach to a dramatic text operates in the same way as the contrast between version and interpretation, between the avowed bias of the version as against the claim of the interpretation correctly, rightly, truthfully to "understand" the text. Throughout the latter half of this discussion, we have seen how this distinction shows up in several forms; throughout, also, we have seen how the notion of "limited authority" colors the sense of "version" as opposed to the more usual literary sense of "translation." For the over-all problems of literary translation as they are usually put, the implications of this distinction are, I think, quite clear. For what is usually wanted of a translation of a literary work is the same kind of total authority that our age feels is characteristic of literary works themselves. And yet such total authority, uniqueness, and integrity as we are wont to claim for literature is achieved through the intense and unquestioned commitment to some sort of bias that only the information and judgment of history can illuminate.

Perhaps, then, this consideration of versions, interpretations, and performances has shed some light on the kinds of relationships between translations and literary originals that are traditionally obscured. Perhaps we have seen how all of the claims of these originals to a privileged inviolability are not equally well founded. And finally, I hope that such traditional demands of translations as that they "get the feel of the original" can now be understood, after all, as meaning one of two things only: a request for some as yet unspecified version, or a demand for the impossible.

NOTES

1. Letter to Mme. du Deffand, May 19, 1754.

2. Reprinted in *Literary Essays of Ezra Pound* (New York, 1954), p. 200.

3. See Charles L. Stevenson, *Ethics and Language* (New Haven, 1944), pp. 210–217. I am perhaps using the notion of persuasive definition in a loose sense by extending its application to what are more strictly stipulative definitions that do not admit to their stipulative role.

4. *Das wüste Land*, first done in 1927, is reprinted in *Die Neue Rundschau*, LXI (1950), 327–345.

5. It is perhaps interesting that the line from *Antony* is given not in the familiar Schlegel-Tieck translation, but in the modern one of Friedrich Gundolf, which might then have had, at the widest, a coterie appeal. In the jazzy lines, incidentally, "*Fetzen*" for "rag" appears like a dreadful howler, except for the fact that Curtius appears to have understood the general tenor of the lines; he may have used "Fetzen" in the sense of "scrap of music" or "strain," without knowing the musical usage of "rag" in English.

6. Joyce derives the title from Stéphane Mallarmé, *Divagations*, note to *Crayonné au Théâtre* (Paris, 1917), p. 371.

ON LINGUISTIC ASPECTS OF TRANSLATION

ROMAN JAKOBSON

ACCORDING TO Bertrand Russell, "no one can understand the word 'cheese' unless he has a nonlinguistic acquaintance with cheese."[1] If, however, we follow Russell's fundamental precept and place our "emphasis upon the linguistic aspects of traditional philosophical problems," then we are obliged to state that no one can understand the word "cheese" unless he has an acquaintance with the meaning assigned to this word in the lexical code of English. Any representative of a cheese-less culinary culture will understand the English word "cheese" if he is aware that in this language it means "food made of pressed curds" and if he has at least a linguistic acquaintance with "curds." We never consumed ambrosia or nectar and have only a linguistic acquaintance with the words "ambrosia," "nectar," and "gods" — the name of their mythical users; nonetheless, we understand these words and know in what contexts each of them may be used.

The meaning of the words "cheese," "apple," "nectar," "acquaintance," "but," "mere," and of any word or phrase whatsoever is definitely a linguistic — or to be more precise and less narrow — a semiotic fact. Against those who assign meaning (*signatum*) not to the sign, but to the thing itself, the simplest and truest argument would be that nobody has ever smelled or tasted the meaning of "cheese" or of "apple." There is no *signatum* without *signum*. The meaning of the word "cheese" cannot be inferred from a nonlinguistic acquaintance with cheddar or with camembert without the assistance of the verbal code. An array of linguistic signs is needed to introduce an unfamiliar word. Mere pointing will not teach us whether "cheese" is the name of the given specimen, or of any box of camembert, or of camembert in general or of any cheese, any milk product, any food, any refreshment, or perhaps any box irrespective of contents. Finally, does a word simply name the thing in question, or does it imply a meaning such as offering, sale, prohibition, or malediction? (Pointing actually may mean malediction; in some cultures, particularly in Africa, it is an ominous gesture.)

For us, both as linguists and as ordinary word-users, the meaning of any linguistic sign is its translation into some further, alternative sign, especially a sign "in which it is more fully developed," as Peirce, the deepest inquirer into the essence of signs, insistently stated. [2] The term "bachelor" may be converted into a more explicit designation, "unmarried man," whenever higher explicitness is required. We distinguish three ways of interpreting a verbal sign: it may be translated into other signs of the same language, into another language, or into another, nonverbal system of symbols. These three kinds of translation are to be differently labeled:

1) Intralingual translation or *rewording* is an interpretation of verbal signs by means of other signs of the same language.

2) Interlingual translation or *translation proper* is an interpretation of verbal signs by means of some other language.

3) Intersemiotic translation or *transmutation* is an interpretation of verbal signs by means of signs of nonverbal sign systems.

The intralingual translation of a word uses either another, more or less synonymous, word or resorts to a circumlocution. Yet synonymy, as a rule, is not complete equivalence: for example, "every celibate is a bachelor, but not every bachelor is a celibate." A word or an idiomatic phrase-word, briefly a code-unit of the highest level, may be fully interpreted only by means of an equivalent combination of code-units, i.e., a message referring to this code-unit: "every bachelor is an unmarried man, and every unmarried man is a bachelor," or "every celibate is bound not to marry, and everyone who is bound not to marry is a celibate."

Likewise, on the level of interlingual translation, there is ordinarily no full equivalence between code-units, while messages may serve as adequate interpretations of alien code-units or messages. The English word "cheese" cannot be completely identified with its standard Russian heteronym "сыр," because cottage cheese is a cheese but not a сыр. Russians say: принеси сыру и творогу, "bring cheese and [sic] cottage cheese." In standard Russian, the food made of pressed curds is called сыр only if ferment is used.

Most frequently, however, translation from one language into another substitutes messages in one language not for separate code-units but for entire messages in some other language. Such a translation is a reported speech; the translator recodes and transmits a message received from another source. Thus translation involves two equivalent messages in two different codes.

Equivalence in difference is the cardinal problem of language and the pivotal concern of linguistics. Like any receiver of verbal messages, the linguist acts as their interpreter. No linguistic specimen may be interpreted by the science of language without a translation of its signs into other signs of the same system or into signs of another system. Any comparison of two languages implies an examination of their mutual translatability; widespread practice of interlingual communication, particularly translating activities, must be kept under constant scrutiny by linguistic science. It is difficult to overestimate the urgent need for and the theoretical and practical significance of differential bilingual dictionaries with careful comparative definition of all the corresponding units in their intension and extension. Likewise differential bilingual grammars should define what unifies and what differentiates the two languages in their selection and delimitation of grammatical concepts.

Both the practice and the theory of translation abound with intricacies, and from time to time attempts are made to sever the Gordian knot by proclaiming the dogma of untranslatability. "Mr. Everyman, the natural logician," vividly imagined by B. L. Whorf, is supposed to have arrived at the following bit of reasoning: "Facts are unlike to speakers whose language background provides for unlike formulation of them." [3] In the first years of the Russian revolution there were fanatic visionaries who argued in Soviet periodicals for a radical revision of traditional language and particularly for the weeding out of such misleading expressions as "sunrise" or "sunset." Yet we still use this Ptolemaic imagery without implying a rejection of Copernican doctrine, and we can easily transform our customary talk about the rising and setting sun into a picture of the earth's rotation simply because any sign is translatable into a sign in which it appears to us more fully developed and precise.

A faculty of speaking a given language implies a faculty of talking about this language. Such a "metalinguistic" operation permits revision and redefinition of the vocabulary used. The complementarity of both levels — object-language and metalanguage — was brought out by Niels Bohr: all well-defined experimental evidence must be expressed in ordinary language, "in which the practical use of every word stands in complementary relation to attempts of its strict definition." [4]

All cognitive experience and its classification is conveyable in any existing language. Whenever there is deficiency, terminology may be qualified and amplified by loanwords or loan-translations, neologisms or semantic shifts, and finally, by circumlocutions. Thus in the new-born literary language of the Northeast Siberian Chukchees, "screw" is rendered as "rotating nail," "steel" as "hard iron," "tin" as "thin iron," "chalk" as "writing soap," "watch" as "hammering heart." Even seemingly contradictory circumlocutions, like "electrical horse-car" (электрическая конка), the first Russian name of the horseless street car, or "flying steamship" (*jena paragot*), the Koryak term for the airplane, simply designate the electrical analogue of the horse-car and the flying analogue of the steamer and do not impede communication, just as there is no semantic "noise" and disturbance in the double oxymoron — "cold beef-and-pork hot dog."

No lack of grammatical device in the language translated into makes impossible a literal translation of the entire conceptual information contained in the original. The traditional conjunctions "and," "or" are now supplemented by a new connective — "and/or" — which was discussed a few years ago in the witty book *Federal Prose — How to Write in and/or for Washington.* [5] Of these three conjunctions, only the latter occurs in one of the Samoyed languages. [6] Despite these differences in the inventory of conjunctions, all three varieties of messages observed in "federal prose" may be distinctly translated both into traditional English and into this Samoyed language. Federal prose: 1) John and Peter, 2) John or Peter, 3) John and/or Peter will come. Traditional English: 3) John and Peter or one of them will come. Samoyed: John and/or Peter both will come, 2) John and/or Peter, one of them will come.

If some grammatical category is absent in a given language, its meaning may be translated into this language by lexical means. Dual forms like Old Russian брата are translated with the help of the numeral: "two brothers." It is more difficult to remain faithful to the original when we translate into a language provided with a certain grammatical category from a language devoid of such a category. When translating the English sentence "She has brothers" into a language which discriminates dual and plural, we are compelled either to make our own choice between two statements "She has two brothers" –"She has more than two" or to leave the decision to the listener and say: "She has either two or more than two brothers." Again in translating from a language without grammatical number into English one is obliged to select one of the two possibilities — "brother" or "brothers" or to confront the receiver of this message with a two-choice situation: "She has either one or more than one brother."

As Boas neatly observed, the grammatical pattern of a language (as opposed to its lexical stock) determines those aspects of each experience that must be expressed in the given language: "We have to choose between these aspects, and one or the other must be chosen." [7] In order to translate accurately the English sentence "I hired a worker," a Russian needs supplementary information, whether this action was completed or not and whether the worker was a man or a woman, because he must make his choice between a verb of completive or noncompletive aspect — нанял or нанимал — and between a masculine and feminine noun — работника or работницу. If I ask the utterer of the English sentence whether the worker was male or female, my question may be judged irrelevant or indiscreet, whereas in the Russian version of this sentence an answer to this question is obligatory. On the other hand, whatever the choice of Russian grammatical forms to translate the quoted English message, the translation will give no answer to the question of whether I "hired" or "have hired" the worker, or whether he/she was an indefinite or definite worker ("a" or "the"). Because the information required by the English and Russian grammatical pattern is unlike, we face quite different sets of two-choice situations; therefore a chain of translations of one and the same isolated sentence from English into Russian and vice versa could entirely deprive such a message of its initial content. The Geneva linguist S. Karcevski used to compare such a gradual loss with a circular series of unfavorable currency transactions. But evidently the richer the context of a message, the smaller the loss of information.

Languages differ essentially in what they *must* convey and not in what they *may* convey. Each verb of a given language imperatively raises a set of specific yes-or-no questions, as for instance: is the narrated event conceived with or without reference to its completion? Is the narrated event presented as prior to the speech event or not? Naturally the attention of native speakers and listeners will be constantly focused on such items as are compulsory in their verbal code.

In its cognitive function, language is minimally dependent on the grammatical pattern because the definition of our experience stands in complementary relation to metalinguistic operations — the cognitive level of language not only admits but directly requires recoding interpretation, i.e., translation. Any assumption of ineffable or untranslatable cognitive data would be a contradiction in terms. But in jest, in dreams, in magic, briefly, in what one would call everyday verbal mythology and in poetry above all, the grammatical categories carry a high semantic import. In these conditions, the question of translation becomes much more entangled and controversial.

Even such a category as grammatical gender, often cited as merely formal, plays a great role in the mythological attitudes of a speech community. In Russian the feminine cannot designate a male person, nor the masculine specify a female. Ways of personifying or metaphorically interpreting inanimate nouns are prompted by their gender. A test in the Moscow Psychological Institute (1915) showed that Russians, prone to personify the weekdays, consistently represented Monday, Tuesday, and Thursday as males and Wednesday, Friday, and Saturday as females, without realizing that this distribution was due to the masculine gender of the first three names (понедельник, вторник, четверг) as against the feminine gender of the others (среда, пятница, суббота). The fact that the word for Friday is masculine in some Slavic languages and feminine in others is reflected in the folk traditions of the corresponding peoples, which differ in their Friday ritual. The widespread Russian superstition that a fallen knife presages a male guest and a fallen fork a female one is determined by the masculine gender of нож "knife" and the feminine of вилка "fork" in Russian. In Slavic and other languages where "day" is masculine and "night" feminine, day is represented by poets as the lover of night. The Russian painter Repin was baffled as to why Sin had been depicted as a woman by German artists: he did not realize that "sin" is feminine in German (*die Sünde*), but masculine in Russian (грех). Likewise a Russian child, while reading a translation of German tales, was astounded to find that Death, obviously a woman (Russian смерть, fem.), was pictured as an old man (German *der Tod*, masc.). *My Sister Life*, the title of a book of poems by Boris Pasternak, is quite natural in Russian, where "life" is feminine (жизнь), but was enough to reduce to despair the Czech poet Josef Hora in his attempt to translate these poems, since in Czech this noun is masculine (*život*).

What was the initial question which arose in Slavic literature at its very beginning? Curiously enough, the translator's difficulty in preserving the symbolism of genders, and the cognitive irrelevance of this difficulty, appears to be the main topic of the earliest Slavic original work, the preface to the first translation of the *Evangeliarium*, made in the early 860's by the founder of Slavic letters and liturgy, Constantine the Philosopher, and recently restored and interpreted by A. Vaillant.[8] "Greek, when translated into another language, cannot always be reproduced identically, and that happens to each language being translated," the Slavic apostle states. "Masculine nouns as ποταμός 'river' and ἀστήρ 'star' in Greek, are feminine in another language as рѣка and звѣзда in Slavic." According to Vaillant's commentary, this divergence effaces the symbolic identification of the rivers with demons and of the stars with angels in the Slavic translation of two of Matthew's verses (7:25 and 2:9). But to this poetic obstacle, Saint Constantine resolutely opposes the precept of Dionysius the Areopagite, who called for chief attention to the cognitive values (силѣ разуму) and not to the words themselves.

In poetry, verbal equations become a constructive principle of the text. Syntactic and morphological categories, roots, and affixes, phonemes and their components (distinctive features) — in short, any constituents of the verbal code — are confronted, juxtaposed, brought into contiguous relation according to the principle of similarity and contrast and carry their own autonomous signification. Phonemic similarity is sensed as semantic relationship. The pun, or to use a more erudite, and perhaps more precise term — paronomasia, reigns over poetic art, and whether its rule is absolute or limited, poetry by definition is untranslatable. Only creative transposition is possible: either intralingual transposition — from one poetic shape into another, or interlingual transposition — from one language into another, or finally intersemiotic transposition — from one system of signs into another, e.g., from verbal art into music, dance, cinema, or painting.

If we were to translate into English the traditional formula *Traduttore, traditore* as "the translator is a betrayer," we would deprive the Italian rhyming epigram of all its paronomastic value. Hence a cognitive attitude would compel us to change this aphorism into a more explicit statement and to answer the questions: translator of what messages? betrayer of what values?

NOTES

1. Bertrand Russell, "Logical Positivism," *Revue Internationale de Philosophie*, IV (1950), 18; cf. p. 3.

2. Cf. John Dewey, "Peirce's Theory of Linguistic Signs, Thought, and Meaning," *The Journal of Philosophy*, XLIII (1946), 91.

3. Benjamin Lee Whorf, *Language, Thought, and Reality* (Cambridge, Mass., 1956), p. 235.

4. Niels Bohr, "On the Notions of Causality and Complementarity," *Dialectica*, I (1948), 317f.

5. James R. Masterson and Wendell Brooks Phillips, *Federal Prose* (Chapel Hill, N. C., 1948), p. 40f.

6. Cf. Knut Bergsland, "Finsk-ugrisk og almen språkvitenskap," *Norsk Tidsskrift for Sprogvidenskap*, XV (1949), 374f.

7. Franz Boas, "Language," *General Anthropology* (Boston, 1938), pp. 132f.

8. André Vaillant, "Le Préface de l'Évangeliaire vieux-slave," *Revue des Études Slaves*, XXIV (1948), 5f.

AUTOMATIC (TRANSFERENCE, TRANSLATION, REMITTANCE, SHUNTING)

ANTHONY G. OETTINGER

THE TITLE of this paper is a crude translation, such as a simple machine might prepare, of the title of a Russian paper, Автоматический Перевод. To understand why the machine translation of languages has grown to be the subject, not of science-fiction tales, but of serious scientific investigation, some understanding of the operating principles of the type of machine under consideration is essential. The first part of this paper is therefore devoted to a brief and, it is hoped, intelligible description of some important basic properties of automatic data processing machines. The attempted application of machine methods to language translation, and its consequences, is the subject of the second part of the paper. Translation from Russian to English is taken as an example throughout.

The use of automatic machines imposes on the investigator of the problems of translation a rigorously objective analytical point of view, a view of language that can be of interest to translators in general. Conversely, translation being a fine art whose origins antedate those of automatic machines by many centuries, the investigator of machine translation has much to learn from the experience of flesh-and-blood translators. Ultimately, no doubt, these two points of view will fuse into a single one from which man, relieved by automatic drudges from tedious routine manual and mental labors, can continue to apply his insight and imagination to new problems.

1. Automatic Data Processing Machines

The physical products of the operation of machines such as stamping presses or cigarette dispensers are of intrinsic value to their user; those of computing or translating machines, on the other hand, are valued not for themselves, but as vehicles for symbols. The tape produced by a cash register at a supermarket has little value except as a record of items purchased and of prices paid, which the housewife may use to make sure she has been charged correctly. Automatic machines of this type are now commonly called data processing machines, to distinguish them from the tools of production.

For more than a decade, automatic calculators have been used to solve with great speed and accuracy mathematical problems which heretofore could have been solved only by the expenditure of many man-lives of effort. Similar machines are replacing less automatic, less versatile machines in the bookkeeping and planning departments of commercial and industrial enterprises. There, they perform a great variety of clerical tasks requiring the transcription and filing of business data, the performance of simple calculations, and the making of routine decisions according to rules of choice which, intricate though they may be, have had to be precisely defined by the machine designer or operator.

It is, in fact, the need for precisely defined rules that makes machine translation a problem not so much of technology as of linguistics. There is only a slight oversimplification in the statement that if explicit rules for translation can be formulated, then a machine can be built to operate according to these rules. As an example of a rule which readily can be translated into machine instructions, the familiar "i before e, except after c" may be cited. There would be no difficulty in instructing a machine to check that the spelling of the words in a list is in accordance with this rule. On the other hand, to instruct a machine to choose between the alternative interpretations of the sentence "he drove here directly after work" on the basis of some characteristics of the context in which the sentence occurs would be a formidable task. The difficulties arise chiefly from the need for explicit specification of the *characteristics of the context*.

To clarify what is meant by instructing a machine to do a given job, some description of the construction and mode of operation of automatic data processing machines will be useful. One outstanding characteristic of these machines is their ability to store large quantities of data such as words or numbers in forms in which they can readily be manipulated by automatic means. In the present state of technology, these forms necessarily differ significantly from such familiar forms as ink patterns on paper or chisel marks in stone. Just as the shape and arrangement of the symbols of cuneiform script was influenced to some degree by the tools and materials available to its Assyrian users, so the materials and techniques now available have circumscribed the range of tokens usable by a machine to represent such symbols as the letters of the alphabet or the decimal numerals. Vacuum tubes are conveniently regarded as capable of assuming two states, conduction and non-conduction; a given spot on a piece of magnetic material may or may not be magnetized; a section of a card may or may not have a hole; a switch may be open or closed; a spot on a photographic plate may be opaque or transparent. The predilection for two alternatives is technological rather than logical. For example, the human eye can readily resolve many shades of gray between opaque and transparent, but the electric eye and its associated electronic circuits are tolerably reliable only when required to distinguish no more than the two extreme cases.

The available means are therefore best suited for the representation of two distinct symbols, commonly labeled *o* and *1*. It need only be demonstrated that any relevant symbol can be represented by properly arranged occurrences of *o* and *1* to establish the principle governing the storage of data in automatic machines. For example, the eight distinct composite symbols *000, 001, 010, 011, 100, 101, 110, 111* may be placed in correspondence with the letters *a, b, c, d, e, f, g, h* of the alphabet, so that *000* stands for *a, 001* for *b*, and so forth. This simple illustration is readily generalized, and should suffice to tear the veil of mystery from the notion of machine *memory*: clearly, if of three consecutive spots on a magnetic material, the first two are magnetized while the last one is not, this segment of a machine can be said to be remembering the letter *g*.

It is a relatively simple technological problem to provide a typewriter with means whereby, when its *g*-key is struck, the corresponding pattern of magnetized spots is produced in an appropriate location on the magnetic material. Conversely, such a pattern of spots can be used to control the printing of the letter *g* by a typewriter connected to the output of the machine. The user of the machine therefore need not even concern himself with the details described in the preceding paragraph. For his purposes, as distinguished from those of the technician, the memory or *data store* of a machine can be fully described in terms of customary symbols.

Storage space for letters or numbers is, in many machines, divided into bins or, as they are called, *registers*, each capable of holding a fixed number of characters. A set of characters fitting into one register is usually called a *word*. Each register is labeled with an identifying number called the *address* of the register. Some properties of a hypothetical machine having a data store with many registers will now be described. The basic instruction calls for the transfer of a word from a register *m* to another register *n*, where *m* and *n* stand for arbitrary addresses. This transfer instruction will be designated by the symbol Tm,n, which should be read "transfer the word in register m to register n." A series of instructions is called a *program*.

Preparing a program of instructions for a machine is hardly an automatic process. Much thought, imagination, and patient labor are required. However, once the program is complete, it can be set into the store like other data. Then the *control unit*, the nerve center of the machine, takes over. The control unit receives an instruction from storage, interprets it, and supervises its execution. Once the operation has been completed, the control unit selects the next instruction, executes it, and continues in this fashion until a stop instruction S is reached. Normally, if the control unit has just used an instruction obtained from register p, it will next select the instruction stored in register $p + 1$. Choices are made by breaking this routine, but more about this important function later.

When a word is typed on the input typewriter, it is momentarily stored in a special register associated with the typewriter, to which the address i (for input) may be assigned. A register o (for output) can store a word transferred into it from an internal register, and then control the printing of this word on the output typewriter. The instruction Ti,n is provided to effect a transfer from the register i to an internal register n, and the instruction Tn,o transfers a word from the register n to the output register o. The program $Ti,6$ $T6,9$, $T9,o$, S will, when obeyed, transfer a word from the input register to register 6, copy it from 6 into 9, transfer it from 9 into o, whence it is printed. The machine then stops. Obviously, such a program has little more than illustrative value, but before more significant illustrations can be given, the repertoire of instructions must be extended somewhat.

An instruction Cm,n which compares the words in registers m and n will be useful. If the words in these registers are identical, the digit 1 is automatically entered into a special *choice register c*, but if the words differ in one or more letter, the digit o is set into the choice register. The electronic circuits which perform such tasks are somewhat complex, but it is sufficient here to take for granted that skillful engineers can construct such circuits. A companion instruction Jn provides for an automatic choice between alternative courses of action, according to the results of the comparison. It has already been stated that the control unit, having obeyed the instruction stored in register 25, for example, will normally select the next instruction from register 26, then that in register 27, and so on. If one

of the instructions, say that in register *27*, is *J26*, the normal course
of action may be interrupted. The instruction *J26* will, if the choice
register *c* holds the digit *1*, simply be ignored, and the instruction in
register *28* obeyed next. If, however, the choice register *c* holds the
digit *0*, the control unit will next obey, not the instruction in register

ADDRESS OF THE REGISTER CONTAINING THE INSTRUCTION	INSTRUCTION	INTERPRETATION OF THE INSTRUCTION
25	T i,5	TRANSFER THE WORD IN THE INPUT REGISTER TO REGISTER 5
26	C 5, 100	COMPARE THE WORDS IN REGISTERS 5 AND 100. IF THEY ARE IDENTICAL, PLACE THE DIGIT 1 IN THE CHOICE REGISTER; OTHERWISE, PLACE THE DIGIT 0 IN THE CHOICE REGISTER.
REPLACE C5,x BY C5,x+2 REPLACE Ty,o BY Ty+2,o		
27	J26	JUMP TO THE INSTRUCTION IN REGISTER 26 IF THE CHOICE REGISTER HOLDS THE DIGIT 0; IF THE CHOICE REGISTER HOLDS THE DIGIT 1, PROCEED IN THE NORMAL FASHION.
28	T101,o	TRANSFER THE WORD IN REGISTER 101 TO THE OUTPUT REGISTER o, AND PRINT IT.
	S	STOP.

Figure 1. Dictionary Search Program

28 as it normally would, but once more that in register *26*! An example should clarify these definitions, and demonstrate the value of the instructions. A program constructed from the instructions defined thus far is given in Fig. 1. Suppose that someone has typed the Russian word перевод on the input typewriter, and that consequently this word is stored in register *i*. The first instruction transfers the word from register *i* to register *5*, freeing the input register for the introduction of the next word. Next, the word is compared with that in register *100*. Then, if the two words are identical, the word in register *101*, assumed to be the English equivalent of the word in register *100*, is printed. Otherwise, the control unit once more obeys the instruction in register *26*. As indicated on the arrow in the first column of Fig. 1, the instruction *C5,100* is automatically replaced by *C5,102*, and *T101,0* is automatically replaced by *T103,0* during the transition represented by the arrow.[1] Hence the word перевод is compared with successive words stored in the machine, until the matching Russian word is found, and the proper English equivalent is printed. This simple machine is seen to be capable of functioning as an automatic dictionary.

The choice by a machine between two alternative sequences of instructions, controlled in the preceding example by a test of the identicalness of two words, can be controlled as well by a test of the validity of one or the other of any precisely defined pair of alternatives. Is a word a noun or is it not? Is its last letter *s* or is it not? Is the preceding word *of* or is it not? All of these questions, if they can be resolved by the machine, can also be used to control the choice of alternative courses of action. The resolution of the question itself is a more difficult matter. The presence or absence of the letter *s* in the last place of the word may be determined by comparing the last letter with an *s* stored in the machine. Nouns like *combination* may be identified by a similar test for the presence of the suffix *-ation*, but *day*, as contrasted to *say* or *pay*, must be identified otherwise, as by comparison with a list of nouns including *day*, and stored in the machine. The restriction to a choice among no more than two basic alternatives has its roots in considerations similar to those governing the range of basic symbols. Again, the limitation is not serious, since a choice among several alternatives can often be realized by a succession of binary choices. Figure 2 illustrates the general selection process. The first choice determines whether procedure 1 or 2, or 3, 4 or 5 is to be followed. If the alternatives corresponding to *yes, yes, no* are valid, the machine eventually will follow the fourth sequence of instructions.

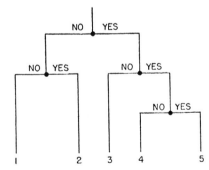

Figure 2. Selection Among Five Alternatives

While this description of machine characteristics is by no means complete — a volume would be required to do the subject justice —

the reader who imagines that the input typewriter is replaced by an automatic device, such as a tape reader, that a score or more of basic instructions are available, and that each of these instructions can be carried out by the machine in as little time as a few millionths of a second and rarely more than a few thousandths of a second, should be able to conjure up an adequate vision of an actual machine. Those wishing to plunge more deeply into the subject can turn to more specialized books.[2, 3, 4, 5]

2. Machine Translation

Research in machine translation requires that all its practitioners subscribe to one common article of faith: that languages obey natural laws as stable as those governing the motions of heavenly bodies. Since the cogency of this tenet appears greater to some than to others, some explanation is in order.

To the literary mind, especially, the composition of a short story or of a poem appears as a creative act of the imagination, often prized in direct proportion to the originality of thought or diction. Originality of diction creates the more difficult problem, which will be examined presently. Original thought, however, can often be conveyed within the bounds of the most rigid rules of syntax. In fact, the very possibility of communication through a language depends essentially on the existence of lexical and syntactical conventions accepted by all speakers of the language. Communication in a language whose rules change daily is most difficult, as long recognized and exploited by cryptographers. A frequent change of rules helps to withhold the sense of vital messages from interceptors, but also burdens the legitimate receiver with the need to remember and to apply correctly a large set of rules. In spite of such efforts, however, the intrinsic regularity of languages is such that few intercepted messages remain undeciphered indefinitely. Regardless of individual variations in style or content, such characteristics of messages as the relative frequency of the letters of the alphabet and the meanings of individual words remain surprisingly constant.

The construction of every message in conventional English, say, is governed by both definite rules, and chance or willful selection. It may be considered a matter of chance that the preceding sentence contains twenty words, and it is a matter of deliberate selection that the word *English* appears in it. On the other hand, *the construction* could have been *the correct construction* but never *the writes*. When all sentences in this paper, or all papers in this book, are viewed together, these seemingly disparate influences acting on the construction of the individual sentences lead to harmonious regularity like that in the behavior of a volume of gas composed of erratically darting individual molecules. The usual distribution of English letters will be present, the word *the* will occur far more frequently than any other word, a limited number of sentence patterns will emerge, various clichés will be found.

No language, however, is a static system. As time goes on, new words are coined, others become obsolete; new technical terms become accepted household words. Yesterday's usage is archaic today, today's vivid phrase is tomorrow's cliché. The novel diction of a young writer, or the spreading influence of a new scientific discovery creates new patterns, new words. But with innovation, communication becomes more difficult. The volume of exegetic writings on the works of Joyce and of popularizations on atomic energy attest to this difficulty. The process of change and assimilation, which has led from the English of Chaucer to that of Churchill, is not yet well understood, though it is now under active study. Whatmough's theory of selective variation,[6] for example, attempts to explain the process by which yesterday's stable, intelligible pattern of a language interacts with perturbing influences to produce a new stable pattern permitting, once again, ready communication. Zipf,[7] two decades ago, observed startling regularities in data describing the relative frequency of occurrence of words and, under attack, stated "I believe that the equilibrating forces suggested by our formulae are wider and deeper than Dr. Thorndike does, and that they are acting to produce equilibrium for equilibrium's sake. Insofar as we know anything of natural processes, we see what is apparently equilibrium for equilibrium's sake everywhere." Recent work by Mandelbrot,[8] based on the mathematical theory of communication developed by Shannon[9] and others, suggests a highly plausible mathematical basis for Zipf's beliefs. Significantly, the mathematical methods employed are similar to those used in relating the regular macroscopic properties of matter to the random behavior of its microscopic constituents. Finally there are studies, like Wexler's,[10] of the linguistic turmoil attending the birth of a new terminology. There is substantial indication, in all of these works, that even linguistic change is patterned, regular. The existence of pattern in form, however, by no means precludes diversity or originality of content. The sentences *Come here!* and *Go away!*

differ in content, but are similar in form. Indeed, while certain patterns are necessarily common to all mutually intelligible writers of a language, others may be characteristic of a single writer, and serve to distinguish him from another. The statistician Yule made use of such distinctive patterns in an attempt [11] to resolve claims that Thomas à Kempis on the one hand, or Jean Gerson, on the other, is the author of *De Imitatione Christi*. Obviously, the more common patterns are of greatest interest where machine translation is concerned.

Since the metamorphosis of language is a very slow, gradual process relative to the time scale of translation, a study of the properties of contemporary language should provide most of the basic design parameters for an automatic translator. The effects of time can be accounted for by designing a machine with sufficient flexibility to permit gradual changes.

Before machine instructions for translation can be formulated, the significant patterns of both the *source* language and the *target* language must be precisely identified and put into correspondence. This requirement effectively precludes any immediate attempt at automatic translation of speech. No practical automatic devices are now available or in sight that can convert the different sound waves produced by different speakers enunciating the same word into a unique symbol for use by a translating machine. Machine translation therefore usually refers to the translation of printed texts only, where patterns are more readily recognizable. For instance, in both Russian and English, words are patterns identifiable as sequences of letters occurring between successive spaces, sentences as sequences of words between successive periods, question marks, or exclamation points.

Placing patterns into correspondence is one major linguistic problem of machine translation; devising recipes for transforming source patterns into target patterns is another. Of the existence of some solutions to these problems there is little doubt, especially for closely related languages. A unique solution seems too much to hope for. While the study of formal linguistic patterns for their own sake interests many investigators, students of information theory in particular, the formal structure of discourse is relevant to translation only as a vehicle of meaning. Corresponding patterns, therefore, must be defined as conveyors of equivalent meanings since, whatever meaning is or means, it is generally agreed that it must be preserved in translation. Consider the following passage from Turgenev's *On the Eve*:

"I would have another bathe," said Shubin, "only I'm afraid of being late.

Look at the river; it seems to beckon us. The ancient Greeks would have beheld a nymph in it. But we are not Greeks, O nymph! We are thick-skinned Scythians."[12]

In the Russian,[13] this is followed by:

— у нас есть русалки, — заметил Берсенев.

— Поди ты с своими русалками! На что мне, ваятелю, эти исчадия запуганной холодной фантазии! Эти образы, рожденные в духоте избы, во мраке зимних ночей?

which Constance Garnett[12] translates:

"We have *roussalkas*," observed Bersenyev.

"Get along with your *roussalkas*! What's the use to me — a sculptor — of those children of a cold, terror-stricken fancy, those shapes begotten in the stifling hut, in the dark of winter nights?"

C. E. Turner[14] translates:

"We, too, have our water-naiads," interrupted Bersieneff.

"Away with you and your naiads! Of what use to me, a sculptor, are these sorry offsprings of an ill-cultured northern fancy, these hideous figures born in the suffocating heat of an *isbah* [a peasant's hut], worthy types of our dark winter nights?"

Moura Budberg[15] translates:

"We have our river-fairies," remarked Bersenev.

"River-fairies, indeed! What good are they to me, a sculptor, these figments of a cold and terror-struck imagination, conceived in the stifling atmosphere of a log-hut in the darkness of winter nights?"

And, finally, Isabel F. Hapgood[16] gives:

"We have water-nymphs also," remarked Berseneff.

"Get out with your water-nymphs! What use have I, a sculptor, for those off-spring of a confused, cold fancy, those images born in the reek of a peasant's hut, in the gloom of winter nights?"

Some of the differences between these versions are interesting. The word русалки, for which Constance Garnett merely gives a slightly altered transliteration, is given by the others as "naiads," "river-fairies," "water-nymphs." The transliteration lends a slightly exotic flavor to the passage, and acts as some unknown quantity x, whose value the reader must determine for himself from the context, somewhat as a native reader meeting the word for the first time might have to do. The actual translations evoke whatever ideas the reader may have associated with the words through previous reading and experience. Образы is rendered variously as "shapes," "figures," "figments," "images," and духоте as "stifling," "suffocating heat," "stifling atmosphere," "reek." In the latter case, where no single English noun corresponds exactly to the Russian, one translator abandons the formal noun to noun correspondence, two of them render the noun by a compound, viz., "духоте" = "suffocating-heat," and one preserves the formal correspondence by taking liberties with the meaning. While the sentence structure in all four versions is acceptable English, no two sentence patterns are exactly alike, each translator hoping, by his particular choice, to approximate as closely as possible the spirit of the Russian original.

Yet, in spite of these differences, the several versions have a close kinship; their underlying meanings are clearly quite similar, although their styles, their "feels" differ. It seems then that an important aspect of meaning can be preserved over quite a range of variation in formal structure. An interesting experiment by van der Pol,[17] in which a passage was translated from English into French by one translator, the French version translated into English by another, this English version into French again and then once more into English, confirms this observation. In van der Pol's words,

> The primary conclusion that can be drawn from this test is that the meaning has been retained to a remarkable degree, though by comparison with the original, the style of [the final English] version is entirely corrupted. Thus a person reading the original, and another reading the final text, should be able to agree on the content and the intent of the paper, although they might not be equally assisted in their appreciation of it by the respective styles.

It is thus reasonable to expect that patterns of the source language and patterns of the target language can be put into correspondence in such a way that certain kinds of meaning will be preserved, and that simple recipes for pattern transformation will emerge as well; ideally, the style of the translations obtained by the resulting process should be of a caliber comparable to the best that human translators produce. What relative roles the recipes should assign to man and machine is still an open question. Should the machine be designed to read a given text automatically, translate it, and deliver for publication a polished version untouched by human hands? Or should it perform only a part of this process and leave the remainder, as authors of mathematical texts are wont to do, "as an exercise for the reader"? The answers to these questions obviously depend on what machines can be made to do, but also on how much it costs, in research and in cash, to make them do it.

Lexical Correspondences

Two sets of elements are said to be in lexical correspondence if they are related by means of a dictionary. Thus, English *yes* is in lexical correspondence with Russian да, for, in an English-Russian dictionary, да will be found listed next to the entry *yes*, and vice versa in a Russian-English dictionary. A correspondence whereby each element of either set is associated with exactly one element of the other set, is said to be *one-to-one*. The words of one language are but rarely in one-to-one correspondence with the words of another. Opening an English-Russian dictionary to the word *rule*, one finds правило, устав, закон, линейка, etc. and conversely, under правило, one finds *rule, maxim, principle* listed. A correspondence whereby an element in one set may correspond to several in the other is labeled *one-to-many*.

It has already been demonstrated, in the first section of the paper, how an automatic machine may be programed to operate as a dictionary. The elements listed as entries in the dictionary need not be words, they may be groups of words, sentences, or even books. The recipe for finding the correspondent of an entry usually depends on juxtaposition: in an ordinary dictionary the target word is found adjacent to the listing of the source word or, in a few cases, a cross-reference index may be given. The recipe is completed by adding a prescription for the method of locating the proper dictionary entry for a given text word. In the program of Fig. 1, the dictionary entry is located by search, and the target word is assumed to be located in the register immediately following the one containing the source word. If sentences are to be listed, more capacious registers may be required, or else the program may be organized so that a group of registers each holding a word of the sentence will be treated as a unit.

In theory, automatic translation may be performed entirely by lexical means. A machine holding in storage the whole passage from Turgenev that we have quoted above, together with one of the four translations, could admirably translate that passage and any others similarly prepared. The absurdity of this procedure in practice is obvious. Lexical translation is practical only when the dictionary entries are used over and over again, as words are in different sentences and in different books. The question is simply one of mass-production; a manufacturer would be foolish to tool up an assembly line to produce one car, and equally foolish not to do so to produce a million cars.

If purely lexical automatic means cannot be used to translate books, what methods are available? An example from arithmetic will suggest the answer. Few men are capable of summing 3,563,257 and 7,201,653 at a glance, while all who have been to school can tell that $2 + 2 = 4$, and many can sum larger numbers given paper, pencil, and time. The sums $2 + 2 = 4$, $2 + 3 = 5$, etc., and products $2 \times 2 = 4$, $2 \times 3 = 6$, etc., of one-digit numbers are memorized at an early stage by all school children. Obtaining the product 8×7, for example, is then akin to a lexical process, in which the question "8×7 makes . . . ?" elicits the prompt response "56." In adding pairs of larger numbers, say 256 and 137, a different process is used. The sum of $6 + 7$, 13, is obtained from the "dictionary," and 3 is marked down as the first column of the sum. A unit is "carried" to the next column, and $5 + 3 = 8$, then $8 + 1 = 9$ are again obtained from the dictionary, and so forth. We see that using the addition table as a "small dictionary" and applying simple rules to each column in turn, is sufficient to define a process for summing any arbitrary pair of numbers. The structure of languages is so much more complex than that of simple arithmetic that an analogous process of equal simplicity is not likely to be found for translation. Nevertheless, we shall see that rules of syntax can be used to extend the power of a small dictionary, just as the rules of arithmetic extend that of the addition table. But first, let us examine lexical processes more closely.

In the early stages of research in machine translation, it occurred to many [18] that since the word dictionary plays so important a role in ordinary translation, some form of automatic dictionary most likely would be an important part of any automatic translating machine. The problems of designing an automatic dictionary have been investigated in some detail, to ascertain whether or not this basic machine itself might produce crude but useful translations, and assist in the development of more sophisticated apparatus. The results of this investigation are fully reported elsewhere; [19, 20] it will suffice here to present a few salient points, beginning with some technological considerations.

The number of different words that can be stored in an automatic dictionary depends chiefly on the cost of automatic storage devices and of the circuits required to perform search operations. The larger, cheaper, and more accessible storage facilities become, the easier the theoretical problems of translation grow, since the lexical process may then be applied to the longest groups of words recurring frequently enough to preclude the absurdity of "automatic" translation of unique passages. The development of photographic storage techniques promises to yield economical means for holding thousands of source words and their target equivalents.

It has been estimated that a vocabulary of the order of 5,000 words is adequate for various limited areas of technical discourse, while estimates of the total number of words current in major Western languages range between 50,000 and 100,000. For an inflected language such as Russian the estimates must be multiplied by a factor somewhere between 5 and 10, since a noun may occur in a variety of distinct forms depending on case and number, and verb forms vary according to tense, person, and number. With a simple matching process like that of Fig. 1, an automatic dictionary can be realized only if every distinct inflected form of every word in the vocabulary is a distinct entry in the dictionary.

If the several inflected forms of a word can all be referred to one standard form listed in the dictionary, the size of the vocabulary that can be held in any given storage device is considerably greater than if space must be allocated to several variants of each vocabulary item. This is done, of course, in the ordinary dictionary; the dictionary user must then rely on his knowledge of the rules of the language to associate word forms as they occur in texts with the standard forms listed in the dictionary. The process of association is so simple, so unconscious for a person familiar with a language, that the complexity of equivalent automatic processes is somewhat startling.

Various processes have been suggested for automatic reduction to standard form. For languages where inflected forms are created by adding different suffixes to a common stem, most writers[21,22] propose to match the word as it occurs in the text with dictionary entries. If an entry identical to the word is found, the process terminates. Otherwise, some letter of the word is deleted, and the matching process repeated. The alternation of matching and deletion continues until either the remainder of the word is found to be identical to a stem listed in the dictionary, or the number of deleted letters exceeds some fixed limit. A number of practical difficulties arise in this process but none are so serious as the fact that the repeated matching process can grow very time-consuming or costly even in a millisecond time scale.

A method has been developed for isolating inflectional affixes directly, without recourse to a matching and deleting process. The

можем	довольно	элементарных
решением	по	многополюсных
выберем	то	контактных
схем	место	эквивалентных
причем	что	аналогичных
запишем	это	обычных
дальнейшем	например	наконец
другим	с	матриц
таким	класс	бы
одним	принадлежат	способы
заметим	аппарат	чтобы
обозначим	бывает	мы
следующим	дает	схемы
рядом	возникает	суммы
образом	будет	равны
полюсником	имеет	законы
целом	следует	пары
самом	характеризует	алгебры
известном	представляет	элементы
матричном	элемент	работы
обычном	от	единицы
некотором	будут	матрицы
этом	замкнут	цепь
успехом	дают	использовалось
двум	отсутствуют	рассматривать
величин	образуют	использовать
о	стоят	называть
множество	между	записывать
общего	синтезу	задать
такого	анализу	обладать
булевского	характеристику	указать
заданного	схему	обозначать
последовательного	одному	изучать
некоторого	тому	получать
этого	поэтому	иметь
несколько	алгебру	предложить
только	классу	положить
число	полюсу	определить
но	работу	заменить
одно	матрицу	получить
можно	матрицах	часть
возможно	всех	есть
релейно	булевских	проводимость
естественно	электрических	возможность
недостаточно	этих	пусть
параллельно	идущих	речь
желательно	слагаемых	лишь
относительно	всевозможных	операцию
значительно	составленных	собою
равносильно	полученных	каждую

Figure 3. End-Alphabetized Words

technique of alphabetizing words according to their terminal letters, rather than, as usually, according to their initial letters, has proved invaluable in the development of this method and in other aspects of the study. Figure 3 is a list of a few end-alphabetized Russian words, on which suffix patterns are discernible. When longer lists are used, as they were in practice, these patterns appear in bold relief, and help in devising rules for separating affixes. These rules take the form of statements such as "If the last letter of the word is y and the penultimate letter is not м, or, if the penultimate letter is м but the third letter from the end is neither e nor o, then the suffix is y." Such statements could be converted into programs for effecting a series of decisions, as in Fig. 2. It is also possible to devise simple circuits that will isolate suffixes according to these rules in approximately the time required for a machine to execute a single instruction, and this is the important advantage of the method. By whatever means inflectional suffixes are separated, not only is a reduction in word storage capacity achieved, but the suffixes themselves are of potential value in the implementation of syntactical rules.

The reader who has tried to apply the rule given in the preceding paragraph to those words in Fig. 3 ending in -y, may have discovered that the rule permits the separation of y from между, which is indeclinable. So long as the remaining stem, in this case межд-, uniquely identifies the word, nothing is lost. Indeed, such cases may be turned to advantage, as an examination of Fig. 4 will reveal. A number of stems, obtained from words in running text according to rules of the type described above, are listed in Fig. 4 in end-alphabetic order. Since the sample from which this list was prepared is larger than that used for Fig. 3, the terminal letter patterns are quite striking. It is clear that the recurrent terminal letters in no way contribute to the identification of the words in which they occur, and hence could be deleted without impairing word identification. If storage space were at a premium, the consequent reduction in storage requirements would be valuable. Some other variations of this approach have been described by Bull, Africa, and Teichroew.[23] Considerations of storage may not prove compelling enough in themselves to warrant the implementation of these ideas, but a further inducement might. Most of the terminal letter patterns of Fig. 4 are characteristic of nouns. Thus, -ени identifies a common class of abstract nouns, most stems in -аци appear in cognates of English nouns in *-ation*. This suggests that storing only the distinctive parts of all stems having a com-

нарастани	выделени	сообщени
возрастани	усилени	помещени
испытани	оформлени	допущени
затухани	накоплени	лини
вещани	замени	удлини
радиовещани	измени	выполни
сравни	примени	напомни
возникновени	распространени	влияни
проникновени	устранени	состояни
соприкосновени	сравнени	строи
падени	уравнени	поступи
совпадени	усреднени	измери
введени	затруднени	критери
воспроизведени	изменени	теори
прохождени	применени	при
подтверждени	соединени	радиопри
возбуждени	дополнени	тригонометри
телевидени	выполнени	эмисси
наблюдени	выяснени	нажати
искажени	строени	обрати
изображени	измерени	замети
отражени	повторени	отмети
выражени	рассмотрени	развити
движени	оцени	приняти
снижени	значени	поняти
продолжени	назначени	реализаци
наложени	послесвечени	сигнализаци
разложени	обеспечени	организаци
приложени	течени	электризаци
положени	истечени	генераци
предположени	увеличени	операци
сложени	ограничени	регистраци
умножени	укорочени	компенсаци
сужени	изучени	флуктуаци
напряжени	получени	экспозици
биени	заключени	функци
ослаблени	включени	самоиндукци
приспособлени	подключени	станци
давлени	решени	радиостанци
направлени	отношени	корреляци
управлени	соотношени	изоляци
сопротивлени	нарушени	модуляци
установлени	улучшени	манипуляци
осуществлени	повышени	обозначи
явлени	уменьшени	обеспечи
появлени	вращени	наличи
проявлени	возвращени	отличи
делени	приращени	ограничи
определени	прекращени	получи
распределени	сокращени	наруши

Figure 4. End-Alphabetized Stems

mon terminal letter pattern in a common section of the store identified by the letter pattern would not only eliminate the need to store redundant letters, but would also suffice to identify the part of speech of the corresponding words. This identification, like that of inflectional suffixes, can be of value in the implementation of syntactical rules.

Frequent one-to-many correspondences between Russian and English words create, as might be expected, one of the most perplexing problems of automatic translation. Since most methods yet proposed for automatic selection among multiple correspondents depend on the application of syntactical rules, their consideration will be deferred. Purely lexical methods are few: the selection may be left to the reader, as it is when ordinary dictionaries are used; it may be made when the dictionary is compiled, as in the making of specialized technical dictionaries; or, a variant of the latter, alternative correspondents may be tagged as relevant to specialized fields of knowledge, and selected according to a field identification accompanying the text to be translated, again a common procedure with ordinary dictionaries.

The selection of correspondents when the dictionary is compiled is susceptible to bias in favor of the selection of those correspondents that best fit a few test sentences to be translated. The results of some highly publicized machine translation experiments [24] are questionable on this and similar counts. This method can be trusted only if many texts, preferably unpublished at the time of selection, can be processed satisfactorily with such a dictionary. Nevertheless, this method, or its variant, eventually may prove to be the only one practicable for most words.

Some limited experiments have been conducted with procedures which an automatic dictionary without selected correspondents could carry out. [19] These procedures too remain to be tested on a large scale, and preparations for such a test are under way. For the limited experiment, the Russian words in a sample text were assigned the correspondents given in a standard Russian-English dictionary. The title of the present paper is typical of the results. The words within parentheses are the English correspondents of the Russian word перевод. Since автоматический corresponds to *automatic* in one-to-one fashion, grouping within parentheses is not necessary.

Is it justifiable to call the product of such an automatic dictionary a translation? The experimental results suggest that for scientific texts the answer is yes. A monolingual reader, expert in the subject matter of the text being translated, should find it possible, in most instances, to extract the essential content of the original from this crude translation, often more accurately than a bilingual layman. He is helped by the fact that Russian word order, in scientific writing at least, is very close to that of English. The absence of number, case, and tense information is no major hindrance, but the great multiplicity of alternatives within parentheses is confusing, and, as the strongest roadblock on the way to comprehension, is responsible for most of the delay in attaining this goal. The simple expedient of ranking alternative correspondents in order of frequency, and printing the most frequent in bold letters, might help matters considerably. The reader, taking the boldly printed words as the translation, could read the text with less confusion than with uniformly presented alternatives, but could, in doubtful cases, examine the other alternatives more closely.

There is every indication that an automatic word dictionary would be a valuable tool. Even in cases where a text as translated by such a dictionary is not wholly intelligible, it is possible at least to decide whether or not it is of sufficient interest to merit more refined treatment. When a polished, literary translation is required, the product of an automatic dictionary should provide excellent raw material. Tedious, time-consuming reference to ordinary dictionaries could be eliminated; an editor presented with the original text and a translated version prepared by an automatic dictionary would be free to devote his attention to historical and literary context, to nuance, to style. A dictionary translation of the sample passage from Turgenev would include all ingredients necessary for the preparation of the four cited translations. It would remain only to select, combine, and season to taste.

The attention of a number of research groups is turned toward the realization of an automatic dictionary, which may be achieved in the not too distant future. The operation of an automatic dictionary would present a number of corollary advantages. In the normal course of operation vast quantities of text would be transcribed on punched cards, magnetic tape, or other automatically readable information storage media. The further development of automatic type readers may even make this transcription automatic. In any case, such texts would be useful in a variety of ways. Concordance making, on this basis, becomes an automatic process that can be completed economically in a matter of weeks, not lifetimes. Likewise, the compilation and revision of dictionaries can be greatly facilitated, since it should prove feasible to place at the disposal of the compiler large samples of contexts for any given word, from which he can determine the range of current usage, the relative frequency of various senses of the word, as well as sharper definitions of these senses in terms of their contexts. Statistical properties of texts of value to linguists, cryptographers, and students of information theory can be computed automatically. Large-scale studies of sentence structure, so essential for the continuing development of machine translation, become possible.

Syntactical Correspondence

It is evident that the automatic word dictionary assumes only a limited share of the burden of translation, one of a routine tedious nature and readily adaptable to simple automatic processes. Whether or not the burden of transcription from the printed page into machine language can also be assumed economically by automatic machines depends on the success of current technological developments. In the meantime, this task can be readily handled by monolingual clerical personnel trained, in the manner of telegraphists, to regard the source text as a coded message to be transmitted into the machine. The burden that remains taxes higher faculties in both men and machines.

It has been suggested earlier that processes analogous in spirit to those of arithmetic may prove useful in extending the power of dictionaries, and this possibility will now be considered. Since experiments indicate that automatic selection among alternative target correspondents of a single source word would be of greater value in improving the quality of dictionary output than other possible refinements, this question alone will be examined in detail.

Among the dictionary words with multiple correspondents, prepositions, conjunctions, and the like are the most troublesome. These are *function* words, carrying little meaning specific to a given text, but all-important in organizing the sentence, in establishing the relations between the other words, the *meaning* words. Meaning words include the nouns, verbs, adjectives, etc., which differentiate an English text on cooking, say, from one on chemistry. Such words may have one correspondent, like автоматический, or four or more, like перевод. Since the function words, although few in number, occur more frequently in texts than any comparable group of meaning words, they are responsible for a good share of the confusion introduced by multiple correspondents into a dictionary translation. The meaning words, however, are so numerous that, although each will occur far less fre-

quently than any function word, as a class they seem to account for
the majority of multiple correspondents in running texts.[25] Words
with multiple correspondents belonging to different parts of speech
create additional problems of their own.

Something like the problem of multiple correspondence exists even
within a single language. For example, *Webster's New Collegiate
Dictionary* lists eleven meanings of the word *for*, the specific interpretation depending, as always, on the context. Translation into a
second language having a word precisely equivalent to *for* would
present no difficulty, since the ambiguity in the translation would be
no more nor less than that in the original. The problem, as Gould [25]
puts it, arises from the fact that "in most Indo-European languages,
prepositions are used in the expression of a large number of different
concepts, and the combination of concepts embodied in a single preposition differs greatly from one language to another. Conversely, a
single general concept is often expressed by a variety of prepositions,
the appropriate choice of which must be considered idiomatic." The
same might be said of many other classes of words.

One way of using context to narrow down the range of correspondents of a word is illustrated by a method developed in Russia for determining a unique correspondent of the word *of*. Figure 5 [26] is what
machine programers call a flow chart; it outlines a procedure for
selecting among alternative Russian correspondents of *of*, and for
generating case indicators for use in the translation of neighboring
words. This procedure is similar to that represented in Fig. 2, and
can be implemented by comparison and jump instruction of the type
used in Fig. 1. The Russian experimenters used an English vocabulary of 952 words; their procedure apparently attempts to take account of all possible significant combinations of *of* with words in that
vocabulary. The evident complexity of the procedure requires no
comment; similar procedures have been prepared for other English
prepositions. This approach, for the few function words which recur
with high frequency, has considerable merit, but cannot be considered
practical without further refinement. For instance, the simple phrase
the result of simple experiments would defeat the procedure of Fig. 5.
The sequence of decisions for this case is indicated by bold lines in
Fig. 5; all goes well until box 21, where the wrong decision is made
because of the interpolation of *simple* between *of* and *experiments*.
The genitive indication is correctly developed, but *of* is translated от
rather than not at all. This is not too serious an error, since the result

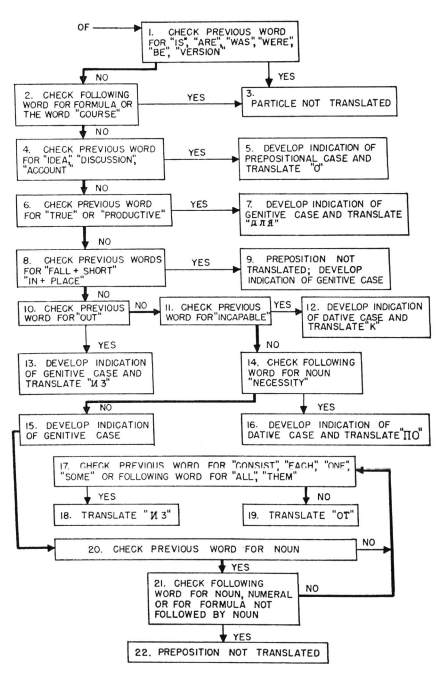

Figure 5. Determination of Russian Correspondent of of

would probably be intelligible to a Russian. The title of the Russian paper, which presumably was not translated by machine, is a case in point. The Russians used *of*, where *in* would be more idiomatic, thereby giving the title a "translated" flavor, but in no way obscuring its meaning. If such mistakes are of no great consequence, the procedure of Fig. 5 may be too elaborate. The consistent use of only one of the alternative correspondents might lead to no more errors than the more complex procedure. On the other hand, the procedure of Fig. 5 could be altered so as to treat the example correctly, by adding *ad hoc*, to the conditions of box 21, a check for a noun preceded by an adjective as well as just for a noun.

The method of Fig. 5 relies on both the identification of specific contexts, e.g., "is the following word *course?*" and the identification of general contexts, e.g., "is the following word a noun?" The first type of identification is simple in principle, but must be limited in application to a few idiomatic constructions, since the number of words that can follow *of* is enormous. The second type of identification permits the use of one procedure for many specific contexts, provided that they can be recognized as belonging to the same class. For example, for the procedure in box 21 of Fig. 5 to be of general value, not only *experiments* and *simple experiments*, but *the experiments, extremely simple experiments, simple, well-designed, accurate experiments, observations, few observations*, etc., must be recognized as belonging to the same class of contexts of *of*. The example of arithmetic suggests a search for simple recursive rules for class identification, and the old-fashioned sentence diagram, now in disrepute, can give a clue as to how such rules may be obtained.

The sentences *Come here!* and *Go away!* of an earlier example may mean different things, but share the pattern *verb adverb!* with many other sentences. The sentence *John loves Mary* may be diagramed as it is in Fig. 6, a diagram characteristic of many sentences. In the sentence *the result invalidated the rule*, the same basic structure can be recognized if the sentence is analyzed as in Fig. 7, where the distinct words *the* and *result*, and *the* and *rule* are first grouped, and then the groups used to take the place occupied by nouns in the diagram of Fig. 6. The more complex sentence *the result of simple experiments invalidated the rule* may be diagramed as it is in Fig. 8. Although the structure of the sentence as a whole is complex, simpler structures recur within it, as, for example, *the result, the rule*, and *simple experiments*; and the whole system { [(the) result] [of (⟨sim-

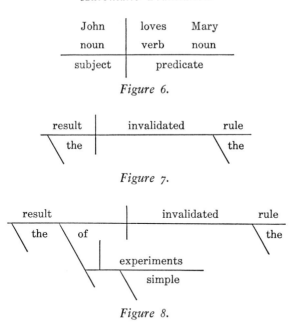

Figure 6.

Figure 7.

Figure 8.

ple⟩ experiments)]} in Fig. 8 plays the same role as *John* in Fig. 6. The same simple structures recur as components of other diagrams, each of which represents a vast number of possible sentences. It is possible then that a small number of rules applicable to these recurrent structures will therefore be valid for a much larger number of sentences. For example, it is the function of the test in box 21 of Fig. 5 to recognize the structure of *result of experiments*, whatever the particular nouns may be, and the test breaks down for *result of simple experiments* only because the recurrent pattern of *adjective modifying noun* has not been taken into account.

The sentence diagram as such cannot be used to identify patterns automatically. One reason for the current disrepute of this once popular teaching aid is that it places the cart before the horse. By some act of intuition, based on experience or on an answer in the back of the book, it has to be guessed that *the result of simple experiments* is the subject, and *invalidated the rule* the predicate. The predicate is then dismembered into the verb *invalidated* and the object *the rule*, where *the* modifies *rule*, and similarly for the subject. Such higher guessing is not possible for a machine. On the contrary, the division of a sentence into subject and predicate, which is the starting point of intuitive analysis, can only be the result of automatic analysis, which must be based on the morphology and on the order of the individual words in a sentence.

A sentence, as given to a machine, is simply a string of individual words. Something of the general pattern of the sentence may emerge if a part-of-speech or *word-class* designation is substituted for at least some words, as assumed in Fig. 5. For the automatic identification of a word with a word class, the class must be recognizable from the morphology of the word, as with nouns in *-ation*, or else the class designation must be stored with the dictionary entry for the word. Membership in a class can be established by the means outlined in the first section, and word classes are used to advantage in the flow chart of Fig. 5 for the definition of general contexts.

The next step, the recognition of patterns of word classes, is more difficult, but necessary for the generalization of procedures like that of box 21, Fig. 5. There are at present, to my knowledge, no methods for automatic word-class pattern analysis that have been tested on any but very limited vocabularies and sentence samples. One method, investigated by Salton,[27] attempts to make use of information supplied by punctuation to identify patterns. Yngve [28] has proposed a method based on the use of a dictionary of short word-class sequences, and illustrated its application with sentences formed from a 52-word vocabulary. These efforts, if successful, will significantly reduce the confusion due to multiple correspondents of function words. We can also expect a dent to be made in the problems of word order rearrangement, and of case, number, and similar indications, since the works of both Muxin and Yngve clearly indicate a close relationship between these unresolved questions and that of multiple correspondents of function words.

Selection among multiple correspondents of meaning words presents a somewhat different problem. While the significance of function words is deducible, at least partially, from their syntactical roles, that of meaning words depends not so much on syntax as on what the text is about. If different correspondents are marked, as they are in ordinary dictionaries, with notes such as *mathematical, nautical, colloquial,* etc., some selection is possible if the text is similarly marked before processing. If the text includes a sufficient number of unambiguous words related to a particular subject, automatic selection among multiple correspondents may be possible on the basis of internal consistency. Gould [25] has investigated this approach, but the evidence is insufficient to justify definitive conclusions.

Idioms create an interesting correspondence problem. In Bar-Hillel's words [29] "a given sentence in a language L_1 is *idiomatic with respect to a language L_2, to a given bilingual word dictionary from L_1 to L_2, and to a given list of grammatical rules* if, and only if, none of the sequences of the L_2 correspondents of the sequence of words of the given L_1 sentence is found to be grammatically and semantically a satisfactory translation, after perusal of the applicable grammatical rules." The italics are Bar-Hillel's, to emphasize the relative nature of idioms. An English expression idiomatic with respect to French may be straightforward with respect to German. An expression may be considered idiomatic if the words in it assume meanings different from those they have in other contexts, and hence whether or not it appears to be idiomatic depends on what senses of these words are given in the dictionary. Finally, what is an idiom with respect to a given set of syntactic rules may not be with respect to a more detailed set. Since idioms are often fossilized metaphors, special treatment may not be necessary if the metaphor is obvious in the target language, and since they are relatively rare in scientific writings, they have not proved seriously troublesome. Most writers conjecture that the extension of the word dictionary to include a small percentage of idiomatic phrases should be adequate to handle most occurrences. The phrases can be recognized by a process such as that indicated by box 2 of Fig. 5.

Any automatically operating machine may also automatically malfunction, and sound design must guard against this eventuality. The Westinghouse air brake is an outstanding early example of a device built in accordance with the *fail-safe* principle, which dictates that machines be built to act safely in the event of likely failures.

A minor mechanical failure that causes an automatic translator to misspell an occasional word is of no great consequence. Most texts are sufficiently redundant to remain quite intzlligiblz in spitz of somz garbling. Mechanical failures serious enough to cause complete garbling are annoying, but there is no danger of misinterpretation. Misinterpretation may arise, however, if the rules the machine is to obey when presented with a new word not listed in its dictionary, or with an unforeseen sentence pattern, are not made in accordance with the fail-safe principle.

New words can be handled relatively simply by transliteration. For cognates such as коммунист (kommunist) or алгебра (algebra) this course is highly satisfactory. For noncognates, e.g., напряжение (naprjazhenie) the transliteration may occur within the text in a number of contexts sufficient to define the meaning of the word. The strange transliteration warns the reader of the danger of misinterpretation and an ordinary dictionary may be consulted in doubtful cases.

Unforeseen sentence patterns present a more difficult problem. The consequences of failure are not easily ascertained. For example, the failure of the procedure of Fig. 5 with the phrase *of simple experiments* does not seem serious, but misinterpretation of more complex phrases is not ruled out. It can only be stated that an incoherent translation would be far less dangerous than a smooth translation that is wrong. It remains to work out methods for insuring that the translation of a sentence of unforeseen pattern will be either substantially correct, or else noticeably incoherent.

Enough has been said to indicate why the automatic translating machine, while not an idle dream, is not yet an operating reality. Meanwhile, the research continuing in many centers will deepen our understanding of the structure of languages and will, in time, lead to the operation of automatic machines whose purpose, in the words of Warren Weaver, is "not to charm or delight, not to contribute to elegance or beauty; but to be of wide service in the work-a-day task of making available the essential content of documents in languages which are foreign to the reader." [30]

NOTES

1. The replacement process must also be programed in practice.
2. B. V. Bowden, *Faster than Thought* (London, 1953).
3. W. J. Eckert, and R. Jones, *Faster, Faster* (New York, 1955).
4. A. D. Booth, and K. H. V. Booth, *Automatic Digital Calculators* (London, 1953).
5. E. C. Berkeley, *Giant Brains* (New York, 1949).
6. J. Whatmough, *Language* (London, 1956).
7. G. K. Zipf, "Homogeneity and Heterogeneity in Language; in answer to Edward L. Thorndike," *Psychological Record*, II (1938), 347–367.
8. B. Mandelbrot, "Structure Formelle des Textes et Communication," *Word*, X (1954), 1–27.
9. C. Shannon, and W. Weaver, *The Mathematical Theory of Communication* (Urbana, 1949).
10. P. J. Wexler, *La Formation du Vocabulaire des Chemins de Fer en France (1778–1842)*, Société de Publications Romanes et Françaises XLVIII (Genève, 1955).
11. G. U. Yule, *The Statistical Study of Literary Vocabulary* (Cambridge, 1944).

12. Constance Garnett translation (New York, 1951).

13. Государственное издательство художественной литературы, Москва (1949).

14. C. E. Turner translation (London, 1871).

15. Moura Budberg translation (London, 1950).

16. Isabel F. Hapgood translation (New York, 1907).

17. B. van der Pol, "An Iterative Translation Text," *Information Theory — Third London Symposium*, C. Cherry, ed. (London, 1956).

18. W. N. Locke, and A. D. Booth (eds.), *Machine Translation of Languages* (New York, 1955); "Historical Introduction."

19. A. G. Oettinger, *A Study for the Design of an Automatic Dictionary*, doctoral thesis (Harvard University, 1954).

20. A. G. Oettinger, "The Design of an Automatic Russian-English Technical Dictionary," Chapter 3 in Locke and Booth.

21. R. H. Richens, and A. D. Booth, "Some Methods of Mechanized Translation," Chapter 2 in Locke and Booth.

22. K. E. Harper, "A Preliminary Study of Russian," Chapter 4 in Locke and Booth.

23. W. E. Bull, C. Africa, and D. Teichroew, "Some Problems of the 'Word'," Chapter 5 in Locke and Booth.

24. L. E. Dostert, "The Georgetown-IBM Experiment," Chapter 8 in Locke and Booth.

25. R. Gould, "Multiple Correspondence in Automatic Translation," *Progress Report No. AF–44, Design and Operation of Digital Calculating Machinery*, Harvard Computation Laboratory, Section 1 (September 1956).

26. From I. S. Muxin, "An Experiment of the Machine Translation of Languages Carried Out on the BESM," Academy of Sciences of the USSR, Moscow (1956) (in English).

27. G. Salton, "A Method for Using Punctuation Patterns in the Machine Translation of Languages," *Progress Report No. AF–43, Design and Operation of Digital Calculating Machinery*, Harvard Computation Laboratory, Section VII (May 1956).

28. V. Yngve, "Syntax and the Problem of Multiple Meaning," Chapter 14 in Locke and Booth.

29. Y. Bar-Hillel, "Idioms," Chapter 12 in Locke and Booth.

30. W. Weaver, "Translation," Chapter 1 in Locke and Booth.

III

A Critical Bibliography of Works on Translation

BIBLIOGRAPHY
46 B. C. – 1958

INTRODUCTORY NOTE

Fifteenth century. "nothing which is harmonized by the bond of the Muses can be changed from its own to another language without destroying all its sweetness" — Dante.

Sixteenth century. "let the critic first find out what it is to translate elegant poems ... without adding or taking away" — Fray Ponce de Leon.

Seventeenth century. "Translation from one language into another ... is like gazing at a Flemish tapestry with the wrong side out." — Cervantes.

Eighteenth century. "Poetry ... cannot be translated." — Samuel Johnson.

Nineteenth century. "a good translation takes us a very long way." — Goethe.

Nineteenth century. "A translation in verse ... seems to me something absurd, impossible" — Victor Hugo.

Nineteenth century. "the live Dog better than the dead Lion." — Edward FitzGerald.

Twentieth century. "One should abandon the effort to translate the untranslatable." — Hilaire Belloc.

The disproportion of these judgments is no accident. For as it is always easier to criticize than to create, the antagonists of translation have consistently outnumbered its advocates. For more than two thousand years (the earliest literary translation, that of Homer's *Odyssey* into Latin by Livius Andronicus, was made about 250 B. C.), men of the western world have been translating, and while most translators like their own work, others have frequently disagreed, some of them categorically. "Translation is sin," said Grant Showerman crisply (1916). On the other hand, one notes this remarkable paradox: whereas critics have repeatedly proved that translation is impossible (Nemiah 1922, Frost 1955) even nonexistent (May 1927, who nevertheless gives advice on how to translate), the plain fact is not only that translation continues to be extensively practiced, but that — as even its severest judges have to admit — no modern civilization can dispense with it. It has been forcefully pointed out (Fitzmaurice-Kelly 1910) that our own world owes to translations an essential part of what it is. The question why so many people undertake the laborious and thankless task of translating has been explored more than once (Thursfield 1936).

The contradictions encountered in the literature are explainable by the very nature of translation, the difficulties of which, insurmountable by any strict standard, are so great that some sort of compromise is inevitable (Larousse 1904). It follows logically that just as one ear enjoys cacophonies in music which another abhors, one critic will demand Homer in prose (O'Neill 1950), while another (Leonard 1921) insists that in translating poetry some form of verse is indispensable.

On the whole, criticism of translations of prose centers on accuracy, which is in theory attainable (Lanier 1897). Yet even here there are pitfalls, particularly when the great writers of Greece and Rome are to be interpreted (Jowett 1871), or when differences in folkways (Smith 1925, Astrov 1946, Ervin 1952) offer verbal or spiritual difficulties. Translators of the Bible point out, for example, that Hebrew has many more words for one idea than English (Knox 1957), or that the Eskimo has no sheep (Chamberlain 1910), so that much fine Biblical imagery is ineffectual as it stands. In translating from modern languages, moreover, a common failing is "translatorese," "that queer language-of-the-study that counts words but misses their living force" (Ciardi 1954).

When we turn to poetry, the channels of controversy open in every direction. Some of the points of contention are purely personal, as when one critic prefers the heroic couplet of Pope, another (Keats) the stately sweep of George Chapman. A further source of confusion lies in the fact, noted by more than one critic, that translations age more than original works. Few verse translations which were approved in their own day show more than a limited survival. Articles which survey English translations in historic sequence usually make it clear that the earlier ones have diminishing appeal, if any (Brower 1947).

In verse translation, as most critics contend, one must distinguish between nearly contemporaneous verse in a language that is widely understood, and poetry more remote either in time or in culture. In the former case, cogent arguments are presented for a close imitation of the original patterns (Roditi 1942, MacNeice 1949), although some close observers find basic differences that can hardly be overcome (Scherer 1878, Grand' Combe 1949) and others feel that a translation can be more faithful by being less exact (Warren 1895). The Schlegel-Tieck translation of Shakespeare is still admired for its fidelity, helped of course by the close affinity of German and English as to vocabulary, syntax, and versification (Fulda 1904). Quite different demands prevailed in Waley's translation of Chinese poetry (1941), as in FitzGerald's recreation of the Persian Omar. Since those originals were closed to most English readers, Rossetti's dictum (1874), "a good poem shall not be turned into a bad one," could be accepted unreservedly. It is recognized by critics, if not by all translators, that in all such cases only poets can produce acceptable translations (Gregory 1944).

Through the entire critical literature runs the demand, not always stated in so many words, that the translation must produce an effect comparable to that of the original work (Cauer 1896). This may take the form that the foreign author should speak as if he were an Englishman (Philips 1663). Only two critics add the reservation which alone would give this requirement true validity: that the translation should affect the reader as the original affects the translator (Thomson 1915, Hamilton 1937). Have we means of knowing what effect the classics of Greece and Rome had in their own day? Without such knowledge, the translator is compelled to make assumptions which are at best plausible, at worst arbitrary. Thus, few critics have considered that Browning's translation of the *Agamemnon* (1877) sounded to English ears as Aeschylus' text did to the Greek playgoers. Certainly the demand that a translation must be readable (Butler 1898) was not met in that case. Moreover, the laws of Greek (and probably Roman) versification differ so radically from our own that a truly comparable effect, as regards line structure and line groupings (as in stanzas), is a physiological impossibility. The resulting compromise is bound to displease someone (see Arnold and Newman 1861 on translating Homer).

The critical opinions set forth in the following books and articles may be summed up under three heads. (1) Good translation requires both knowledge of the foreign language (and world) and skill in the native tongue, and the translator needs the ultimate in both. It is generally acknowledged that translation is as much an art as is original composition, and partakes of its nature. (2) The law of comparable effect, sound in principle, means in practice that the translator's taste and skill must be his guide, since he has no objective criteria either of the effect of the original work on its audience, or of his success in matching it with his own public. (3) Like actors on the stage, or performers on the platform, the translator appeals to a living audience and seeks its approval. While this precludes the success of anything which that audience cannot understand, appreciate, or enjoy, a necessary corollary is that the translations of yesterday will eventually yield to those of tomorrow.

Few bibliographies can be exhaustive, and the present one does not even claim to be complete, but attempts to present a selection, controlled but generous, which will serve the needs of any student of the subject. On the other hand, in place of a dead list of names and titles, we have chosen to bring our material to life by critical comment intended to reveal the basic character of most of the titles listed. It is in the same spirit that we have prefixed to this introduction — in itself an enlargement of the conventional bibliography — a chronologically arranged *florilegium* calculated to show that the field of translation has generated its share of witty sayings and sage observations.

While theoretically it might be desirable to quote from either the first or the standard edition of an author, we have considered that many smaller libraries do not possess either first editions or the latest critical ones. Thus in the case of Goethe, for instance, the edition probably owned by the largest number of libraries is the *Jubiläums-Ausgabe*, from which we quote. For another sort of case, take Jowett's translation of Plato: his remarks on translation do not appear in the first edition and were doubtless added to the second edition in response to comment and criticism.

It will be noted that the bibliography is much more copious in its recent listings. This is not due to an overweighting of the present — for which arguments could be advanced — but reflects the actual increase of interest in the theory of translation shown by critics, translators, and other writers. It also reflects our growing awareness of the importance of communication in a shrinking, interdependent world. Nothing shows more clearly than this bibliography that national isolationism is a thing of the past.

46 B.C. CICERO. *Libellus de optimo genere oratorum* IV:14. — "I did not translate them as an interpreter but as an orator . . . not . . . word for word *(verbum pro verbo)*, but I preserved the general style and force of the language."

20? B.C. HORACE. *Ars poetica* I:33. — *Nec verbum verbo curabis reddere fidus / Interpres.* (Nor will you as faithful translator render word for word.) — (Cf. Sherburne 1701 and Huet 1661 on the interpretation of this passage.)

1530. LUTHER, Martin. *Ein Sendbrief vom Dolmetschen. Werke.* Weimar. xxx Abt. II: 627–646. — The importance of writing not a latinized German, but a native idiom. (For English tr., see Carruth 1907.)

1576?. MONTAIGNE, Michel de. "Apologie de Raimonde Sebonde." *Essais.* Paris 1874. II:149. — "It is easy to translate authors like this one, with hardly anything but subject matter to transfer; but it is risky to undertake those who have given their language much grace and elegance, particularly with a language of less power."

1611. CHAPMAN, George. Pref. to tr. of Homer's *Iliad*. London. (Cf. Bartlett 1942.)

1656. COWLEY, Abraham. Pref. to the *Pindarique odes*. (In his *Works*.) London. — "I have . . . taken, left out, and added what I please; nor make it so much my aim to let the reader know precisely what he spoke, as what was his *way* and *manner* of speaking."

1656. DENHAM, John. Pref. to *The destruction of Troy* (i.e., tr. of *Aeneid*, Book II). London. — "translate Poesie into Poesie" "if Virgil must needs speak English, it were fit he should speak it not only as a man of this Nation, but as a man of this age."

1661. HUET, Pierre Daniel. *Petri Danielis Huetii de Interpretatione Libri duo, quorum prior est de optimo genere interpretandi, alter de claris interpretibus.* Paris. (Cf. Sherburne 1701.)

1663. PHILIPS, Katherine F. *Letters from Orinda to Poliarchus.* 2d ed. London 1729. Letter XIX (not in 1st ed.). — "I think tr. ought not to be used as musicians do a ground, with all the liberty of Descant, but as Painters when they copy; and the Rule that I understood of Trs. . . . was to write to Corneille's Sense, as it is to be supposed Corneille would have done, if he had been an Englishman not confined to his lines, nor his Numbers . . . but always to his meaning."

1680. DRYDEN, John. Preface to Ovid, *Epistles*. In *Essays*, ed. W. P. Ker. Oxford 1900. — Three types: (1) metaphrase, word for word, line for line (Ben Jonson's *Ars poetica* of Horace); (2) paraphrase . . . words not so strictly followed as the sense, which may be amplified but not altered (Waller's tr. of Virgil, *Aeneid* IV); (3) imitation (which he admits may not be tr. at all).

1684. ROSCOMMON, Wentworth Dillon, Earl of. *An essay on translated verse.* London. — Gives advice to the "well-bred" tr.; admired by Dryden.

1701. SHERBURNE, Edward. *The tragedies of L. Annaeus Seneca . . .* London. — "A brief discourse concerning translation" quotes Huetius as authority for disputing the idea that Horace favored a free rather than a word-for-word tr. (Cf. Huet 1661.)

1711. DACIER, Mme Anne. *L'Iliade d'Homère*. Traduite en François. Amsterdam. — Advocates prose tr. of Homer. (Cf. Mazon 1935.)

1714. LA MOTTE, Antoine de. *L'Iliade, avec un discours sur Homère* . . . Paris. (Cf. Rigault 1856.)

1715. POPE, Alexander. Pref. to the tr. of Homer's *Iliad*. London. — "it is the first grand duty of an interpreter to give his author entire and unmaimed" "the diction and versification only are his proper province" "above all things to keep alive that spirit and fire which makes his chief character."

1760. BATTEUX, Charles. *Principles of tr.* Edinburgh. — Tr. of pt. 3, sec. 4, of *Cours de belles lettres*.

1778?. CONDORCET, Antoine, 1743–1794. Quoted in Alfred Neymarck, *Turgot et ses doctrines*. Paris 1885. II:287. — "Condorcet était pour une version franche et sans réticence. 'Il faut dire dans la traduction ce qu'a dit Tibulle ou Catulle et non point ce qu'ils auraient dû dire s'ils avaient eu des moeurs plus pures.' "

1778?. TURGOT, Anne Robert Jacques, 1727-1781. See Alfred Neymarck, *Turgot et ses doctrines*. Paris 1885. II:293. — "Turgot ne transpose pas mais il amplifie volontiers, esquive parfois certaines difficultés et s'écarte souvent du texte." (For a contrary view see West 1932.)

1779. JOHNSON, Samuel. *Lives of the poets*. London 1890. I:437. — "A tr. is to be like his author: it is not his business to excel him."

1790. TYTLER, Alexander Fraser. *Essay on the principles of translation*. London. Also in Everyman's Library. — "A good tr. . . . that, in which the merit of the original work is so completely transfused into another language, as to be as distinctly apprehended, and as strongly felt, by a native of the country to which that language belongs, as it is by those who speak the language of the original work."

1791. COWPER, W. Preface to *Iliad*. London. — "Fidelity indeed is of the very essence of tr. and the term itself implies it." "The tr. which partakes equally of fidelity and liberality. . . promises fairest."

1796. HUMBOLDT, Wilhelm v. Letter to A. W. v. Schlegel, 23 July; in *Briefwechsel* . . . Halle 1908. — "All translating seems to me simply an attempt to accomplish an impossible task."

1800?. NOVALIS, *pseud. Fragmente*. Dresden 1929. Pages 617–618. — Three types of tr.: (1) grammatical, (2) modified (*verändernd*), (3) mythical (*mythisch*). (1) designates the usual type, which demands much learning, few abilities. (2) demands supreme poetic power, otherwise travesty results, as in Pope's Homer, most French trs. (3) are trs. in the highest sense, which give not only the actual work of art but also its ideal picture. No complete model exists, but bits are in evidence.

1811. GOLITSYN, Prince B.V. *Réflexions sur les traducteurs russes*. St. Petersburg. — Earliest book discussing the cardinal problems of Russian tr. technique, especially in respect to poetry.

1813. GOETHE, J. W. v. *Dichtung und Wahrheit*, III, 11. *Jubiläums-Ausgabe*. Stuttgart. XXIV: 56–59. — Argument in favor of prose tr., including Homer; Luther's Bible tr. as example.

1813. SCHLEIERMACHER, Friedrich. "Über die verschiedenen Methoden des Übersetzens." *Werke*. Berlin. III. Abt. II:207–245. — Three types: (1) paraphrase; (2) informative, like Goethe's first type; (3) emigration of foreign author, like Fulda's second type; S. rejects this. (Cf. Fulda 1904.)

1816. HUMBOLDT, Wilhelm v. Preface to Aeschylos, *Agamemnon*. Leipzig. — Simplicity and faithfulness striven for. A tr. can and should not be a commentary. When the original merely hints and is obscure, the translator has no right to give the text an arbitrary clarity. (Cf. Humboldt 1796.)

1816. STAËL-HOLSTEIN, Anne L. G. *baronne* de. "De l'esprit des traductions." *Oeuvres*. Paris 1820-1821. XVII:387-399. — Remarks on particular trs., little theorizing.

1819. GOETHE, J. W. v. "Übersetzungen," in "Noten und Abhandlungen zum West-östlichen Divan." *Jubiläums-Ausgabe*. Stuttgart. V:303–306. — Three types: (1) informative, like Luther's Bible; (2) adaptation ("parodistisch"); (3) reproduction (Voss's tr. of Homer).

1820. FRERE, J. H. Review of Mitchell's *Aristophanes*. *Quar R* 23:474–505. — (1) *Spirited Translators* substitute "a modern variety or peculiarity for an ancient one." (2) *Faithful Translators* render into English all the conversational phrases according to their grammatical and logical form. "The language of tr. ought never to attract attention to itself."

1820?. SHELLEY, Percy Bysshe. "In defence of poetry." *Shelley's prose in the Bodleian MSS*, London 1910. p. 71. — "It were as wise to cast a violet into a crucible, that you might discover the formal principle of its color and odor, as seek to transfuse from one language into another the creations of a poet."

1827. GOETHE, J. W. v. Letter to Carlyle, 20 July. *Goethe-Briefe*. Berlin 1902–1905. — "Say what one will of the inadequacy of tr., it remains one of the most important and worthiest concerns in the totality of world affairs."

1837. ANON. (Jas. D. Knowles). "Principles of translation." *Chr R* 2:596. — Baptists' argument for tr. of "baptize" by a native word meaning to immerse.

1851. SCHOPENHAUER, Arthur. "Über Sprache und Worte." In *Parerga und Paralipomena*. Leipzig 1888. II:624-640. — One difficulty in tr. is that a word in one language seldom has a precise equivalent in another one; S. uses overlapping circles as analogous.

1855. LEWES, George Henry. *Life of Goethe*. London. II:315. — "In its happiest efforts, tr. is but approximation, and its efforts are not often happy. A tr. may be good *as* tr., but it cannot be an adequate reproduction of the original."

1856. RIGAULT, H. *Histoire de la querelle des anciens et des modernes*. Paris. — Trs. of *Iliad* by La Motte (12 books, rhyme) and Mme Dacier (prose). (Cf. Mazon 1935.)

1858. MOMMSEN, Tycho. *Die Kunst des deutschen Übersetzers aus neueren Sprachen*. Leipzig. (Cf. 1886.)

1859. FITZGERALD, Edward. *Works*. New York. II: 100. — "Better a live sparrow than a stuffed eagle."

1860. PATTISON, Everett W. "Translation." *Univ Q* 2:124-135. — Values of translating to the translator explored and illustrated.

1861–1862. ARNOLD, Matthew. "On translating Homer" (two essays). London. Also in *Essays literary and critical* (Everyman's Library). — Insists on hexameters, tries to prove their appropriateness by examples, which are very bad. (Cf. Benson 1924.)

1861. CONINGTON, John. "The English translators of Virgil." *Quar R* 110:73–114. — "a tr. ought to endeavor not only to say what his author has said, but to say it as he has said it."

1861. NEWMAN, Francis W. *Homeric translation in theory and practice.* London. — Reply to Matthew Arnold. (Cf. Newman 1875.)

1869?. CALVERLEY, C. S. "On metrical translation: the *Aeneid* of Virgil." *Complete works.* London 1901. pp. 496–508. — Critical comments on attempts to translate classical meters into English ones. Specific criticism of Conington's tr. of Virgil. (Cf. Conington 1861.)

1874. ROSSETTI, Dante Gabriel. Pref. (1861) to *Dante and his circle.* London. — "a good poem shall not be turned into a bad one."

1875. NEWMAN, Francis W. "Essay on poetical translations." *Fraser* 92:88–96. — Examples from Greek and Latin, with comment.

1877. BROWNING, Robert. *Works.* London 1889. XIII:261–267. Pref. to tr. of *Agamemnon.* — "There is abundant musicality elsewhere, but nowhere else than in his poem the ideas of the poet."

1878. FITZGERALD, Edward. *Letters* . . . London 1894. Letter to J. R. Lowell, 22 Dec. — "I am persuaded that . . . the Translator . . . must re-cast that original into his own Likeness . . . the live Dog better than the dead Lion."

1878. SCHERER, Edmond. *Etudes sur la littérature contemporaine.* Paris. V:319–340. — "Deux choses font obstacle à la traduction en vers . . . les différences de grammaire et vocabulaire . . . la nature même de la poésie . . . notre vers n'a pas les mêmes qualités mélodiques que le vers étranger . . . il ne réproduit pas." "La traduction ressemble toujours un casse-tête chinois . . . on est sûr d'avance que l'adaptation laissera à désirer."

1881. ĆWIKLIŃSKI, Ludwik. *Homer i homerycy* (Homer and Homeridae). Lwów. — A survey of Polish Homer trs.

1886. GUMMERE, E. B. "The translation of Beowulf . . ." *Amer J Philol* 7:46–79. — He quotes Conybeare: "Poetry can alone reflect . . . the images of poetry." Three possible methods: (1) retelling in prose; (2) modern meter and diction; (3) adoption of original meter. Gummere votes for (3).

1886. MOMMSEN, Tycho. *Die Kunst des Übersetzens fremdsprachlicher Dichtungen ins Deutsche.* Frankfurt am Main. — Three types: (1) formless ("stillos"), like Goethe's "informative" type; (2) in foreign style, like Fulda's colonization; (3) formal ("stilhaft"), like Goethe's "reproduction." (Cf. Goethe 1819, Fulda 1904.)

1891. JOWETT, Benjamin. Pref. to *The dialogues of Plato.* London. 2d ed. — The first requisite of an English tr. is that it be English. Thoroughgoing comparison of Greek and English diction, with resulting problems for the translator.

1895. ANON. *Essays in translation.* Repr. from *J of Ed.* (London).

1895. WARREN, T. H. "Art of translation." *Quar R* 182:324–353. Also in *Essays of poets and poetry*. New York 1909. — (1) A good tr. should be rather faithful than exact. (2) "a tr. must read like an original," while preserving the differentiating character of the original.

1896. CAUER, Paul. *Die Kunst des Übersetzens*. Berlin. — Comparable effect is the desirable goal; a perfect tr. would be identical with the original.

1896. ERMATINGER, Emil, and HUNZIKER, Rudolf. "Die Kunst des Übersetzens . . ." In *Antike Lyrik in modernem Gewand*. Frauenfeld.

1897. LANIER, Sidney. *The English novel*. New York. pp. 290–291. — "it is words and their associations which are untranslatable, not ideas; there is no idea . . . which cannot be adequately produced as idea in English words."

1898. BUTLER, Samuel. Pref. to tr. of Homer's *Iliad*. London. — The English must be idiomatic, it must flow, and it must keep as near as it can to the original. "The genius of the language into which a tr. is being made is the first thing to be considered; if the original was readable, the tr. must be so too."

1900. ANON. "Translating the Arabian nights." *Nation* 71:167–168, 185–186. — Historic survey of the various versions in English, then one in German, one in French.

1900. BEYER, C. *Deutsche Poetik*. Stuttgart. III:184ff. — "Kurzer Abriss von der Geschichte der Übersetzungskunst." He calls for fidelity and readableness, sets up a long list of demands on the translator.

1900. BUTLER, Samuel. Pref. to tr. of Homer's *Odyssey*. London. — "Liberty of translating poetry into prose involves the continual taking of more or less liberty throughout, for much that is right in poetry is wrong in prose."

1901. CHAMBERLAIN, Alexander F. "Translation: a study in the transference of folk-thought." *J Amer Folk-Lore* 14:165–171. — Examples from Amerindian languages; Bible stressed.

1901. TOLMAN, H. C. *The art of translating*. Boston. — Virtually identical with Cauer 1896.

1902. CROCE, Benedetto. *Aesthetic*, tr. Douglas Ainslie. London 1922. pp. 68, 73. — "Faithful ugliness and faithless beauty" proverbial; we cannot reduce what has already possessed aesthetic form to another form also aesthetic. Unaesthetic trs. are simple commentaries. But there is relative possibility of trs.; not as reproductions, but as productions of similar expressions. The tr. called good has original value as a work of art.

1902. MURRAY, Gilbert. *Euripides translated into English rhyming verse*. London. — Preface gives account of his procedure and his ideal in translating. (Cf. Eliot 1920.)

1902?. WILAMOWITZ-MOELLENDORFF, Ulrich v. "Was ist Übersetzen?" In *Reden und Aufsätze*. Berlin. — "The new verses should produce the same effect upon their readers as the originals did upon their contemporaries."

1903. BEERBOHM, Max. "Translation of plays." *Sat R* 96:75–76 — "advice to those about to tr. plays" A natural diction essential. Archer's tr. of Ibsen not good on the stage.

1903. MERCIER, Ernest. *L'Art de la traduction*. Alger.

1904?. ANON. "Traduction" in Larousse, *Grand dictionnaire*. — Two general types: (1) a sort of photographic reproduction, cold and precise, (2) an attempt at color and emotion at the expense of literalness.

1904. FULDA, Ludwig. "Die Kunst des Übersetzens." In *Aus der Werkstatt.* Stuttgart. — Two choices: (1) colonize the foreign world, (2) make the foreign poet an immigrant. To make him a native is the highest goal (Schlegel's Shakespeare).

1907. CARRUTH, W. H. "Luther on translation." *Open Ct* 21:465–471. — A tr. of Luther's *Sendbrief vom Dolmetschen* (1530).

1907. HEADLAM, Walter. *Book of Greek verse.* Cambridge. — "Untranslatable . . . is applied too readily" "Greek poets wrote native metre . . . we must write what is really verse."

1908. HASKELL, Juliana. *Bayard Taylor's translation of Goethe's "Faust."* New York. — Taylor's failure to "meet the demands which may reasonably be made upon" his translation.

1909. BONE, Karl. *Peirata Techne.* Über Lesen und Erklären von Dichtwerken. Leipzig. pp. 58–72. — 4 types: interlinear, literal, free, recreation; close analysis of Latin examples.

1909. STORR, Francis. "The art of translation." *Educ R* 38:359–379. — Presidential address to (British) MLA 1908. Urbane, chatty discussion, with numerous examples.

1910. CHAMBERLAIN, Alexander F. "Some difficulties in Bible tr." *Harper* 121:726–731. — Anthropologist draws on primitive languages: male and female terms, endings, and speech; taboos which rule out certain episodes; "lamb of God" translated for Eskimo as "seal of God." See also Chamberlain 1901.

1910?. FITZMAURICE-KELLY, James. "Translation." In *Encyclopaedia britannica*, 11th ed. (No such article in 14th ed.) — Much space devoted to the history of tr. in England, i.e., the historic importance of tr.

1910. WARTENSLEBEN, Gabriele V. "Beiträge zur Psychologie des Übersetzens." *Zs f Psych u Physiol d Sinnesorgane*, Abt. I:57:89–115. — Attempt to probe the reactions of the translator (using Latin to German).

1913. CROMER, E. B. "Translation and paraphrase." *Edinb R* 218:102–114. Also in *Political and literary essays*, 1st ser. London. — Review of four volumes of verse, three from Greek, one into Greek. Resort to paraphrase is problematic, but on the whole it is approved for verse.

1914. BURTON, Richard. "Difficulties of translation." In *Little essays in literature and life.* New York. — "the form of the original is of its very essence" He prefers "prose to any substitute in verse."

1914. COWL, R. P. *Theory of poetry in England.* London. — Virtually a restatement of Dryden's theories.

1914. FRÄNZEL, W. *Geschichte des Übersetzens im 18. Jahrhundert.* Leipzig. — His chief concern is with the theory of tr.

1914. TARNAWSKI, Władysław. *O polskich przekładach dramatów Szekspira* (On Polish translations of Shakespeare's dramas). Cracow.

1915. SPAETH, Sigmund. "Translating to music." *Mus Q* 1:291–298. — Need for tr. as interpretation of words and music. Difficulties set forth and illustrated. Ways of solving problems suggested.

1915. THOMSON, J. A. K. "Some thoughts on translation." In *The Greek tradition*. London. — His "version must produce upon the English reader the effect which the original has produced upon himself." The two dangers are overtranslation and undertranslation.

1916. LEONARD, William Ellery. Pref. to *Lucretius*. New York. —Defense of verse: (1) "verse permits a wider and more apposite choice of syntactical constructions; (2) "verse gives to the many repetitions . . . their proper relevance"; (3) "verse, by its very cadence . . . possesses . . . an instrument scarcely available in . . . prose." (Quoted from 1935 ed.)

1916. SHOWERMAN, Grant. "The way of the translator." *Unpop R* 5:84–100. — Tr. is sin. Many examples of tr. difficulties, with citations from several languages, ancient and modern.

1918. PHILLIMORE, J. S. *Some remarks on translating and translators.* Engl. Assn., No. 42. London 1919. — There are right periods for superior trs. (cf. Orage 1922). "is the ancient to come in on his own terms or ours?" "A tr. should be read for pleasure." Hence he rejects Browning (1877), seconds FitzGerald (1859, 1878).

1918. SCHOLZ, K. W. H. *The art of translation* . . . Americana Germ. 33. Philadelphia. — Special reference to prose drama. He demands "a complete transcript of the thought and spirit."

1919. BATJUŠKOV, F., ČUKOVSKIJ, K., GUMILEV, I. *Principy xudožestvennogo perevoda* (Principles of artistic translation). Petersburg. — First Russian attempt toward a systematic discussion of tr. problems.

1919. HUGHES, Helen S. "Notes on 18th century fictional translation." *Mod Philol* 17:225–231. — Excessive liberties taken with style and content, often on moral grounds.

1919. WHIBLEY, Charles. "Tudor translators." In *Literary studies*. London. First printed in *Cambridge history of English literature*. 1907–1927. — Personal and critical appraisals. "In general, the trs. of the heyday were accurate neither in word nor in shape." But they aimed "to discover new worlds of thought and beauty."

1920. AMOS, Flora R. *Early theories of translation*. New York. — Theory of tr. cannot be reduced to a rule of thumb; it must again and again be modified to include new facts.

1920. ANDERTON, Basil. "Lure of translation." In *Sketches from a library window*. Cambridge 1923. — Tr. is a mode of self-expression, springs from a desire to instruct and to enrich literature.

1920. ELIOT, T. S. "Euripides and Professor Murray." In *The sacred wood*. London. — "Greek poetry will never have the slightest vitalizing effect upon English poetry if it can only appear masquerading as a vulgar debasement of the eminently personal idiom of Swinburne."

1920. SOUTER, Alexander. *Hints on translation from Latin into English*. London. — "Every word should be represented somehow in the tr., except where . . . the omission of a word improves the English and takes nothing from the meaning." (Quoted by Frost 1955.)

1920. TOKSVIG, Signe. "The mutilation of a masterpiece." *New Repub* 25:113–114. — Tr. of Nexö's *Ditte* scrutinized.

1921. ARNS, Karl. "Über die Kunst der Übersetzung englischer Verse." *Zs f frz u engl Unterricht* 20:12–27.

1921. DENT, Edward J. "Song translations." *Nation* (London) 29:482–484. — German songs: problems of the singer.

1921. DRAPER, John W. "The theory of translation in the 18th century." *Neophilol* 6:241–254. — Extensive bibliography.

1921. FOX-STRANGWAYS, Arthur H. "Essay on principles of tr." In *Music and letters.* July.

1921. HARRISON, Frederic. "The art of translation." *Forum* 65:635–647. — Review of trs. from Latin, Greek, Italian, Spanish, French, German, with comment on particular works or writers. Laws: (1) exact rendering of the full meaning; (2) some echo of the original form; (3) clarity, grace, and vigor.

1921. MORITZEN, Julius. "Is the translator without a literary conscience?" *Bookm* 53: 133–135. — Pros and cons of retaining "offensive" matter in a tr., starting off with Nexö's *Ditte.* (Cf. Toksvig 1920.)

1922–1940. *Index translationum.* Répertoire international des traductions. Paris. — Resumed in 1948 under auspices of UNESCO. Not always accurate.

1922. NEMIAH, Royal Case. "Shall we read literature in translation?" *Educ R* 64:135–141. — He undertakes to "explain why no tr. can in any sense be considered as a substitute for the original."

1922. ORAGE, Alfred R. "When shall we translate?" In *Readers and writers.* New York. pp. 48–50. — He thinks "our period for perfect tr. has not yet come; he expects it about 1970.

1922. PEYSER, Herbert F. "Some observations on song text and libretto translation." *Mus Q* 8:353–371. — "Perfect tr. of song text or opera libretto is impossible." Peculiar difficulties of opera: literal renderings sound ludicrous when sung.

1922. POLLAK, Roman. *"Goffred" Tassa-Kochanowskiego.* Poznań. — A detailed analysis of a seventeenth-century Polish tr. of *Gerusalemme Liberata.*

1922. POSTGATE, J. B. *Translation and translations, theory and practice.* London. — "The prime merit of a tr. is faithfulness" "The Faithful Translator" will give the letter where possible, but in any case the spirit." "The Transfuser is only too prone to sacrifice the letter and the spirit as well."

1923. MURRAY, Gilbert. "On translating Greek." *Liv Age* 318:420–423. — Principles and examples.

1924. BELLOC, Hilaire. "On translation." *Lond Merc* 10:150–156. — Need for *good* trs. in our day. Requirements are (1) knowledge of native tongue, (2) rebirth of the spirit of the original. The spirit must take precedence of the letter. Examples, hand-wringing. (Cf. Belloc 1931.)

1924. BENSON, A. C. "Verse translation." *Cornhill M* 57:586–598. — Verse tr. preferred for the Greek anthology, but a diversified meter recommended. Arnold's Homer tr. violated all his own canons.

1924. GRANVILLE-BARKER, Harley. "On translating plays" in *Essays by divers hands.* Transactions of the R.S.L., New series 5:19–42. London. — The demand for a comparable effect and its results in French versions of Shakespeare. "dramatic tr. is a matter of makeshift" "we must seek for each . . . play the likeliest compromise."

1924. RILKE, R. M. Letter to Lou Andreas Salomé, 22 Apr. *Briefe aus Muzot, 1921 bis 1926.* Leipzig 1935. — His experience with bilingual composition "would seem to indicate that trs. are not natural."

1925. SMITH, J. M. Powis. "Some difficulties of a translator." *J Relig* 5:163–171. — Divergence in mental outlook, inadequacy of English vocabulary.

1926. MUNSTERBERG, Margaret. "Gift of tongues." *JEGPh* 25:393–406. — The peculiar genius of a language appears best in the process of tr.

1926. PETERSEN, Julius. *Die Wesensbestimmung der deutschen Romantik.* Leipzig. p. 64. — The tr. as work of art can never be a true image of the original; a rebirth in the translator's tongue of products of another language, it will always impose a new form.

1926. PORTIER, L. "A propos des traductions de Giacomo Zanella." *R Litt Comp* 5:455–470. — Advice given by Zanella: tr. freely, as if transposing music for a different instrument. "A tr. demands a certain moral attitude at least as much as an effort of intelligence."

1927. ANON. "Transformation by translation." *Liv Age* 333:1117–1118. Also in *Bul Pan Am Union* 62 (1928): 375–376. — Report of experiment: J. V. Jensen (Dane) wrote 700-word sketch; this was translated into Swedish, German, English, French, Danish again. Each translator a master of both languages. Final product was unrecognizable.

1927. MAY, J. Lewis. "Concerning translation." *Edinb R* 245:108–118. — Review of seven titles. "there is . . . no such thing as tr. . . ." as proved by the wedding of words and thought.

1928. CHAPMAN, John Jay. *Two Greek plays* . . . Boston. — Perceptive remarks on tr. Greek poetry.

1928. DUBEUX, Albert. *Les traductions françaises de Shakespeare.* Paris.

1928. LEPPLA, R. "Übersetzungsliteratur" in Merker-Stammler, *Reallexikon der deutschen Literaturgeschichte.* Berlin. 3:394–402. — Five categories: (1) contemporary literature; (2) dead languages; (3) contemporary but alien culture; (4) older stages of native tongue; (5) native works in foreign speech. Bibliog. of German literature dealing with tr.

1928. WELLARD, James H. "The art of translating." *Quar R* 250:128–147. — Many examples, especially from Latin, some into Latin. Some critical discussion of particular problems: humor, word play, proverbs, etc.

1929. BELLOC, H. "On translation" in *A conversation with an angel and other essays.* London. — His formula: (1) read the original thoroughly, (2) render into your own tongue the effect on your mind, (3) recheck with the original to get closer to it without sacrificing naturalness.

1929. DICKINSON, G. Lowes. "On translation." *Nation* (London) 46:282–283. — Review of tr. of Tu Fu by Florence Ayscough. What is left of poetry in tr. from Chinese to English, and vice versa? "things," he says.

1929. FINKEL', A. *Teorija i praktika perevoda* (Theory and practice of translation). Khar'kov. — A useful manual for translators.

1929. FISCHER, Otokar. "O překládání básnických děl" (On the translation of poetical works) in *Duše a slovo* (Prague): 263–283. — The prominent translator outlines the vital and difficult tasks of poetic tr.

1929. POUND, Ezra. "Guido's relations." *Dial* 86:559–568. Experiments in poetic tr., with shrewd and acid comment.

1930. JAKOBSON, R. "O překladu veršů" (Translation of verses). *Plán* II:9–11. Prague. — The seemingly identical form may have a quite divergent function in two different languages.

1930. JIRÁT, V. *Dva překlady Fausta* (Two translations of Faust). Prague. — Careful formal analysis of trs. made by two eminent Czech poets of different times and schools, in relation to the German original.

1931. ALEKSEEV, M. "Problema xudožestvennogo perevoda" (The problem of artistic translation), *Sbornik trudov Irkutskogo Gos. Universiteta* 18:149–196. — Pivotal stylistic questions of tr. raised by an outstanding literary historian; comprehensive bibliography added.

1931. BELLOC, Hilaire. *On translation.* The Taylorian lecture. Oxford. Also in *Selected essays.* Oxford. Also in *Bookm* 74:32–39, 179–185. — Two types: (1) tr. for instruction calls for exactitude; (2) literary tr. adds color. Three requirements: (1) tr. into native tongue; (2) command foreign tongue; (3) tr. must be free from restriction (a) of space, (b) of form.

1931. HECK, Philipp. *Übersetzungsprobleme im frühen Mittelalter.* Tübingen. pp. 1–32. — Importance for the interpretation of legal documents of extempore, oral, unrevised Latin-German and German-Latin tr. as frequently practiced.

1931. MAGNUS, Laurie. "Hours in undress: translation." *Cornhill* 71:244–254. — Discussion of Arnold "On translating Homer," also Pope's tr. of Homer (defended). Argument for adaptation of tr. to its age; argument for tr. in a wider sense, bringing in new ideas to fructify.

1931. MATTHIESSEN, F. O. *Translation: an Elizabethan art.* Cambridge, Mass. — Study of trs. made from the Italian, French, Latin, and Greek. Careful comparison with the originals.

1932. RICHARDS, I. A. *Mencius on the mind; experiments in multiple definition.* London. — Can we in attempting to tr. a work which belongs to a very different tradition do more than read our own conceptions into it? A pioneer work in exploring difficulties in the tr. of Chinese; important for questions it raises about the nature of tr.

1932. VOSSLER, Karl. *The spirit of language in civilization.* Tr. Oscar Loeser. London. — "the philosophic justification of tr. is the maintenance of the autonomy of language taste" "If one denies the concept of tr. (e.g., Croce 1902) one must give up the concept of a language community."

1932. WEST, Constance B. "La théorie de la traduction au XVIIIe siècle . . ." *R Litt Comp* 12:330–355. — Engl. into French treated. She quotes Le Tourneur: "Tirer de l'Young anglais un Young français qui pût plaire à ma nation."

1933. PETERSEN, Julius, and TRUNZ, Erich. *Lyrische Weltdichtung in deutschen Übertragungen.* Berlin. — The taste of an age is reflected in its (favorite) trs.

1933. THÉRIVE, André. "Le prix des traductions." *Ann Pol et Litt* 100:79–80. — Mentions a proposed prize for the best tr. of a novel, saying that most published trs. are "scandaleuses et ridicules" and give the impression that foreigners can neither think nor speak.

1934. MOROZOV, M. *Texnika perevoda naučnoj literatury s anglijskogo jazyka na russkij* (Technique of translating technological literature from English into Russian). Moscow. — Important methodological observations.

1934. USOV, D. *Osnovnye principy perevodčeskoj raboty* (Basic principles of translation work). Moscow.

1934. ZALESKI, Z.-L. "Le mouvement des traductions." *Mercure Fr* 254: 189–194. — Study of the *Index translationum* affords interesting comparative figures for the countries included. British and American provincialism indicated.

1935. BÜTOW, Hans. "Übersetzen — eine edle und schwere Kunst." *Zs f Bücherfreunde* 39, 3. Folge IV:23–29. — Inadequacy of many trs. Tr. of a poem by Rupert Brooke, with discussion.

1935. FUCHS, Gerhard. *Studien zur Übersetzungstheorie und -Praxis des Gottsched-Kreises.* Freiburg diss.

1935. MAZON, Paul E. *Mme Dacier et les traductions d' Homère en France.* Oxford. — Zaharoff lecture. — "alternative: renoncer au style formulaire pour conserver le mouvement . . . ou conserver le style formulaire et renoncer au mouvement . . . n'est plus Homère . . . ce n'est plus rien." "La véritable exactitude . . . produire sur ses lecteurs la même impression . . ." Mme Dacier (who bowdlerized and "ennobled") made Homer palatable to her society.

1936. BATES, Ernest Stuart. *Modern translation.* London. — Chapter IV contains a good discussion of theory and practice.

1936. ČUKOVSKIJ, K. *Iskusstvo perevoda* (The art of translation). Moscow-Leningrad. — Challenging discussion of typical blunders in trs.

1936. EASTMAN, Max. "Pushkin and his English translators." *New Repub* 89:187–188. — Tr. of P. by Yarmolinsky and Deutsch "is a calamity both in literature and in our cultural relations with Russia." Other translators of his poetry equally bad.

1936. NEWALD, Richard. "Von deutscher Übersetzungskunst." *Zs f Geistesgeschichte*: pp. 190–206.

1936. THURSFIELD, Hugh. "Translation." *Cornhill* 153: 482–486. — An attempt to answer the question: why do men (want to) translate?

1937–1941. FEDOROV, A. *Teorija i praktika perevoda nemeckoj naučno-texničeskoj literatury na russkij jazyk* (Theory and practice of translating German technological literature into Russian). Moscow.

1937. HAMILTON, Edith. *Three Greek plays.* New York. — "On Translating": "The best a tr. can hope for . . . is to convey something of the impression the poem made upon him."

1937. ORTEGA Y GASSET, José. "Miseria y esplendor de la traducción." *Obras completas.* Madrid 1947. 5:429–448. — Only when we oblige the reader to move within the linguistic habits of the author will there be worthy trs.

1937. SZUREK-WISTI, Maria. *Miriam tłumacz* (Miriam as translator). Cracow. — A study of a versatile translator of Symbolist poets, Zenon Miriam–Przesmycki (1861–1944).

1938. GRASSET, Bernard. "Traduction et traducteurs." *R d Deux Mondes* 46:459-466. — Much about Goethe's views in connection with his tr. of Diderot, *Le neveu de Rameau.*

1938. HERTER NORTON, M. D. *Translations from the poetry of . . . Rilke.* New York. — Argues for a "literal" and unrhymed version facing the original.

1938. HIGHAM, T. F. Pref. to *Oxford book of Greek verse in translation.* London. Pp. xxxiiiff. — Two sects of translators, (1) Hellenizers, (2) modernists. "All tr. is a kind of illusion . . . . Those trs. are always best in which the illusion is most complete and the idiom least suggestive of tr."

1938. UNDERHILL, Ruth. *Singing for power.* Berkeley, Calif. — Translating songs of the Papagos (Arizona). "One can hope to make the tr. exact only in spirit, not in the letter."

1940. PEGGRAM, Reed Edwin. "First French and English translations of *Utopia. M L R* 35:330-340. — Careful examination. Robynson's tr. has never been supplanted. (Cf. Binder 1947.)

1941. ČUKOVSKIJ, K. *Vysokoe iskusstvo* (The high art). Moscow. — Highlights of tr. art.

1941. FEDOROV, A. *O xudožestvennom perevode* (Artistic translation). Leningrad. — Tr. of belles-lettres, discussed by the chief Russian specialist in tr. technique.

1941. NABOKOV, Vladimir. "The art of translation." *New Repub* 105:160-162. — Three grades of evil: (1) errors; (2) slips; (3) wilful reshaping. Examples from Russian in both directions. Analysis of an opening line of Pushkin. (Cf. Eastman 1936.)

1941. WALEY, Arthur S. *One hundred seventy Chinese poems.* — Chinese poetry is rhymed and resembles traditional English verse. Rhyme omitted in order to keep more of the sense.

1942. BARTLETT, Phyllis B. "Stylistic devices in Chapman's *Iliad.*" *PMLA* 57:661-675. — Analysis of Chapman's preface (verse) on principles of tr., and examination of his tr., particularly what Chapman calls "the free grace of his natural dialect" as opposed to a literal word-for-word version.

1942. BELL, Harold Idris, and BELL, David. "The problem of translation," in *Fifty poems translated*, with essays. London. pp. 63-103. — "The ideal of tr. is this: to make a poem whose form is as seemingly spontaneous as the poem it seeks to translate, and to put into that form the whole wealth of the original conception." Special attention paid to the tr. of Welsh poetry, with analysis of its peculiarities.

1942. FUERST, Norbert. "Rilke's translation of the sonnets of Elizabeth Barrett Browning, of Louise Labé, and of Michelangelo."*Stud Philol* 39:130-142. — In the first two cases Rilke's trs. surpass the originals; he fails to equal the hugeness of Michelangelo.

1942. GREEN, Julien. "Translation and the 'fields of scripture.' " *Amer School* 11:110-121. — Discovery that various trs. of the Bible (English, French, German, Latin) do not agree, and that Hebrew is in part inaccessible.

1942. HUEBSCH, B. W. "Cross-fertilization in letters." *Amer Schol* 11:304-314. — Movement of ideas by means of tr.

1942. RODITI, Edouard. "Poetics of translation." *Poetry* 60:32–38. — "the spirit of poetry resides entirely in its body." He favors the closest possible reproduction; the tr. should meticulously reconstruct its body in another language.

1943. BATES, Ernest Stuart. *Intertraffic. Studies in tr.* London. — Survey of tr. (of poetry) done in Italy and the Far and Near East. Special appendices with examples.

1943. BISHOP, John Peale. "On translating poets." *Poetry* 62:111–115. — Review of three Spanish-American poets' tr. by several hands. Why tr. a poem? Two modes: (1) produce an English poem; (2) get close to the original.

1943. KOYRÉ, Alexandre. "Traduttore-traditore; à propos de Copernic et de Galilée." *Isis* 34, 3:209. — The word "orbium" (spheres) tr. as "Himmelskörper" (heavenly bodies); "by experiment" added to Galileo's text.

1943. PELLEGRINI, A. M. "Giordano Bruno on translations." *ELH* 10:193–207. — Bruno on tr. as promoting knowledge of science.

1943. VITTORINI, Elio. *Americaia: Raccolto di narratori.* Milan. (Introduction by Emilio Cecchi).

1944. GREGORY, Horace. "On the translation of the classics into English poetry." *Poetry* 64:30–35. — Review of Allen Tate's *Vigil of Venus*. He advocates a sort of paraphrase — by a first-rate poet.

1945. GIDE, André. "Lettre-Préface." *Hamlet: Edition bilingue.* New York.

1945. MICHAUD, C. "Traduction: matière et forme." *Bibliog f Roy Soc Can Trans* 3d ser 39, Sect 1: 127–141. Ottawa. — Special reference to Canada, French and English. Analysis of British, American, French lang. "Ideal tr. would be that which, reversed, would produce the original text." "Quel parti prendre? . . . celui du juste milieu."

1945. OWEN, Walter. Pref. to tr. of *La Araucana.* Buenos Aires. — "I have tried . . . to present . . . a version . . . that reads like an original English poem." Detailed analysis of his procedure with Ercilla's opening stanza.

1945. SCHWARZ, W. "Theory of translation in 16th century Germany." *M L R* 40:289–299. — Emphasis on theorizing, apart from Bible tr., which offers special problems. Trs. into German or Latin considered.

1945. UNWIN, Stanley. "On translations." *Life & Letters To-Day* 47:139–143. — Problems of a publisher with respect to translators and trs.

1945. URZIDIL, John. "Language in exile." *Life & Letters To-Day* 45:22–23. — Article tr. by M. M. Kallir (from Czech). Tr. should approach the original as an infinite decimal number approaches infinity. Tr. an ethical function, can mean enrichment.

1946. ASTROV, Margaret. "The word is sacred." *Asia* 46:406–411. — Problems of the tr. of Amer. Indian texts. Characteristics of various Indian languages to be observed by the translator.

1946–1947. ISAČENKO, A. "Marginalie k problému básnického překladu" (Marginal notes to the problem of poetic translation). *Literaria historica slovaca* 1–2:148–163. — General problems of poetic tr. exemplified in the Slovak tr. of Puškin's *Eugene Onegin*.

1946. LEWISOHN, Ludwig. *Thirty-one poems* by Rainer Maria Rilke. New York. — "as in all great . . . poetry, form *is* meaning."

1947. BINDER, James. "More's *Utopia* in English: a note on translation." *MLN* 62:370–376. — Robinson throws More's approach to human living off balance: extravagant coloring, "gorgeous" ten times, all this false and misleading.

1947. IGLAUER, Edith. "Housekeeping for the family of nations." *Harper* 194:295–306. — Tr. problems (and solutions) in the UN Secretariat.

1947. NIDA, Eugene A. *Bible translating — an analysis of principles and procedures*. New York.

1948. ASPINWALL, Dorothy B. *The art of translating French verse*. Diss. U. of Washington.

1948. BROWER, R. A. "The Theban eagle in English plumage." *Class Philol* 43:25–30. — "The aim . . . is . . . to draw attention to what makes Pindar's poetry . . . almost untranslatable." Praise for Lattimore and Wade-Gery and Bowra as translators of Pindar.

1948. COWLEY, Malcolm. "American books abroad." *Literary history of the United States*. New York.

1948. GRIERSON, Herbert. *Verse translation*. Oxford. With special reference to tr. from the Latin. — Wide-ranging survey, with much quotation and comment; not so much critical as appreciative.

1948. POLLAK, Seweryn. "Z zagadnień przekładu poetyckiego" (Some problems of poetic translation). In *Prace Polonistyczne* 6:191–210.

1948. SZUMAN, Stefan. *O kunszcie i istocie poezji lirycznej* (About the art and nature of lyrical poetry). Łódź. — The second half of the book, pp. 137–293, deals with problems of tr. of lyrical poetry.

1949. COCKING, J. M. "Mr. Day Lewis and the tr. of Valéry." *19th Cent* 145:311–318. — *Le cimetière marin* analyzed and Lewis' tr. dissected. "If they cannot have the orig., they want a near substitute, not a new poem." "No issue from the dilemma of the translator of poetry: prose with its obvious limitations, or poetry with its obvious dangers."

1949. GRAND' COMBE, Félix de. "Réflexions sur la traduction." *French Studies* 3:345–350; 5(1951):253–263. — (1) pedagogical tr. a kind of playing with dice; (2) absorption followed by re-creation. — Remarks on precision and logic of French, looseness of thought and wording in English.

1949. HIGHET, Gilbert. "The Renaissance: translation." In *The classical tradition*. New York. pp. 104–126. — Importance of translated works to any culture, illustrations. Tr. "does not usually create great works; but it often helps great works to be created."

1949. KNOX, Ronald. *Trials of a translator*. New York. — Defense and explanation of his practice in translating the Bible and the Latin Psalms. Follows Belloc in stating that "Bible should speak to Englishmen . . . in English idiom." Criticism of un-English character of both Authorized and Douay versions.

1949. MACNEICE, Louis. *Radio Times*, Nov. — The ideal demand (e.g., for Goethe's *Faust*): (1) literal faithfulness; (2) connotative faithfulness; (3) line for line; (4) retain the order of words and images; (5) exact equivalents of rhythmical patterns; (6) exact equivalents of the rhyme patterns; (7) exact equivalent of the "texture" (sequence of consonants and vowels).

1949. MATHIEU, George J. "Words before peace; translators and interpreters." *UN World* 3:58–59. — UN problems: tr. plus interpretation a constant requisite.

1949. PUTNAM, Samuel. "Translating isn't all beer and skittles." *Books Abr* 23, 3:235f. — Facility is not enough. Blood and sweat are the secret.

1949. PUTNAM, Samuel. Pref. to tr. of Cervantes, *Don Quixote*. New York. —History of English versions and of Spanish text. Translator's detailed apologia. "I have striven to avoid . . . an antiquated style and vocabulary, and . . . any modernism that would . . . savor of flippancy."

1949. TEELE, R. E. *Through a glass darkly: A study of English translations of Chinese poetry*. Ann Arbor. — Very useful analysis of problems in tr. Chinese poetry into English.

1950. DRINKER, Henry S. "On translating vocal texts." *Mus Q* 36:225–240. — Plea for tr. as conveying better understanding of the text to the singer. Words must be adapted to the music. Six requirements stated, with examples. Since these will conflict, tr. must choose. Practical hints.

1950. GANŠIN, K., KARPOV, I. (editors). *Voprosy teorii i metodiki učebnogo perevoda* (The critical and methodical questions of translation as means of teaching). Moscow. — Problems of understanding text and of interlingual correspondences; role of tr. in language teaching.

1950. O'NEILL, Eugene, Jr. "On translating Homer." *New Repub* 123:18. — Review of Rieu's *Iliad* and that of Chase and Perry. Only prose will do; English of King James Bible supplies the right language.

1950. PICK, Robert. "Precarious profession: literature's greatest challenge." *Sat R Lit* 33 S 30:8–9. — Datedness of older trs. Problems of tr. are those of communication.

1950. POUND, Ezra. *The letters of* . . . ed. D. D. Page. New York. — Letters to W. H. D. Rouse on the tr. of Homer. Practical illustrations of Pound's aims as a tr.

1950. TUWIM, Julian. "Traduttore - traditore," *Pegaz dęba*. Warsaw. pp. 165–190. — An outstanding Polish poet discusses striking errors of translators.

1950. VAN DOREN, Mark. "Uses of translation." *Nation* 170:474. — The literature of the world has exerted its power by being translated.

1950. WINSTON, Richard. "The craft of translation." *Amer Schol* 19:179–186.

1951. BROWER, R. A. " . . . And of recent translations . . . " In *Yearbook of comparative and general literature*. Chapel Hill, N.C. — Review of Kinchin Smith's *Antigone* (compared to that of Fitts and Fitzgerald) leads to a discussion of what constitutes good tr. of (great) verse drama.

1951. GALANTIÈRE, Lewis. "On translators and translating." *Amer Schol* 20:435–445. — Needed: (1) command of own lang.; (2) broad general culture; (3) knowledge of for. lang. (life and culture). "A tr. ought to . . . make upon the reader . . . the same impact as that made by the original text upon its reader."

1951. KNIGHT, Douglas. *Pope and the heroic tradition*. New Haven, Conn.

— A unique study of the translator's relation to poetic tradition. "For the adequate tr. in Pope's terms is a special kind of artist, in a double relation to the tradition by virtue of his duty to another poem as well as his debt to it."

1951. MANCHESTER, Paul T. "Verse translation as an interpretive art." *Hispania* 34:68–73. — Chilean epics tr. by M. and Lancaster; explanation and defense of their procedure.

1952. BARZUN, Jacques. "Trial by translations: plays of Corneille." *New Repub* 127 (Dec 8): 20–21. — Lacy Lockert's tr. of Corneille's "chief plays" passed under expert scrutiny.

1952. BOROWY, Wacław. "Boy jako tłumacz" (Boy as translator). *Studia i rosprawy* 2:73–178. Wrocław. — A masterly short study of a great Polish translator of French classics, Tadeusz Boy-Żeleński (1874–1941).

1952. ERVIN, Susan, and BOWER, R. T. "Translation problems in international surveys." *Pub Opin Q* 16, 4:595–604. — Tr. distortion (and perhaps garbled data) caused by differences (1) in meaning; (2) in syntactical context; (3) in cultural context.

1952. LEDNICKI, Waclaw. "Some notes on the translation of poetry." *Am Slavic R* 11:304–311. — Apropos of Pushkin's lyrics in tr. Valéry, Pushkin, Słowacki; analysis of work of two trs. of Pushkin.

1952. PIRES, Armando S. "At best an echo." *Américas* 4 S 13–15. — Subtitle: "Soul-searching of a translator."

1952. RUSH, F. A. "Standards of translation and the status of translators." *PEN International Bulletin of Selected Books*, III, 3 (October–December). — Brief, but includes further bibliographical references.

1952 —. *Yearbook of comparative and general literature*. Chapel Hill. — Each issue contains reviews of recent trs.

1953. BAR-HILLEL, Yehoshua. "Some linguistic problems connected with machine translation." *Philos Sci* 20:217–225.

1953. BAR-HILLEL, Yehoshua. "The present state of research on mechanical translation." *Amer Documentation* 2:229–237.

1953. BARZUN, Jacques. "Food for the N.R.F., or, My God, what will you have?" *Partisan R* 20:660–674. — Misconceptions of France fostered by ineptitudes of tr. Requirements: (1) clear to readers and idiomatic; (2) must sound like the original author; (3) must not mislead in substance or implication. The tr. must have two minds with twin thoughts.

1953. FEDOROV, A. *Vvedenie v teoriju perevoda* (Introduction to the theory of translation). Moscow. — History of Russian views on tr. problems; linguistic questions of tr. Tr. of documentary texts and verbal art in prose and verse.

1953. HIGHET, Gilbert. "The art of translation." In *People, places and books*. New York. — A radio speech sponsored by Oxford Univ. Press. Tr. is difficult . . . and neglected. Poor trs. rob us of foreign masterworks. Examples from Greek and Latin.

1953. *Kniha o překládání* (A book about translating). Prague. — Grammatical and lexical questions of tr. from Russian into Czech are discussed by several Czech philologists; brief bibliography.

1953. MACFARLANE, J. W. "Modes of translation." *Durham Univ J* 45:

77-93. — His intent is "to underline the need for some new, provisional theory of tr. — new in the sense that it should be diagnostic rather than hortatory . . . concerned . . . with actualities . . . It is not the principles of tr. that need re-adjusting . . . but rather our ideas about them."

1953. POUND, Ezra. *The translations of Ezra Pound*. With an introduction by Hugh Kenner. New York. — "Pound has had both the boldness and the resource to make a new form, similar in effects to that of the original" "Tr. does not, for him, differ in essence from any other poetic job"

1953. RICHARDS, I. A. "Toward a theory of translating." In *Studies in Chinese thought*, ed. A. F. Wright. Chicago. — Exploration of a "comprehensive view of comprehending" as a basis for a theory of tr. Raises the important question, "What is synonymy?"

1954. ALEGRÍA, Fernando. "How good is a translation?" *Américas* 6 My 36-38. — Tr. of English, German, and Russian novels poorly paid, done hastily from French, often with unannounced pruning.

1954. BAR-HILLEL, Yehoshua. "Can translation be mechanized?" *Amer Sci* 42:248-260. — He thinks so for scientific texts under certain conditions.

1954. CIARDI, John. "Strictness and faithfulness." *Nation* 178:525. — Review of Fitts's *Lysistrata* and Marianne Moore's *La Fontaine*. Moore follows Pound: "a superb theory but an impossible one." Fitts aims at faithfulness rather than strictness. C. remarks on "translatorese," a queer language-of-the-study that counts words but misses their living force.

1954. KENNER, Hugh. "Hellas without Helicon." *Poetry* 84:112-118. —Tr. of Aeschylus by Lattimore, of Greek poets by Gow in prose, and in trs. selected by Hadas, leads to discussion of the faults of tr. from the Greek, with acute suggestions and reference to Pound's Sophocles.

1954. MATHEWS, Jackson. "Campbell's Baudelaire." *Sewanee R* 62:663-671. — Review of R. C.'s tr. of *Fleurs du mal*. Detailed criticism, with illuminating comment and remarks on both languages.

1954 — . MT, *Mechanical translation*, devoted to the translating of languages with the aid of machines. Cambridge, Mass. (Sponsored by M.I.T.)

1954. MOORE, Marianne. *Fables of La Fontaine*. New York. — "practice of Ezra Pound has been for me a governing principle"

1954. POUND, Ezra. *Literary essays of Ezra Pound*. Norfolk, Conn. — Includes "Translators of Greek." "Early translators of Homer." An influential expression of twentieth-century taste in tr. Pound recalls to English readers the virtues of earlier trs. and offers excellent practical criticism of more recent ones, especially Browning.

1954. VELLACOTT, Philip. *Four plays of Euripides*. Penguin. — "The highest aim of a tr. is to persuade the reader to dispense with it." "If Engl. . . . cannot achieve accuracy, universality, and force without loss of dignity, then Engl. is not a language into which it is worth while to translate Greek plays. There is no doubt that it can."

1955 — . *Babel*. Revue internationale de la traduction. Publiée par la Fédération Internationale des Traducteurs avec le concours de l'UNESCO, Bonn. — Each issue contains international bibliography.

1955. BAR-HILLEL, Yehoshua. "Can translation be mechanized?" *J Symbol Logic* 20:192–194. — Critique of Abraham Kaplan.

1955. BIEBER, Konrad. "The translator — friend or foe?" *French Review* 28:493–497. — Chiefly a list of errors in the tr. of Camus' *The Rebel*.

1955. BODDE, D. "On translating Chinese philosophical terms" (in Fung Yu-lan's History of Chinese Philosophy) *Far East Q* 14:231–234.

1955. FROST, William. *Dryden and the art of translation*. New Haven, Conn. — An attempt to describe the process of tr. in terms acceptable to recent critical theory (e.g., "pillar symbols" and "local symbols"). Analysis of Dryden's trs. based on the theory that "a verse tr. is a commentary on the original."

1955. GARVIN, P. L. *A Prague school reader in esthetics, literary structure, and style*. Washington. — Valuable material on translation.

1955. ISHIKAWA, K. I. "Difficulties in translating Japanese into English and vice versa." *Pac Spec* 9:95–99. — Engl. to Japanese is easier. Plea for "teamwork in tr. such violently different languages as Engl. and Japanese."

1955. KENNER, Hugh. "Problems of faithfulness and fashion." *Poetry* 85: 225–231. — Review of trs. by Henry Hart, John Ciardi (Dante's *Inferno*), and A. E. Watts (Ovid's *Metamorphoses*).

1955. LEOPOLD, W. F. Review of tr. of Ernst Cassirer, *The philosophy of symbolic forms*, in *Language* 31:73–84. — "every act of tr. is an act of interpretation."

1955. LOCKE, W. N. "Speech typewriters and translating machines." *PMLA* 70:23–32. — Theoretical discussion of the problems; possible ways to a solution.

1955. LOCKE, W. N., and BOOTH, A. D. *Machine translation of languages*. New York.

1955. LOWE-PORTER, H. T. "Translating Thomas Mann." *Symposium* 9:260–272. — Personal experiences which throw light on her handling of Mann's texts.

1955. MOUNIN, Georges. *Les belles infidèles*. Paris. — First-rate defense and illustration of the art of tr. Refutation of arguments against the possibility of tr.: historic, theoretical, linguistic, semantic, etc.

1955. NABOKOV, Vladimir. "Problems of translation: *Onegin* in English." *Partisan Rev* 22:496–512. — "The clumsiest literal tr. is a thousand times more useful than the prettiest paraphrase." Analysis of Pushkin's verse novel; all four Engl. versions are "grotesque travesties." (Cf. Eastman 1936, Nabokov 1941.)

1955. POSIN, Jack. "Problems of literary translation from Russian into English." *ATSEEL Journal*, 13:9–15. — Advocate of the theory of comparable impression.

1955. RUSINEK, Michał (ed.). *O sztuce tłumaczenia* (On the art of translation). Wrocław. — A collection of twenty-four essays by various authors, the most general among them being: Wacław Borowy, "Dawni teoretycy tłumaczeń" (Old theoreticians of translations), Zenon Klemensiewicz, "Przekład jako zagadnienie językoznawstwa" (Translation as a linguistic problem), Roman Ingarden, "O tłumaczeniach" (On translations). — The last one, a fairly large study by the well-known Polish phenomenologist philosopher, the author of *Das literarische Kunstwerk* (Halle, 1931). On pp. 534-549 there are short English summaries of all the papers.

1955. *Voprosy xudožestvennogo perevoda* (Questions of artistic translation). Moscow. — Symposium dealing with realistic traditions of Russian translators, the place of trs. in a national literature, attitude to the national peculiarities of the original.

1956. ANON. "Translating classical poetry." *TLS* 2 Nov. — Leading article. Review of six items, half of them from Greek. Approval of "modern" style in tr., with examples.

1956. AUSTIN, R. G. *Some English translations of Virgil.* An inaugural lecture. Liverpool. — Survey, with examples, of four centuries of Virgil tr. Praise for Dryden and Gavin Douglas, guarded commendation of C. Day Lewis.

1956. BURKHARD, Arthur. Review of E. H. Zeydel, *Goethe the lyrist,* in *Yearbook of comparative and general literature.* Chapel Hill, N. C. — Recognizing that Zeydel "has here attempted a . . . self-defeating task," Burkhard nevertheless finds much to commend.

1956. CARY, E. *La traduction dans le monde moderne.* Genève. — General survey, including machine tr. He thinks "Il n'existe pas d'ouvrage d'ensemble consacré à la traduction."

1956. GOULD, R. "Multiple correspondence in automatic translation." Progress report no. AF-44, Design and operation of digital calculating machinery. Harvard Computation Laboratory. Cambridge, Mass.

1956. LEISHMAN, J. B. *Translating Horace.* Oxford. — "Business" of tr. of Horace's stanzas is not to recall their movement "to those who already know the original and do not require to have it recalled, but to communicate it to those who cannot read the original for themselves" "the syllable pattern of the lines, their . . . sequence of long and short . . . syllables can be reproduced exactly."

1956. MAYMI, Protasio. "General concepts or laws in translation." *MLJ* 40:13-21. — Three types: (1) literal, (2) idiomatic, (3) paraphrasical. "a set of 33 principles of tr. . . . established and tested" Motteux and Ozell considered to have preserved Cervantes' style.

1956. MORGAN, B. Q. "On translating feminine rhymes." *On Romanticism and the art of translation,* studies in honor of E. H. Zeydel. Princeton, N.J. — A verbal problem in English.

1956. MORGAN, B. Q. "What is translation for?" *Symposium* 10:322-328. — Answer: for the enrichment of our literature and life.

1956. ROSENBERG, Justus. "Constant factors in tr." In Zeydel volume (see under Morgan). — "The current school of thought . . . maintains that poetic tr. is . . . the transmigration of poetic souls from one lang. into another."

1956. SALTON, G. "A method for using punctuation patterns in the machine translation of languages." Progress report no. AF-43. Harvard Computation Laboratory. Cambridge, Mass.

1956. WIRL, J. "Erwägungen zum Problem des Übersetzens." *Anglo-Americana* (Festschrift . . .). Wien.

1957. HORÁLEK, K. *Kapitoly z teorie překládání* (Chapters from a translation theory). Prague. — A linguist analyzes the essence and role of tr.

1957. KNOX, R. A. *On English translation.* The Romanes Lecture. Oxford. — "the first quality of a book is that people shall . . . want to go on reading it."

1957. LEVÝ, J. *České theorie překladu* (Czech theories of translation). Prague. — History of Czech translation art and theory from the Middle Ages; selected essays with comments and notes on tr. problems by Czech writers, translators, and critics of XVI–XX centuries; detailed international bibliography.

1957. SAVORY, Theodore H. *The art of translation.* London. — The best book on the subject in English. New is his principle of reader analysis as affecting the kind of tr. desired.

1957. WOJTASIEWICZ, Olgierd. *Wstęp do teorii tłumaczenia* (Introduction to the theory of translation). Wrocław. — A short, elementary book; there is an English summary, pp. 121–128.

1958. *Cumulative List No. 5 (1952–1957) of translations in the fields of meteorology, astronomy, geophysics, oceanography, and physics.* American Meteorological Society. — Translations from German, Russian, French, Spanish, Italian, Japanese, Greek, Hungarian, Dutch, Czech, Swedish, and Bulgarian. Chiefly from Russian and German. These translations are sponsored by the United States Air Force Cambridge Research Center, Air Research and Development Command under Contract AF 19(604)–1936 and are made at the request of scientists actively engaged in research at AFCRC, Geophysics Research Directorate.

1958. JACOBSEN, Eric. *Translation: A traditional craft.* Copenhagen. — An historical study of tr. as a humanistic discipline, together with a detailed analysis of Marlowe's versions from Ovid.

1958. PASTERNAK, Boris. "Translating Shakespeare." *20th Cent.* 164:213–228. — Brief interpretations of plays which Pasternak has translated.

1958. *Tezisy konferencii po mašinnomy perevodu (15–21 maja 1958 g.)* (Papers of the conference on machine translation). Moscow. — A stimulating linguistic discussion of the cardinal problems connected with automatic tr.

INDEX TO BIBLIOGRAPHY

Sherburne, 1701
Showerman, 1916
Smith, 1925
Souter, 1920
Spaeth, 1915
Staël-Holstein, 1816
Storr, 1909
Szuman, 1948
Szurek-Wisti, 1937

Tarnawski, 1914
Teele, 1949
Tezisy konferencii po mašinnomy perevodu, 1958
Thérive, 1933
Thomson, 1915
Thursfield, 1936
Toksvig, 1920
Tolman, 1901
Trunz and Petersen, 1933
Turgot, 1778?
Tuwim, 1950
Tytler, 1790

Underhill, 1938

Unwin, 1945
Urzidil, 1945
Usov, 1934

Van Doren, 1950
Vellacott, 1954
Vittorini, 1943
Voprosy xudožestvennogo perevoda, 1955
Vossler, 1932

Waley, 1941
Warren, 1895
Wartensleben, 1910
Wellard, 1928
West, 1932
Whibley, 1919
Wilamowitz-Moellendorff, 1902?
Winston, 1950
Wirl, 1956
Wojtasiewicz, 1957

Yearbook of comparative and general literature, 1952–

Zaleski, 1934